SEEKING GLOBAL JUSTICE & PEACE

CATHOLIC-INSPIRED NGOs
AT THE UNITED NATIONS

Emeka Xris Obiezu

PACEM IN TERRIS PRESS

Devoted to the global vision of Saint John XXIII,
prophetic founder of Postmodern Catholic Social Teaching,
and in support of the search for a Postmodern Ecological Civilization,
which will seek to learn from the rich spiritual wisdom-traditions
of Christianity and of our entire global human family.
www.paceminterrispress.com

2019

Pacem in Terris Press publishes scholarly books directly or indirectly related to Catholic Social Teaching and its commitment to justice, peace, ecology, and spirituality, and on behalf of the search for a Postmodern Ecological Civilization.

In addition, in order to support ecumenical and interfaith dialogue, as well as dialogue with other spiritual seekers, Pacem in Terris Press publishes scholarly books from other Christian perspectives, from other religious perspectives, and from perspectives of other spiritual seekers that promote justice, peace, ecology, and spirituality for our global human family.

Opinions or claims expressed in publications from Pacem in Terris Press represent the opinions and claims of the authors and do not necessarily represent the official position of Pacem in Terris Press, the Pacem in Terris Ecological Initiative, Pax Romana / Catholic Movement for Intellectual & Cultural Affairs - USA or its officers, directors, members, and staff.

PACEM IN TERRIS PRESS
is the publishing service of

PAX ROMANA
Catholic Movement for Intellectual & Cultural Affairs
USA
1025 Connecticut Avenue NW, Suite 1000,
Washington DC 20036
www.paceminterris.net

This book shows convincingly that, despite any failures, contradictions and bad decisions, the UN is carried by a social philosophy that deserves the support of Catholics and, more generally, of all people committed to universal cooperation in favor of peace and justice. The greater the public support for the UN, the more likely will be its institutional reform. The author asks Catholics to become interested in the work of the UN, enter into dialogue with its thinking, and promote its values in their society.

GREGORY BAUM, *a world-famous and recently deceased Catholic theologian, had been a distinguished professor at St. Michael's College in the University of Toronto and later at McGill University in Montreal.*

This informative and inspiring work on Catholic NGOs at the United Nations celebrates the long history of Catholic teaching on peace through international law and solidarity. It belongs in the classes of every Catholic university and seminary.

JOSEPH J. FAHEY, *Ph.D., retired Professor of Theology at Manhattan College, co-founder of Pax Christi USA and of Catholic Scholars for Worker Justice, and a long-time Catholic activist in and justice and peace. in relation to the UN.*

I predict that this important book by Emeka Xris Obiezu will become the definitive contemporary study of Catholic-inspired non-governmental organizations (NGOs) at the United Nations. His impressive book contains a treasury of scholarship and insight into the invaluable work of these organizations on behalf of global justice and peace.

JOE HOLLAND, *Ph.D., Emeritus Professor of Philosophy & Religion at St. Thomas University, President of Pax Romana / Catholic Movement for Intellectual & Cultural Affairs - USA, and past Pax Romana NGO Representative to the United Nations Economic & Social Council.*

Emeka Xris Obiezu has written a deeply researched and most helpful book for understanding and appreciating the large-scale presence of Catholic-inspired non-governmental organizations (NGOs) at the United Nations. All leaders, members, and especially UN representatives of Catholic-inspired NGOs need to read this book and can learn from it.

MARK J. WOLFF, *J.D., LL.M., Professor of Law at Saint Thomas University School of Law, Vice-President of Pax Romana / Catholic Movement for Intellectual & Cultural Affairs - USA, and past Pax Romana Main NGO Representative to the United Nations Economic & Social Council*

TABLE OF CONTENTS

FOREWORD

Professor Gregory Baum

(1923-2017)

W hile the Catholic Church has favored the United Nations Organization from the very beginning, Catholics, including their theologians, have shown little interest in the global institution founded to promote peace in the world, protect peoples' human rights, and stimulate development in poor countries.

The founders of the UN after World War II were aware that, at the beginning of the war, Pius XII had called for the creation of a world organization empowered to protect the peace among the nations. Because of its support for non-violent resolutions of international conflicts, the Holy See sent a Permanent Observer to the UN to defend principles of Catholic social ethics in debates on several levels within this world organization.

When the UN dedicated the year 1999 to "the dialogue of civilization" as a reply to Samuel Huntington's destructive theory of "the clash of civilizations," John Paul II supported the UN by advocating "the dialogue of civilizations" in his message for the World Day of Peace of 2001.

1

I remember how impressed I was by the speech given at the UN by Archbishop Rafael Martino, the Holy See's Permanent Observer, on October 15, 2001, spelling out how to respond to the terrorist attack September 11, 2001. Catholic wisdom made him propose what no one else dared to say. Here are two sentences from his carefully argued speech: "We do a disservice to those who died in the tragedy of September 11, if we fail to search out its causes..." and at the end, "Global disparity is fundamentally incompatible with global security."

Despite the failures and the incompetence of the UN, and despite the internal contradictions of this vast organization, the UN does produce an admirable critical literature on peace and justice — reports, reflections and recommendations — that have an affinity with Catholic social teaching.

The ethical ideal of an international world based on the cooperation of the nations is shared by the UN and the Catholic Church, but it is at odds with the foreign policies of the powerful nations based on competition and collective self-interest. National governments tend to assume that loving concern for others and ascetical self-limitation are ethical ideals for individuals, not for political organizations. States must strive for self-promotion and triumph in a competitive world, arming themselves for protection against their enemies.

The literature produced by the UN and by researchers associated with the UN constitutes an intellectual tradition consistent with Catholic social teaching (and Protestant social ethics) and differs substantially from the presuppositions of today's dominant culture. This tradition deserves the attention of theologians.

While Catholics and their theologians have paid next to no attention to the UN, a number of Catholic groups, among them teams belonging to religious orders, have sought accreditation at the UN as Non-Governmental Organizations (NGOs). The task of the accredited NGOs is twofold: they supply information to various UN departments based on their experience and their research; and they promote the policies on peace and justice endorsed by the UN in their own milieu and in this way influence public opinion. This is how John Paul II described the work of these NGOs:

> No organization ... not even the United Nations ... can alone solve the global problems which are constantly brought to its attention ... It is then the privileged task of the NGOs to help brings these concerns into the communities and the homes of the people, and to bring back to the established departments the priorities and aspirations of the people. (Address at the UN, October 2, 1979).

This present book deals with the work of Catholic NGOs affiliated with the UN and, more especially, with their theological reflections justifying their solidarity and cooperation with a secular organization. The author of the book, Emeka Obiezu, is an Augustinian priest, a member of the Augustinian NGO team accredited to the UN. He believes that Catholics should be well informed about the policies of peace and justice adopted by the UN, relate them to the Catholic ethical tradition and promote them in their society.

He reminds Catholics that the popes have supported the UN and its vision of the human future. They have addressed the UN's General Assembly at various occasions, expressing their approval and support as well as raising critical questions that challenge certain UN policies. Yet in this book Emeka Obiezu does not introduce the reader to the evolving policies of the UN on international peace, economic development, human rights, weapons control, decolonization, and other public issues. What interests him primarily is the theological understanding of the ministry exercised by the Catholic NGOs at the UN.

Emeka Obiezu documents the evolution of the Catholic Church understanding of itself and its mission in the world. He pays primary attention to the religious experience and theological reflection of the members of the Catholic NGOs at the UN. He shows that the understanding of their ministry has changed significantly over the years. His study suggests that the Church's doctrinal development is

3

grounded in the evolving religious experience of dedicated Catholics living in new historical situations. The Church's renewal begins at the base. The author shows that the Catholics who see their mission in a new light have a dialogical relation to the ecclesiastical authorities: they speak to the magisterium of their local experience, hoping to influence its thinking; and they learn from the magisterium, whose concern is the Church universal.

In the early years, the Catholic organizations accredited as NGOs at the UN, Caritas Internationalis among them, understood their mission as the promotion of Catholic values at the UN, which meant that they argued against certain UN policies on issues of gender and procreation. Their aim was to Catholicize the UN. The Catholic NGOs of more recent origin, including those sponsored by the Augustinians and other religious orders, understand their mission in more secular terms as support for universal cooperation in favor of justice, peace, liberty and the protection of the environment.

The interviews of the author with members of these NGOs reveal their conviction that in today's world the aim of the Church's mission transcends the *bonum ecclesiae*, pointing instead at the *bonum humanitatis*. Is this theologically legitimate? Is the secular engagement of these Catholic NGOs in keeping with their religious vocation defined by the Gospel of Jesus Christ? This book offers a positive answer to this question.

One theological concept that has led the Church to rethink its mission in the world is "social or structural sin." We resist the divine will and damage human beings not only by personal sins but also, and more especially, by collective actions and social structures such as wars, genocide, oppression, exploitation, discrimination and unemployment. The Gospel that accuses us of sin and promises to recue us from sin addresses us as individuals and, at the same time, communicates a socio-political message. Catholics are divinely summoned to be critical of the institutions to which they belong.

Emeka Obiezu argues therefore that Catholic NGOs that cooperate with the UN are obliged by the Gospel to become aware of and critique the structural sins of the UN, its internal contradictions and its violations of its own principles. Catholic NGOs at the UN, he writes, must be both loyal and critical. Their critique must be expressed in dialogical form, not aggressively, so that their cooperative activities continue undisturbed. He calls this "dialogical confrontation" and argues that Catholics, made responsible subjects by God's grace, are called upon to exercise this critical task in the institutions to which they belong.

The final chapter of the book actually deals with the internal contradictions of the United Nations Organization. The greatest of these is the supreme power of the Security Council allowing it to overrule decisions made by the General Assembly in matters of peace, security and military force. The permanent members of the Security Council are China, France, Great Britain, Russia and the United States of America, the great powers that can veto any resolution made by the General Assembly. It is ironic that the five nations responsible for peace in the world are in fact the major producers of arms and military equipment and therefore profit economically from the wars outside their own territory.

It seems to me—and to the author himself—that his theological arguments in favor of "dialogical confrontation" apply to the duties of religious in their congregations and of Catholics in their Church.

This book shows convincingly that despite its failures, contradictions and bad decisions, the UN is carried by a social philosophy that deserves the support of Catholics and, more generally, of all people committed to universal cooperation in favor of peace and justice. The greater the public support for the UN, the more likely will be its institutional reform. The author asks Catholics to become interested in the work of the UN, enter into dialogue with its thinking and promote its values in their society.

T his book explores an urgent, complex, contemporary debate about the proper relationship between the Church and the world, viz. the active participation of Catholic-inspired non-governmental organizations (NGOs) in the United Nations (UN). Since 2006 when I attended my first UN Department of Public Information/Non-Governmental Organization Conference in New York as one of the Order of St. Augustine NGO delegates, I developed a keen interest in Catholic-inspired NGO UN activities. Observing their activities out of my academic background of systematic theology aroused my further interest and a question. How can we understand these NGO activities as truly Christian not just on the basis that the representatives of these NGOs themselves are Christians but primarily because their very activities pertain to the economy of salvation? I discovered that many others were asking the same question.

Many people I encountered during these ten years of my Catholic NGO involvement wanted to know why Christians, especially Catholics and more so those belonging to institutes of religious life, should take up a UN ministry. What is the point of such a relationship? They wanted to know if we introduce prayer at UN meetings, if we speak of Christ to the system, if we hope to "Catholicize" the UN and if we can see to it that the UN listens to what the pope has to say. Sometimes these questions come with a tone of hopefulness and sometimes with a hint of criticism. Whatever they imply, these simple, real life questions can be summed up in one single sincere enquiry. They all ask how we can evaluate the catholicity of the Catholic NGO UN presence.

The Catholic Church has supported the UN from its very beginnings and laid the foundation for Church members to participate in it both as individuals and in groups. By its social justice theology developed in Vatican II's *Gaudium et Spes* and other Catholic social teaching documents, the Church expanded the scope and principles upon which this involvement could be judged as legitimately Catholic. Our work undertakes an exploration of Catholic social teaching development from the privileged experience of Catholic-inspired UN NGOs and insists that their UN presence and activities are consistent with, and flow from, the Catholic Church's understanding of the UN and the Church's mission in the Modern World. Concentrating on Catholic NGOs, lay and religious, we can observe a living Vatican II collaborative ministry theology, its mandate, modernity, practicality, prospects, challenges and limitations.

This book further seeks within the boundaries of specifically Catholic theological principles a paradigm that can deepen Catholic NGO UN presence so as to realize its intended goals and aspirations. We also attempt to investigate these principles themselves as to what extent they can be extended to embrace a critique of Catholic activity in global institutions. Specifically pertaining to our project, when we name unfair UN organizational elements as structural injustices that can be evaluated within a theology of structural sin and we urge Catholic-inspired NGOs to see these organizational elements through that lens, we work within and in accord with Catholic theological principles.

Though this book is Catholic in outlook and in its theological focus, it presents an exploration and a case study of the significance of religion within social relations today, specifically the practical realities and possibilities of religious institutional participation in a major secular-political institution in the modern world like the UN. This approach to religious studies, political science, international relations and kindred areas should be of interest to scholars as well as to the general reading public.

The first chapter presents an overview of the UN within the landscape of humanity's search for some form of international arrangement for global governance to pursue global peace, security and development. A section of this chapter presents the UN in Catholic perspective. It looks at why the Church has encouraged a Catholic engagement with that organization from its inception. The second chapter studies Catholic-inspired NGOs at the UN, the dynamics of their journey to, and activities in, that organization. The third chapter takes on the proper theological assessment of these NGOs and their activities based on their various self-understandings and evaluating these self-understandings through theological principles empowering Catholic social activism. Solidarity is our overarching operative theological hermeneutic here, especially in its incarnational aspects.

Incarnational solidarity yields for us the paradigm of dialogical confrontation, which we propose as basis for authentic Catholic UN participation in the modern world of the Second Vatican Council. This paradigm holds together the two essential complimentary roles demanded of a Catholic, or any Christian, UN participant: dedicated support of the UN with its programs in pursuit of its goals and courageous constructive criticism of that same UN with its systemic imbalances hindering the achievement of those goals. The fourth chapter discusses the meaning, implications and challenges of dialogical confrontation, our proposed paradigm for authentic Catholic-inspired NGO UN participation. This last chapter also explores how this paradigm could help NGOs respond to some of the institutional dynamics and limitations also discernible in the Church and in their own various institutions.

Acknowledgment is due to a list of people who have identified with me throughout the writing of this book. I am grateful to John Paul Szura, OSA who introduced me to the UN mission and supported me all the way. His generosity with his time and knowledge in the editing of this work is immeasurable. I thank Richard Nahman, OSA for also helping me with the copyediting of the draft. Professor Gregory Baum was so good to me not just for providing the F oreword to the book but in seeing this work through to the publishers. Rest in Peace a rare gem. My colleagues at the UN, especially the members of Religious at the UN (RUN) and other NGO committees, have been strong support groups for me. I want to single out Professor Joy U Ogwu, Nigeria Ambassador to the UN, an ardent Catholic whose faith subtly yet consistently radiated in her dealings at the UN. My interviewees, I thank you. Equally, I appreciate the love and kindness of Traci Barrow and family, Benedeth Aluele Amao, and many others I am not able to mention here.

INTRODUCTION

I n the precarious aftermath of the Second World War, global stability demanded the creation of a world body for international organization and for the development of international law. There was
need to resolve major international conflicts without violence and to
preserve the human and material resources needed to confront world-
wide problems. Out of this reality on October 24, 1945 the United Nations (UN) was born: "a political instrument responding to the interdependence of nations to build the conditions for world peace
through the acceptance of world law."[1]

The universal foundational UN values and principles proclaimed in
its Charter gave hope to a similar concurrent Judeo-Christian vision
of a peaceful world described as the reign of God in the prophecy of
Isaiah. This would be a world where lion and lamb lie together in
peace, where nations forgo all hostilities and where weapons of warfare are converted into tools for farming (Isaiah 11:7-9; 65:25). Such a
world, envisioned by both the UN founders and the Judeo-Christian
scriptures, would be characterized by universal human rights, enhanced human dignity, justice, good neighborliness, and freedom.[2]

---

[1] Douglas Roche, *United Nations: Divided World* (Toronto: NC Press, 1984), 7.
[2] See *Basic Facts – About the United Nations* (New York: United Nations Publications,
2005), 5.

With admixtures of successes and failures throughout its seventy years of functioning, the "UN has been called everything from 'the best hope of mankind' to 'irrelevant and obsolete.'"[3] Structural problems such as the apparent tyranny and inefficiency of the Security Council, "the tension between sovereignty and internationalism"[4] and glaring inconsistencies in its founding documents stand out as major causes of UN weaknesses.

There are a number of other significant defects in the UN system that may impede the organization from realizing the principles it was instituted to uphold. For instance, in an insightful article in the March 18, 2016 *New York Times* entitled "I Love the UN, but It Is Failing," Anthony Banbury, a former UN Assistant Secretary-General for field support and head of UN Mission for Ebola Outbreak, alluded to its dysfunctional, colossally mismanaged, minimally accountable and inefficient personnel system. It is because of this system that the organization is unable to attract and deploy the best talent to those parts of the world where it is needed the most – such as the Ebola crisis in Western Africa. In view of this defect he compares the UN systems "to a black hole into which disappear countless tax dollars and human aspirations, never to be seen again."[5]

But despite its limitations and fragility, the UN has throughout the years deservedly won the admiration and support of many Christian communities, the Catholic Church in particular. In the early days of its formation, Pope Pius XII described the UN as a justified response to a plea coming "from the depths and [calling] for justice and a spirit

---

[3] Jussi M. Hanhimäki, *The United Nations: A Very Short Introduction* (New York: Oxford University Press, 2008), 1.

[4] See Paul Kennedy, *The Parliament of Man: The Past, Present, and Future of the United Nations* (New York: Vintage Books, 2006), xiv.

[5] Anthony Banbury, "I Love the UN, but It is Failing," *New York Times* (March 18, 2016), online edition, *http://www.nytimes.com/2016/03/20/opinion/sunday/i-love-the-un-but-it-is-failing.html?_r=0*, accessed April 15, 2016.

of collaboration in a world ruled by a just and compassionate God."[6]
The Church was represented in the various conferences that drafted
the UN Charter and the Universal Declaration of Human Rights
(UDHR). Catholics actively participated, some even as delegates of
their nations, in the 1944 Dumbarton Oaks Washington, D.C. meeting,
the drafting of the 1945 UN Charter in San Francisco, and the drafting
of the Universal Human Rights document that was adopted in 1948.[7]

In 1964 the UN granted the Catholic Church official recognition as a
non-member state with Permanent Observer Status.[8] This status allows the Church to solicit, encourage and promote the pursuit of the
universal common good and the integral good of humanity.[9] To the
present day, the Catholic Church, both as an institution represented
by the Holy See and as the people of God through their Church-inspired nongovernmental organizations (NGOs), continues to support
and participate in UN projects and agencies. In recent times official
visits to the UN General Assembly were made by four popes: Paul VI
(October 4, 1965), John Paul II (October 2, 1979 and October 5, 1995),
Benedict XVI (April 18, 2008) and Francis (September 25, 2015).

This favorable official disposition of the Catholic Church toward the
UN has not been fully accepted with enthusiasm in every part of Catholicism. Likewise, the positive regard toward the UN officially
adopted in many instances by Christian communion leaderships has
not been totally accepted in some parts of the wider Christian community. Some Christian fundamentalists describe the very idea of the
UN as a utopian vision from which every Christian should strive to

---

[6] See John Courtney Murray, *The Pattern for Peace and the Papal Peace Program*, 4-5, Joseph Rossi, *Uncharted Territory: The American Catholic Church at the United Nations,
1946-1972* (Washington D.C.: The Catholic University of America Press, 2006), 37.
[7] Joseph Rossi, *Uncharted Territory*, 37.
[8] See, *Paths to Peace: A Contribution, Documents of the Holy See to the International Community*, (New York: Liturgical Publication in partnership with the Permanent Observer Mission of the Holy See to the United Nations, 1987), 65.
[9] See Paul VI, "Address to Holy See Representatives to International Organizations" (4
Sept, 1974), *Path to Peace*, vi.

extricate humanity.[10] Other Christians, including Catholics, wonder how a relationship with the UN, often fraught with systemic limitations and contradictions, could enrich, reaffirm or even contribute to a witnessing to Christ consciously and deliberately understood as an element in the economy of salvation—God's "plan for salvation accomplished through the Church."[11] Another group of Christian critics of the Catholic Church's UN relationship are convinced that the Church's presence in the UN is a theologically inappropriate fit and at times even an obstruction to adopting progressive decisions on issues of population, status of women and the right to choices.

In response to these concerns, this book explores and analyzes the state and role of the Catholic Church through Catholic-inspired NGO UN participation. Though it is Catholic in outlook and in its theological focus, this work can be of interest to those studying or working within other religious traditions as well as to scholars of the UN and NGOs more broadly. Catholic-inspired NGOs, as NGOs in general, work at the UN in collaboration with those of the several Christian communities, of other faith traditions and of no faith tradition whatsoever. Focusing on Catholic NGOs presents a case study of the significance of religion within social relations today, specifically the practical realities and possibilities of religious institutional participation in a major secular-political institution in the modern world like the UN.

Even though the UN is a secular organization with no common religion, its decision-making is sometimes shaped by religious values and concerns. To understand the dynamics of this paradoxical reality we must recognize "the religious actors' involvement, value and contribution as to how the UN pursues justice, peace and reconciliation on a wide range of policy issues." UN involvement of religious NGOs,

---

[10] See Joseph Loconte, "The United Nations' Disarray," *Christianity Today* (February, 2007), 1-3.

[11] Alister McGrath, *Christian Theology: An Introduction,* (Malden, MA.: Blackwell Publishing, 2007), 267.

such as those of Catholic inspiration, is one prime way that religion is visible within the UN system. Further, readers with little or no UN interest can find our work valuable as it can illustrate and exemplify a dilemma growing ever more salient in the modern world — how can students, scholars or practitioners cope with and serve in institutions doing critically important work while these institutions are burdened with structural injustice.

Though it has this wider scope, our project is nevertheless sharply focused upon Catholic-inspired NGOs, both lay and religious. These present a significant, unique way of speaking with the Church's voice and of manifesting a collaborative ministry that stamps them as authentic –though not official – representatives of the Church herself. We are of course aware that the Holy See is the authoritative and formal representative of the Church at the UN.

Holy See refers to the supreme administrative body of the Roman Catholic Church under the pope and his cabinet known as the Roman Curia.[12] It has the responsibility of discharging the duties of the Vatican State, as provided in the Lateran treaty of 1929 that recognized its sovereignty by granting it the geographical territory of Vatican City.[13] It is on account of this sovereign right that the Catholic Church enjoys in the UN the singular and unique privilege which no other religion has in its status of Permanent Observer State. In other words, the Vatican is a sovereign state and the Holy See is its government.

We also observe that many Catholics serve at the UN in various capacities as staff or as diplomats representing their countries. But these individuals do what they do as their career, and, even while graced by authentic Christian gospel-inspired motivation, they do not work

---

[12] Canon 360, 361 of the 1983 *Codex Iuris Canonici – Code of Canon Law*. See *Code of Canon Law*, Latin-English Edition (Washington D.C.: Canon Law Society of America, 1983), 130, 131.

[13] Hyginus Eugene Cardinale, *The Holy See and the International Order* (Gerrards Cross, Buckinghamshire, England: Colin Smythe, 1976), 101, 124. See also

in an official, or even quasi-official, capacity to witness at the UN for the Church out of the gospel imperative.

Focusing on NGOs, our book examines the Church-UN project considering the following questions: What theologically descriptive, normative, bases provide the impetus and sustenance for the activity of Catholic NGOs and so justify their designation as Christian discipleship? How can one evaluate the NGO's representation of Catholic interest in such a public forum? On what bases do they choose what to address and how to operate? How should their decisions and activities be critically evaluated? Can their performance, based on the theological principles justifying their participation in the UN, be improved? Is there any way that academic theology can contribute to these practical activities?

This book argues that our call as Christians to be co-redeemers of the world today includes activities on both national and international levels, as exemplified by the participation of Catholic-inspired NGOs at the UN. A call such as theirs places on these participants the complementary twin demands to support the mission of the UN and to be vocally critical against structural sin inherent in the UN system inhibiting its efficiency and efficacy. Considering salvation as a foundational notion that can be linked directly to the UN's language of peace, this work demonstrates that soteriology, 'salvation,' is the basis of the encounter between Christian *mythos* and state *mythos*.[14]

This approach finds support in the Second Vatican Council teaching that salvation is not a matter just of the human soul alone but concerns the well-being of the entire human person. This revitalized soteriology is a guarantor of human dignity, identifying everything human along with its entire history as places where God can be encountered, as places in need of God's salvation.

---

[14] William Cavanaugh, *Theopolitical Imagination: Discovering the Liturgy as a Political Act in an Age of Global Consumerism* (New York: T & T Clark, 2002, 2004 reprint), 18.

Contrary to a pre-Vatican II mentality that viewed the Church as essentially separate from, unconcerned with and thus unchanged by "the sea of temporal life," *Gaudium et Spes* (*Joy and Hope*), the Pastoral Constitution of the Church in the Modern World, proposes a Church which focuses its mission not on disembodied souls but on human persons as historical beings. This constitution affirms that "nothing that is genuinely human fails to find an echo in the hearts of the followers of Christ" (*Gaudium et Spes*, 1). This document insists that the Church is not set at odds against the world, for it is in the world that the God of history will be encountered.

In accord with the Vatican II renewal thrust, the Church's social documents have promoted enriched theological and pastoral principles that provide support for Catholic social engagement and action. This development can be explored within the context of such categories as anthropology, Christology, Pneumatology, ecclesiology, soteriology and solidarity. Each theological category now promotes a more universal, limit-breaking approach than did its previous perspectives. Anthropology is considered in terms of the whole person, his or her relatedness and historical context. Christ is understood to be beyond all institutional constraints, as is the Spirit and the Church. Salvation is recognized as open to all people and all creation, as well as a hope for all while encompassing all aspects of life. Solidarity is promoted among the unorganized masses of the poor and not limited to specific organized social groups. The developments in these categories reflect the trajectory of Vatican II and influence the broad history of Church-inspired UN NGOs.

In its all-embracing dynamics, solidarity embraces the other categories, offers us the opportunity to appreciate the contributions of NGO activities, and provides a tool to assess the fidelity of these NGOs to the articulated vision of their self-understandings. As used in this work, solidarity is to be understood more specifically as *incarnational*

solidarity[15] based on the mystery of God entering into history and becoming one like us, chastising us even while gently leading us to our
full glory. Understood in this way and as outlined above, it is solidarity that imposes on Catholic participants in the UN the complementary twin demands for visible support for the UN mission and for a
corresponding critical voice against the structural sin and systemic injustices within the UN itself.

As one example of this complementarity, these twin demands would
require a commitment to the UN struggle to eliminate world hunger
and poverty and to ensure world peace, human rights and dignity of
all people while simultaneously joining the growing clamor to democ-
ratize the UN itself – such a democratization not being a merely political project but rather a struggle for an equal and open UN access to
all people irrespective of size, color or power. Both this democratizing
struggle and the struggle against hunger and poverty are aspects of
UN ministry promoting the common good of all.

Active participation of the over one hundred fifty (150) Catholic-inspired NGOs promoting UN initiatives for alleviating the sufferings
of our time presently witnesses powerfully to the first demand of *incarnational solidarity* mentioned above. Their ministry is indeed a really effective and eloquent expression of Christian solidarity and respectful affection for the whole human family. However, as a resource
in confronting UN structural injustices, the full integration of Catholic
social teaching into Catholic-inspired NGO ministry still leaves much
to be desired. An example is a powerful yet a still incipiently used
lens through which Augustinians are learning to view their UN participation, viz., as an *empire-community* encounter.[16] By visioning

---

[15] Incarnational solidarity as used here is borrowed from Christine Firer Hinze's work,
"Straining Toward Solidarity in a Suffering World: *Gaudium et Spes* 'After Forty
Years,'" in William Madges, ed., *Vatican II: Forty Years Later* (Maryknoll, New York:
Orbis Books, 2006), 165-195.
[16] See John Szura "The Augustinians: Promoters of Justice and Peace," *Augustinians and
Promotion of Justice and Peace* (Roma: Secretariat of Justice and Peace, 2004), 8.

through this lens, they hope to confront the imperial tendencies within the UN system of unbridled self-interest, accumulation and domination, countering them with the communitarian values of development promotion, friendship and collaboration. For nations participating in global governance, their work is not a zero-sum game.

Yet a question—perhaps a dilemma—arises. At what level should Catholic Church-inspired NGOs participate in those societal institutions which are sometimes, and in some measure, responsible for inflicting the very wounds they are called upon to heal? In the face of the obvious structural weaknesses of the UN, how do these Church representatives respond compassionately in a transformative way to give proper witness to both of the complementary demands of *incarnational solidarity*? To this end, we confidently propose the paradigm of *dialogical confrontation* as an approach that responds to the obvious structural deficiencies of the UN while continuing to support those policies and programs that foster the general welfare or common good.

By dialogical confrontation we mean a prophetic presence that responds prudently and effectively to the UN defects, whether operational or structural, while engaging in UN ministry for worthy UN goals. This critique calls on Church representatives to be observant, to recognize and to challenge those elements of injustice or contradiction in the structures of the UN that may undermine the promotion of the common good. However, care must be taken to ensure that this critique transcends mere socio-political analysis and is able to decipher moments of sin and grace that do not promise any false utopian optimism.

Such a critique demands a consciousness of the paradox of grace and sin simultaneously existing in the UN with a ready and appropriate response to each. Success in this environment requires an ability to undertake a sound critical analysis, which can be accomplished only in collaboration with critical social theory. The way to achieve this is by entering into or strengthening the partnership many Catholic NGOs already enjoy with other groups in a genuine dialogical mutuality that respects all partners as bearers of God. Hence the approach is dialogical in as much as it is open to mutual conversation with the UN system and all collaborating stakeholders. It is confrontational in as much as it consistently calls the system and its collaborators to be aware of the need for a systemic change countering structural imbalances.

Ultimately, it is hoped that the paradigm of dialogical confrontation might inspire in these Catholic NGOs a critical self-reflexive engagement with their own systems. In this way we believe that dialogical confrontation in the way we suggest here not only encourage Christians to take seriously their role in the socio-political sphere but has already provided them with the 'how.' This 'how' highlights the validity of critiquing the structures of the institutions in which we participate without necessarily abandoning them. Such a critique is also extended to their own institutions. They are to search within their own systems for the presence of similar traits and to face the challenges that are raised. By "their own systems" is meant both their individual 'home' institutions and the Church as whole. As advocates for justice, the Church-inspired NGOs are to be dispensers of justice, lest they incur the biblical reproach of not removing the plank from their own eye before trying to remove the splinter from the eye of another.

This study undertakes an evaluation of the activities of Catholic Church-inspired NGOs officially recognized by the United Nations and an analysis of these activities from the dual perspectives of the United Nations and the Catholic Church. The socio-political analysis utilizes inter-disciplinary literature across history, politics and international relations, religion and philosophy in relation to NGOs and the United Nations. Undertaking a theological interpretation of NGO activities, we plan to articulate creatively and critically the theological framework and the hermeneutical basis for promoting and assessing a relationship between the Catholic Church and the UN. We plan to establish the relevance of a UN apostolate in the context of the salvific mission of the Catholic Church today. Relying upon personal interviews with individuals who have played key roles in UN-Church relations and upon the theological analyses of a spread of Catholic authors ranging through St. Augustine, Karl Rahner, Gregory Baum, Christine Firer Hinze and Richard Gaillardetz, our approach attempts to transcend sociological and historical descriptions as it constructs a theological analysis that appreciates the NGO role as a genuine Christian apostolate and confronts its challenges and limitations.

This method in its originality significantly provides a healthy link between academic and practical or lived theology. It analyzes and evaluates the way conceptual resources, normative frameworks and historical knowledge help guide moral prioritizing and energize Church-inspired NGO performance. It adds to the currently available literature in this area by undertaking a study of Christian and specifically Catholic activities in the UN. Most importantly, it is hoped that the systematic study provided here will evoke further studies on this aspect of Christian witness. The method employed here, which situates our analysis within the economy of salvation, attempts to link orthodoxy and praxis. This approach is in full accordance with recent scholarship that seeks an integral theology through a method that retains fidelity to 'creedal Christianity'[17] while rethinking tradition in a way that challenges its earlier weaknesses as it attempts a positive repositioning of the Church in its relationship with the world which the Lord has commissioned her to renew.

Brief mention should be made of some significant issues which cannot be treated fully here simply because they are outside the limits of this project. First, this book does not treat the activities of the Holy See Permanent Observer Mission to the UN, the official Catholic Church presence at this 'Community of Nations.'

---

[17] See John Milbank, et. al, eds., *Radical Orthodoxy* (New York: Routledge, 1999, reprint 2006), 2, 3.

Second, neither does it study NGOs of other Christian communities, the World Council of Churches, and/or other faith traditions in the UN. This does not in any way deny or belittle the presence of these others in the UN or their equally significant contributions in this regard. Though sometimes in this work the word "Church," often capitalized, may appear in a generic sense referring to all Christian communities, it is used here specifically with reference to the Catholic Church though without any bias.

Third, this book does not embark on a detailed historical account of the Catholic Church-inspired NGO presence in the UN. This has been studied by other works such as Joseph Rossi's *The Uncharted Territory: The American Catholic Church at the United Nations, 1946-1972* and his *American Catholics and the Formation of the United Nations* as well as Jean Gartlan's *At the United Nations: The Story of the NCWC/USCC Office for United Nations Affairs 1946-1972*.

Fourth, a detailed scholarly treatment on the UN and NGOs is beyond the scope of this work. Explored here are only those aspects of the UN and NGO nature, structure and activity that provide a sufficient framework for the main task of this project, specifically the exploration and assessment of the participation of Catholic Church-inspired NGOs.

It is important to mention too that the theological analysis offered here is not targeted at the UN itself. Its focus is rather the Catholic participants in the UN system, particularly those of the NGOs. Finally, the proposals offered here for transformative structural change pay heed to the wisdom of effective and substantial incremental change that guard against the frustrating tendency of all-or-nothing approaches identifiable with some advocacies for social and structural change. This does not take away from the radicalism of our approach characterized by its fearless and hopeful engagement with the root cause of the issues at hand, in the manner that justifies the prophetism of this aspect of Christian witnessing.

This book is divided into two major parts preceded by this introduction with its project overview including methodology, objectives, scope and limitations. The first major part deals with practical description and analysis, the second with theological interpretation and assessment. These two major parts are in turn subdivided to deal with specifics issues, the first major part embracing Chapters One and Two, the second major part embracing Chapters Three and Four.

The first major part focuses on the UN in general: its structure, agencies and projects, as well as the general understanding of Catholic-inspired NGOs and their activities at the UN.

In this part, Chapter One treats the UN specifically. It explores as succinctly as possible the history, purpose, structures and procedures of the UN and the Catholic Church's view of that organization. In this chapter the issues of the UN's weaknesses are identified as inherent within its structures, a form of structural sin, thus making our argument for an alternative model of presence that would include challenging those structures within the scope of the Catholic-inspired NGO activities.

In this part, Chapter Two examines the history and activities of the Catholic Church-inspired NGOs that enjoy official recognition by the UN. It begins with some general understanding about NGOs. Specific examples of the Catholic-inspired NGOs studied are IMCS-Pax Romana, Caritas International and the Order of St. Augustine or *Curia Generalizia Agostiniana* as it is formally known in the UN. IMCS-Pax Romana, an association of Catholic university students, illustrates the role of Catholic youth at the UN, while Caritas International models an example of NGOs that have the full support of Church authority. The Order of St. Augustine's NGO, even with a brief history of UN participation, provides insight into the role of NGOs of religious institutes of men and women in the UN and the impact this involvement has on their religious life commitment.

There are religious institutes with longer UN participation histories such as Franciscan International, Dominicans for Justice and Peace and the Congregations of St. Joseph among many others. Our choice to focus on the Augustinians is strictly based on my membership in the Order and personal involvement in its UN apostolate which indeed motivated this study.

Included in the issues treated in Chapter Two is an appraisal of the relationship between the Holy See and Catholic-inspired NGOs, which probes powerful dynamics affecting the assessment of this representation from Catholic theological perspectives.

The second major part of this book takes up a theological interpretation and assessment of the Catholic Church-inspired/UN relationship. It attempts to establish a theological basis for such a Christian encounter that justifies these activities as valid by the standards of both academic theology and Christian living.

This part pursues the following four goals: first, to articulate the various theological self-understandings that enable the Catholic-inspired NGOs to engage in this project; second, to undertake a theological assessment of the activities of these NGOs in the light of these various theological self-understandings and their articulated vision; third, to propose from this theological assessment a position that would address areas of conspicuous neglect in the work of these NGOs — that is, the brushing over of this participation in the structural injustices inherent in the UN system; fourth, to inquire how this relationship would enable the Church-inspired NGOs as other international institutions to deal with their own institutional issues at variance with their vocation to embody God's love for all.

In this second major part, Chapter Three treats in general the theological self-understandings of these Catholic-inspired NGOs and the pastoral principles for a Christian social encounter in the public arena that necessitate and justify the participation of Catholics in an international organization such as the UN. This chapter also evaluates the works of these Catholic-inspired NGOs in the light of these principles and self-understandings. The analysis takes into account our claim that this relationship is an expression of the Church's commitment to the common good and therefore participates in the economy of salvation. Finally, in the light of the dynamics of the UN system and activities, this chapter proposes that the work of these NGOs includes a constructive critique of the present structure of the UN.

The fourth and final chapter considers what is referred to here as *dialogical confrontation*, an alternative model of presence expected of the Catholic-inspired NGOs in all their varied forms of their UN participation. This chapter discusses the nature and challenges of this new paradigm. It again insists that, for Christian participation in the UN to be seen as truly salvific within the demands of *incarnational solidarity*, challenging the unjust structures in the UN system should not remain a subordinate clause but must become a constitutive part of, and a key priority in, the work of Catholic-inspired NGOs. This is based on the already identified structural imbalances in the UN system recognized here as belonging to the category of social or structural sin.

The book concludes by drawing the lessons of this model for the individual NGOs as international institutions with similar traits and constraints as the UN itself.

PART ONE
Practical Description & Analysis: The United Nations & Catholic Non-Governmental Organizations

W hile many Christians today understand Catholic Church participation in the United Nations to be obviously appropriate, some still do ask with Tertullian *quid Athenae Hierosolymis – what has Jerusalem to do with Athens?* Some Christian fundamentalists regard even the very idea of the UN to be a utopian dream supporting multilateralism and a multiculturalism that are spreading confusion among the Churches. From their standpoint, the only obligation a Christian has regarding the UN is to guard humanity against what they consider being its treacherous utopian vision "that rewards the world's most repressive governments with membership and voting privileges."[1]

Speaking specifically of human rights, especially the right to religious freedom, Joseph Loconte maintains that the UN's original sin was that it confused "inalienable human rights with social and economic

---

[1] See Joseph Loconte, "The United Nations' Disarray: The Decline of the Human-Rights Agenda, and What Evangelicals can do about it," *Christianity Today* (February 2007), 1-3.

aspirations."[2] He seeks to restore the sacred basis of human dignity by reconnecting it to a biblical view of the human person, claiming that the salvation of the human soul and mind is the only sure step towards the salvation of humanity and its society.[3] Such committed opposition may be sociologically informed, but its theological and anthropological bases lie in a resurgence of the pre-Vatican II ecclesiological attitude of "holy Church and sinful world." Further, it relies on a theology of salvation keeping sin and redemption within the narrow limits of the self-project of the individual and directing the salvific mission of the Church to the soul but not to the body. It focuses Church concern only on the heavenly—'spiritual'—without a glance at earthly, socio-political matters.

In stark contrast, the American Jesuit theologian John Courtney Murray regards the motive for the UN even from its earliest days to be a "compassionate charity" addressed to the human race which was gravely "dehumanized in its spirit and institutions."[4] This "universal love [inspiring the UN] is the apex and the most generous expression of the Christian ideal … [that] bridges the gap between us and those who have not the blessing of sharing the same faith with us."[5] Indeed, participation in the UN can positively contribute to the integral response of the Church to the call for interfaith dialogue based on mutual respect and co-responsibility.

Murray considered the UN a noble and great cause, though failing in some aspects of Catholic ethical standards, which the Church cannot deny without betraying her saving mission. In a 1946 article, the British Catholic journalist John Eppstein echoed Murray's stand as he

---

[2] Ibid.

[3] Ibid., 3.

[4] John Courtney Murray and Wilfrid Parsons, *International Co-operation* (Washington, D.C.: Catholic Association for International Peace, 1943), 2. in Joseph Rossi, *Uncharted Territory: The Catholic Church at the United Nations, 1946-1972* (Washington, D.C.: The Catholic University of American Press, 2006), 39.

[5] Ibid.

called on the European Church to support the UN initiative, adopting what he referred to as *politique de presence* or "getting into the game." To continue with the attitude of *politique de bouderie* or "strategy of grumbling," he said, would be interpreted as the Church grievously turning a deaf ear to the cries of her children.[6]

Murray's position anticipated Vatican II's expansion of the theologies of sin and redemption beyond the individual to include collective human history and structures, as well as its commitment to the Church's solidarity with "the joys and hopes, and the sorrows and anxieties of people of our time."[7] The Council observed that the Church "can find no more eloquent expression of its solidarity and respectful affection for the whole human family…than to enter into dialogue with it about all these problems."[8] This observation is based on the Council's Christological anthropology that the Spirit of God is not absent from positive modern developments.[9] It also reflects the Council's view that this is the only way the Church can bear true witness through the same Holy Spirit to Christ, who has come not to condemn the world but to save it, not to be served but to serve. It is renewed theological outlooks such as these that ground Catholic participation in the UN.

Yet history shows opinions do diverge on the position the Church should take on her relationship with the United Nations. Murray did note that Pope Pius XII's letter on post-World War II society, *The Peace Program*, suggested that the new world order could survive only if built on two indispensable pillars: "spiritual leadership and worldwide collaboration." Spiritual leadership belonged to the Pope, whose primary duty is "to illuminate the conscience of the world…"[10] By extension this responsibility would include the entire Church with the Pope and his teaching authority, though collaborative participation of

---

[6] See John Eppstein, in Joseph Rossi, *The Uncharted Territory,* 17.

[7] See *Gaudium et Spes,* 1.

[8] Ibid., 3.

[9] Ibid., 26.

[10] John Courtney Murray in Rossi, *Uncharted Territory,* 38.

others in world affairs would also be required. But at the time this letter was issued, it could be understood only in the context of the prevalent ecclesiology of *societas perfecta*, "perfect society," which posited a self-sufficient Church without whose assistance and guidance the world could not recognize the divinely willed cosmic order of things.

This ecclesiological understanding of the Church as the "perfect society" was previously evident in Pope Pius XI's *Quadragesimo Anno (Fortieth Year)*, his 1931 encyclical on the reconstruction of the social order celebrating the forty-year anniversary of the 1891 encyclical of Pope Leo XIII on the rights and duties of capital and labor called *Rerum Novarum (of Revolutionary Change)*. (*Rerum Novarum* is considered the foundational text in the history of Catholic social teaching.) Addressing a world at the point of despair, Pope Pius XI states in paragraph 7 of *Quadragesimo Anno* that "the eyes of all, as often…turn toward the chair of Peter, sacred repository of the fullness of truth whence words of salvation are dispensed to the whole world."[11] Thus, Murray claims that *The Peace Program* reserved to Catholics without sufficient justification the "rank of preeminent entitlement, the place of discrete responsibility. Catholics, because of the gift of the Holy Spirit given to the Church by Christ … were obliged to aspire to an even more unified stand, to choose an even more valiant devotion on behalf of this initiative …"[12]

This outlook was understood by the first Catholics at the UN as a mandate to hold fast to the Church's superiority over other participants. They saw their mission solely to propagate Catholic principles, particularly the Pope's principles of peace. It was to be "a crusade to

---

[11] Richard R. Gaillardetz, "The Ecclesiological Foundations of Modern Catholic Social Teaching," Kenneth R. Himes O.F.M., ed., *Modern Catholic Social Teaching: Commentaries and Interpretations* (Washington D.C.: Georgetown University Press, 2005), 72, 73, 74.

[12] Joseph Rossi, *The Uncharted Territory*, 45, 38.

catholicize the UN charter," as Joseph Rossi puts it.[13] He writes that Edward A. Conway, S.J., special correspondent for the National Catholic Welfare Conference (NCWC) to the UN conference, requested Monsignor Howard J. Carrol, general secretary of NCWC, on May 30, 1946 to appoint a full-time observer of the Catholic Church in the United States to the UN. The observer, above other things, was to make sure "that the Catholic viewpoint was advanced whenever critical issues were being deliberated and opinions requested at the appropriate United Nations agencies."[14]

There are some Catholic NGOs today that still see their UN work through this lens. So do some other Catholics at the UN, as evidenced by questions sometimes asked of Catholic NGO representatives as mentioned in this book's preface. An example of such questions is whether or not the Catholic NGOs support at the UN the pro-life agenda of the Church regarding abortion and birth control. Nevertheless, this attitude is challenged by the humble Vatican II recognition that the Church not only teaches the world but learns from it as well. As Michael Himes would say, "authentic conversation is not governed by either of the participants; it is governed by the question under discussion. This is why the conclusion of a conversation can never be premeditated."[15] Later groups of Catholic participants would insist that it is appropriate to participate in programs the UN itself initiated.

This more recent position, which is also the position of our book, is supported by Pope Paul VI's insistence that the sole aim of Church participation in international organizations such as the UN is "to solicit, encourage, and promote the pursuit of the universal common

---

[13] Ibid., xii.

[14] AMU, series 11, box 1, Conway to Carroll, [New York], May 31, 1946, 1-3, copy, quoted in Joseph Rossi *Uncharted Territory*, 1.

[15] Michael Himes, "'The Church and the World in Conversation:' The City of God and 'Inter Urban' Dialogue," *New Theology Review*, 18.1 (February 2003), 31.

good and the integral good of [humanity]."[16] The tension caused by these diverse opinions and their effect on the entire dynamic of the Catholic Church-inspired NGO relationship with the UN is treated later in this book.

Being positive and hopeful about the world outside of set Church boundaries is not the same as being naively optimistic. As Joseph Komonchak writes, this outlook "does not refrain from often quite critical remarks on imbalances and failures in the modern world and on the mistaken views of God and humans that frequently lie behind them."[17] That means seeking to "preserve an uneasy tension between affirming legitimate human endeavors and insisting on the world's need for transformation."[18]

Thus in terms of the Catholic participation in the UN it means, as proposed in our book, a dialogical confrontation in which a prophetic stance places upon Catholic UN participants the complementary responsibilities of effectively supporting the UN mission and at the same time critiquing equally effectively the structural deficiencies in the UN system that are an obstacle to its mission. In accord with these above considerations, we intend to address a theological challenge of deep importance to the Church in the modern world: How are we to interpret, justify and evaluate the United Nations participation of Catholic Church-inspired NGOs as to their integration into the salvific mission of the Church?

Summarily, the primary focus in this Part One is to set the foundation for the entire project of this book. It contains a fairly substantial

---

[16] Paul VI, "Address to Holy See Representatives to International Organizations," (September 4, 1974), *Path to Peace: A Contribution, Documents of the Holy See to the International Community* (New York: Liturgical Publications in partnership with the Permanent Observer Mission of the Holy See to the United Nations, 1987), vi.

[17] See Joseph Komonchak, "The Significance of Vatican Council II for Ecclesiology," in *Gift of the Church: A Textbook on Ecclesiology,* Peter C. Phan, ed. (Collegeville, Minnesota: The Liturgical Press, 2000), 89.

[18] Richard R. Gaillardetz, "The Ecclesiological Foundations of Modern Catholic Social Teaching," 75.

knowledge of the UN and its operations, as well as the perception and role of its Catholic Church actors, especially the Catholic NGOs. Most significantly, it highlights those structural issues of the UN that may constitute obstacles to its goal. It is these structural issues seen through the prism of the theological category of structural evil/sin that provides the basis for the theological assessment undertaken in the second part of this work.

UNDERSTANDING THE UNITED NATIONS
FROM A CATHOLIC PERSPECTIVE

T he UN was formed in 1945 with the asserted purpose of ensuring world peace and security through the nonviolent resolution of world conflicts. It is recognized as the most realistic and successful result in a series of human attempts for universal and international governance. However, the reality of the organization could still be described analogically in terms of the elephant in the ancient story of the four blind people who described one and same animal according to their various limited perspectives.

Different people, depending on their angles of experience, have perceived the UN quite differently. To some, the significant feature of the UN is the Security Council and its peacekeeping mission or the Secretary-General and his bureaucracy. To others, the UN is understood primarily as the body that advances the human rights common to everyone in the world. Many perceive it as an organization of relief and humanitarian workers responding to various calamities and consequent sufferings that afflict humanity and the environment – as a virtual union of specialized agencies and NGOs. There are those for whom it is essentially a meeting place for world leaders.

The assessment of the UN's efficacy is likewise diverse, even polarized. While some view it as the best hope for humanity, others see it as imprisoned within the "tyranny of the majority."[1] This view is in line with two poles popular with UN analysts – the idealistic and the cynical.

Among the cynics is former United States UN Ambassador Daniel Patrick Moynihan, who actually describes the UN as "the tyranny of the majority" in his scholarly article "The United States in Opposition."[2] Owen Harries, the former Australian Ambassador to UNESCO, dismisses the UN as promoting vague concepts of human rights like "the right of solidarity" and "the right to cultural identity," which he considers to be anti-western.[3] The Georgetown University Professor of Government Joshua Muravchik, in the introduction to his book, *The Future of the United Nations: Understanding the Past to Chart a Way Forward*, charges that the UN in its sixty years history is a failure and an illusion. He feared that it could be a source of much harm.[4]

But for those who sing its praises, this following observation says enough and needs no proof: if the UN did not exist, we would have to invent it. It is humanity's most visible commitment to a world of justice, peace and progress for all people of the earth.[5]

In this chapter, we undertake a study of the factual history of the UN, its operational dynamics and its potential for ensuring the common good and security of all. We trace the evolution of the UN and attempt

---

[1] See Douglas Roche, *United Nations: Divided World* (Toronto: NC Press, 1984), 8, 81, 89.

[2] *Commentary*, March 1975.

[3] Ibid.

[4] See Joshua Muravchik, *The Future of the United Nations: Understanding the Past to Chart a Way Forward* (Washington, D.C.; The AEI Press, 2005), 1, 5.

[5] Ida Urso, "The New World Order and the Work of the United Nations," A talk given at the World Goodwill Symposium. *Let the Future Stand Revealed: Envisioning the World We Choose*. New York City (October 28, 1995). 4; Ida Urso, "Let Purpose Guide the Little Wills of Men: The Spiritual Impulse Behind the United Nations," A talk at the Arcane Scholl Conference (Saturday, May 13, 1995, New York), 1.

to clarify its various structures and procedures. Because of their complexities and of the wide scope of UN operations, our limited work cannot possibly cover every detail of this mammoth organization. We are rightly limited to a concise narration that nevertheless does provide an analytical overview of the UN's specific place in global governance within its normative mandate — to ensure world peace and security. In terms of our book, this mandate means to seek "the global common good."

Our narration is made within a Catholic perspective and, to set a secure foundation for the study of Catholic-inspired NGO UN participation, it is guided by these two questions. "What lies behind the founding of such a broad and potentially powerful global organization? Why, despite much criticism, does it continue to survive and win the support of a prominent group such as the Roman Catholic Church?"[6]

History & Purpose of the UN
in the Context of the Quest for Global Governance

The quest for some form of international or global governance had consumed the heart and mind of humanity since the dawn of civilization. Against conventional presumption, this desire was not originally merely political. Historians of international relations, such as the renowned British scholar Paul Kennedy, point out that during the vast range of human history, the idea of a global federation had been considered by such thinkers as ancient Chinese philosophers, Greek sages and medieval Catholic theologians.[7]

Certain Christian political analysts would claim that this desire is built upon the relics of the Judeo-Christian dream of a peaceful world

---

[6] This set of questions is adapted from Jussi M. Hanhimäki's account of the history of the UN. See, Jussi M. Hanhimäki, *The United Nations: A Very Short Introduction* (New York: Oxford University Press, 2008), 7.

[7] Paul Kennedy, *The Parliament of Man: the Past, Present and Future of the United Nations* (New York: Vintage Books, 2007), 3.

where lion and lamb would lie down together in friendship and where nations would discard warfare. Instead, all would advance together in the way of peace under the shadow of Almighty God (Isaiah 2: 1-5; 11:7-9; 65:25). Symbolically, a plaque inscribed with this text of Isaiah is placed on the wall of a building housing UN agencies and organizations as well as civil society organizations. It is at 777 UN Plaza, across the street from UN headquarters in New York.

The Church's idea of a worldwide human community was first thematized by St. Augustine in his *City of God*. It was further developed in the philosophical and theological thought of St. Thomas Aquinas, whose medieval synthesis was a basis for the harmonious cooperation of pope and Catholic emperors. Despite not simplistically identifying state and Church with the city of earth and the city of God respectively, Augustine did hold that the visible Church and the city of God are closely interrelated. This view enabled him to focus on the institutional aspects of the Church with its universal mandate embracing all humanity — a Christian sovereignty inclusive of the citizens and nations of the entire world. This was an ideological foundation for the unification of the Papal States and the establishment of Christendom.[8]

In his work *The Parliament of Man: the Past, Present and Future of the United Nations*, Paul Kennedy notes that various disciples of Confucius and authors such as Dante, William Penn, and the Abbe de St.-Pierre, at one point or another, mulled over the proposal of "a mutual state of dependence." The call for "the United States of Europe" was advocated by Lenin. Immanuel Kant's 1795 *Perpetual Peace* also had an undertone of global fellowship. We may add to this list Arnold Toynbee, who pleaded "for a new form of an international system of affairs."[9]

---

[8] See Eric O. Hanson, *The Catholic Church in World Politics* (Princeton, New Jersey: Princeton University Press, 1987), 24-25, 53.

[9] Kennedy, *The Parliament of Man*, 3.

Irrespective of their different backgrounds, these earlier advocates of an international community mentioned in Paul Kennedy's work share some significant common characteristics in context, aspiration and approach. Most wrote either in anticipation, in the heat of, or at the end of a horrendous war. For instance, Kant wrote *Perfect Peace* on the threshold of Napoleon's raid on Europe. In their ideas, they express an aspiration for an international solution that would ensure lasting peace. Their approach can be described as critical yet optimistic. While they take into account the human proclivity to conflict and war, they also express an unwavering hope in the human capacity for peace. These characteristics are integral to the formation of the UN.

Common perspectives of these early writers regarding global governance are the intellectual framework of the Enlightenment, the rise of free trade, and the advance of Western liberalism--veritable UN cornerstones. As we read in Paul Kennedy, these thinkers did not themselves accomplish a universal monarchy or a parliament of humanity. Yet their contributions did help put in place cultural and economic movements promoting peace, tolerance and interdependence, *e.g.* the abolition of "slavery and slave trade, the emancipation of Catholics in Britain and of Jews in France and in the Habsburg Empire, and the reduction or elimination of protectionist tariffs such as the Corn Laws."[10]

Moreover, we may note their influence in some nineteenth-century successes at international legal and commercial structures to forestall international anarchy and advance economic development. Numerous examples include the 1894 formation of the Red Cross and two peace conferences at The Hague, 1899 and 1907.[11]

---

[10] Ibid., 4.

[11] Ibid., 5.

The Twentieth Century, the League of Nations, & the Birth of the UN

The closest the world came to a systematic form of a universal commonwealth before the formation of the UN was the 1919 founding of the League of Nations. The UN was built upon its ashes. Characteristic of past suggestions and steps toward structurally sustainable world peace, the League was born out of war, World War I (1914 - 1918). This worldwide conflict wreaked havoc of immeasurable economic disaster and the slaughter of millions of people. The world was ready for the League.

Indeed, the twentieth century from its earliest beginnings was faced with choosing two decisive but divergent paths: hope or pessimism — "the promise of life" and "the threat of death."[12] Along with the hope of a universal abundant life enriched by rapid scientific and technological developments, there loomed the dreaded specter of universal death emerging from those same developments. When there entered fear, hunger for power, and pride associated with the philosophical and political relationships between the "Great Powers" and other nations, the result was domination and subjection. [13]

This culminated in the Balkan conflict of 1908 when Bulgaria took advantage of the Turkish revolution to overthrow Turkish suzerainty while Austria annexed the provinces of Bosnia and Herzegovina. The manner in which this annexing occurred angered the Russians who, to make matters worse, were told by their German ambassador to "recognize it under the pain of a combined Austrian and German attack."[14] With the involvement of the "Great Powers" of Germany, Russia, France, Italy, Britain and Austria, the hostilities escalated and

---

[12] See Douglas Roche, *United Nations: Divided World*, 11.
[13] Ibid., 1.
[14] See Liddell Hart, *The History of the First World War* (London: Pan Books, 1976), 13.

expanded beyond regional boundaries to an international crisis. The subsequent result was World War I, the "Great War."

Both post-war hunger for lasting world peace and a realistic hope for its attainment begot aspirations for an international body to secure that peace through arbitration and consultation. From these initial inspirations, the League of Nations was born in 1919 under the Treaty of Versailles in order "to promote international cooperation and to achieve peace and security."[15] It became the first internationally organized and constituted association with membership open to all sovereign nations across the globe regardless of size or power. It did make some notable achievements toward global peace and mutual international cooperation. It offered new opportunities for small nations to confer with dominant powers. It also imposed accountability on the great powers, with the threat of sanctions and even dismissal in some cases.

Russia was the test case, dismissed in 1940 following its invasion of Finland. Other powers, like Japan and Germany in 1933, would withdraw on their own because of perceived threats to their imperial territories. The League also insisted on the recognition and protection of ethnic rights, and it established the first treaty on arms and ammunition when the five "Great Powers" entered into a detailed agreement to limit naval strength, regulating classes of warships, and numbers and sizes of guns.[16]

The enthusiasm for the League with its fond hopes for guaranteeing lasting peace was cut short by World War II which brought to light the League's glaring weaknesses and lack of efficiency. The collapse of the League is often conveniently attributed to the absence of great powers (The United States, Russia and Japan) and the lack of military strength to enforce its decisions. It is more realistic to cite as contributions to its failure the selfishness of nations, the triumph of national

---

[15] Paul Kennedy, *The Parliament of Man*, 6, 7.
[16] Paul Kennedy, *The Parliament of Man*, 10-12, 13, 19.

sovereignty over internationalism, and the exclusion of socio-economic and human development as priorities.

Paul Kennedy's observation lends support to this viewpoint. He writes that with the persistent "economic dislocation, ideological hatreds and primal passions" that lingered in the world, especially in Europe, neither the Locarno optimism, the 1925 treaties, a host of attempts by allies of western and eastern Europe at a post-war territorial settlement nor any global machinery could ensure the anticipated peace.[17]

Even the internationality of the League was questionable. Most of the issues it dealt with were just Eurocentric even though many nations were at the time still colonies of the Great Powers. For example, when Italy committed atrocities and even attempted genocide in Libya between 1911 and 1930[18] and later in 1934 and 1935 attacked Ethiopia, a member of the League, the super-powers were too occupied with their own domestic and imperial interests to intervene effectively.

Again, another weakness of the League of Nations was that it was hijacked by national governments which had little or no representation by, or consultation with, their ordinary citizens. Only a few civil society organizations were permitted to attend League proceedings, and then under very limited and restricted participation.[19] Unfortunately, most of the elements cited here such as selfishness of nations, triumph of sovereignty over internationalism and the limited participation of civil society remain the giant "elephants in the room" of global governance today. The UN has its share of these defects.

---

[17] See Ibid., 12.

[18] See *Arab Times*, (Thursday, September 4, 2008),1, *http://www.arab-timesonline.com/pdf08/sep/4/page%2009.pdf*.

[19] See Hilkka Pietilä, *The Unfinished Story of Women and the United Nations* (New York: United Nations, Non-Governmental Liaison Service (UN-NGLS), 2007), 1-5.

The precarious state of the world and the fear of anarchy in the aftermath of World War II renewed desires for another attempt to create a world body with the universal law to resolve major international conflicts without violence and to preserve and mobilize the human and material resources needed to address global problems.

The initiators of the UN would adopt many of the League's ideals and structures, building on its achievements while avoiding its mistakes. When initial discussions began in London in June 1941, their focus went beyond military victory in the Second World War to the consideration of the postwar future. This meant asking serious questions about the root causes of war and the enduring characteristics of genuine peace: Would we win only to live in dread of another war? Should we not define some purpose more creative than military victory? Is it not possible to shape a better life for all countries and peoples and eliminate the causes of war at its roots?

Responding to these questions, world leaders formally declared at St. James Palace on June 12, 1941: "The only true basis of enduring peace is the willing cooperation of free peoples in a world in which, relieved of the menace of aggression, all may enjoy economic and social security. It is our intention to work together, and with other free peoples, both in war and peace, to this end."[20] Significant improvements recognized since the time of the League of Nations are discernible in this resolution. There was the recognition that peace cannot be achieved without corresponding economic, human and social development as

---

[20] The meeting held in London that issued the famous St. James' Palace declaration was attended by representatives of Great Britain, Canada, Australia, New Zealand and the Union of South Africa, and the exiled Governments of Belgium, Czechoslovakia, Greece, Luxembourg, the Netherlands, Norway, Poland, Yugoslavia, and that of General de Gaulle in France. See *Basic Facts – About the United Nations*, (New York: News and Media Division of United Nations Department of Public Information, 2004), 3.

well as the willingness of nations to cooperate and support an international agenda.

As a matter of fact, promotion of social and economic progress stands out as a major difference between the League of Nations and the UN. The League only briefly referred to this progress, a priority mentioned late in its Covenant—Article 23. In contrast, the UN explicitly recognized it as a central goal and thus cited it in its preamble.[21] Likewise, the St. James Palace declaration displayed a remarkable concern for the entire world, as opposed to the League's narrow focus on Western sovereigns. But regrettably, UN reliance solely on national governments' political will and policies for its decision making would remain a major obstacle in implementing its projects –just as it was for the League.

The London resolution was solidified when United States President Franklin D. Roosevelt and British Prime Minister Winston Churchill signed the *Atlantic Charter* declaration on August 14, 1941. On June 26, 1945, the UN Charter was signed by representatives of the fifty countries present at the United Nations Conference on International Organization in San Francisco. The event was preceded by other series of meetings including one at Dumbarton Oaks, Washington, D.C. in 1944. Subsequently, the United Nations Organization was officially established on October 24, 1945, with the ratification of the Charter by the majority of its original fifty member nations, led by the P5: China, France, Great Britain, the Union of Soviet Socialist Republics and the United States of America.[22] The term P5 is frequently used in this book to refer to the five permanent members of the UN Security Council.

UN membership was and still is declared open to all "peace-loving states which accept the obligations contained in the present Charter and, in the judgment of the Organization, are able and willing to carry

---

[21] See Hanhimäki, *The United Nations,* 16.
[22] Ibid.

out these obligations."[23] There are one hundred ninety-three member nations of the UN today and two non-member states with Permanent Observer Status, namely the Holy See and the State of Palestine.[24] Details on the Holy See, which also refers to the Roman Catholic Church, are treated later in this chapter.

Ida Urso, an integrated psychologist associated with the UN, described the UN Charter's inception as the divine purpose guiding the "little wills of men [sic]."[25] Around the world, cynics and doubters, or "Armageddonites" as Urso aptly called them, were more than convinced that the San Francisco Conference had failed even before it was convened and that a third world war was imminent. It was indeed a miracle that surprised even the conveners themselves that in nine weeks the men and women delegates from fifty nations who gathered in San Francisco would be able to chisel out the ten-thousand-word UN Charter, despite their many differences.[26]

The aims of the UN are embodied in a set of purposes and principles contained in Articles 1 and 2 of the Charter. The aims are summarized as follows: "maintenance of international peace and security through non-violent means; development of friendly relations among nations, achievement of cooperation in solving international economic, social, cultural and humanitarian problems through promotion of respect for human rights and fundamental freedom for all, and to be center for the harmonization of the actions of nations in attaining these common ends."[27] The guiding principles in achieving its aims include: sovereign equality of all member states; state agreement to settle international disputes by peaceful means; assisting the UN to realize its goal and the implementation of the Charter; noninterference of the

---

[23] See UN Charter Chapter 4: 1.

[24] *Intergovernmental Negotiations and Decision Making at the United Nations* (New York: NGLS, 2003), 3.

[25] Ida Urso, "Let Purpose Guide the Little Men," 2.

[26] Ibid.

[27] *Facts About the UN*, 5.

UN in domestic matters of the member states except in the threat to or the breach of peace.[28]

Structures & Operational Procedures of the UN

A brief survey of the main UN structures (organs) will show diverse competencies, each important for attaining a peaceful world, somewhat lacking to the League of Nations. The UN at its founding was structured by the Charter with six main organs, namely the General Assembly, Security Council, Economic and Social Council, Trusteeship Council, International Court of Justice and Secretariat. These have grown to include fifteen agencies and numerous other programs and organizations. The list also includes some UN adopted specialized agencies that may be older than the UN itself, such as the International Labor Organization (ILO).

The functioning of these several structural components, whether coordinated or not, underpin UN efforts that maintain humanity's hope that threat to global peace and security would not prevail or lead to another world war. We noted "whether coordinated or not" simply to acknowledge the alleged silo mentality describing the operation of some parts of the UN system. Conceding diverse procedural processes, powers and privileges to various UN entities offers the best attempt at striking a balanced approach toward world governance for peace, development and security.

It was an arduous task to weave together the variables and intricacies of international relations to empower the UN toward these goals. The compromises and concessions necessary to achieve an effective balance still mark the modus operandi at the UN today. A brief survey of the six major UN organs shows the wisdom of attaining this balance and their challenges as well.

---

[28] Ibid.

The General Assembly is the main deliberative organ of the UN, composed of all the member states plus the non-member states with Permanent Observer status. Each enjoys equal voice and voting power. The Holy See, the official representation of the Catholic Church at the UN, maintains a non-voting Permanent Observer status. The General Assembly's many functions include considerations and recommendations related to the principles of cooperation in the maintenance of international peace and security as well as discussions of issues relating to international peace.

In being determined to see the UN succeed in deterring any threat of another war and recalling the League of Nations' failure to prevent the carnage of World War II, the founders of the UN vested the Security Council with immense power in dealing with violations of peace. Its functions include the maintenance of international peace and security in accordance with the principles and purposes of the UN, facilitating peace negotiations among disputing members and favoring measures not involving armed power, such as sanctions, to enforce its decisions.

The Economic and Social Council (ECOSOC) functions as the central forum for addressing international economic and social affairs and for the formulation of policy recommendations addressed to member states and the UN systems. It initiates and produces studies, reports, and recommendations on international issues such as economic, social, cultural, educational and health matters. It promotes respect for, and the observance of, human rights and fundamental freedoms.[29]

The Secretariat serves as the hub around which all the other principal UN organs work. It administers their programs and policies, with duties as varied and complex as the UN systems and the world problems themselves. Some of the varied Secretariat responsibilities include "administering peacekeeping operations, mediating international disputes, surveying economic and social trends, preparing studies on

---

[29] Ibid., 11.

human rights and sustainable development, informing the world's communications media about the work of the UN, organizing international conferences on issues of worldwide concern, interpreting speeches and translating documents into the UN's official languages."[30]

The International Court of Justice is the judicial arm of the UN charged with the duties of settling disputes within the principles of international law as may be referred to it by member states. It also provides legal advice to the UN organs and specialized agencies.

Lastly, the Trusteeship Council saw that territories and colonies are protected. This UN organ also helped them to achieve independence and self-determination. Following the October 1, 1994 independence of Palau, the last UN trust territory, the Trustee Council suspended its operation on November 1, 1994.[31]

The assessment of UN activities in the light of its mandate to ensure world peace, security and development will bring to light some of the strengths and weaknesses of UN structures that make advocacy for systemic change a constitutive part of NGO UN participation.

Assessment of the UN

The years of the UN's history tell an ambiguous tale, a mix of success and failure. The success comes in the ways it has acted as a moral force in dangerous times. The UN has mediated peace among disputing member states, stationed peacekeeping forces in warring nations, inspired post-conflict reconstruction in some of these nations and brought many guilty perpetrators to justice. It paved the way and facilitated the dismantling of colonialism and the independence of many countries. The UN response in time of crisis cannot be measured. Imagine how many displaced people would have been left

---

[30] Ibid., 14-15.

[31] *http://www.un.org/en/mainbodies/trusteeship/*, accessed March 22, 2016.

unaided if there were no UN relief agency. Through its High Commission for Refugees (UNHCR), the UN has provided shelter and care for more than thirty-four million refugees driven out of their homes by war, famine, natural disaster and persecution. Also, in the recent crisis in Syria, over two hundred thousand displaced people were cared for by the *United Nations Relief and Works Agency* for Palestine (UNRWA)[32] in about eighty schools. Even in the thick of the conflict the UN still sought opportunities for humanitarian services negotiated between the warring parties. Some may comment, and rightly so, that it is better to prevent a war than to provide relief. But though the UN may not have prevented a war, it still deserves commendation for bringing warring parties to the negotiation table more effectively than any other organization or world power.

Several UN entities operate throughout the world providing for people in need, especially for children and the disadvantaged. Prominent examples include the UN Development Program (UNDP), the UN Children's Fund (UNICEF) and other kindred programs and agencies such as the World Health Organization (WHO) and the World Food Programme (WFP), a joint program of the UN and the Food and Agriculture Organization (FAO). These and similar organizations of the UN system have responded promptly and efficiently in times of world crisis. We may recall the 2004 tsunami, the 2005 Hurricane Katrina, the 2008 Nargis cyclone, the 2010 Haiti earthquake and the 2011 Japanese earthquake and tsunami.[33] Also, the UN International Atomic Energy Agency (UN IAEA) continues to monitor and regulate the acquisition and use of nuclear power. It might not be out of place to

---

[32] The *United Nations Relief and Works Agency* for Palestine was formed by "United Nations General Assembly resolution 302 (IV) of 8 December 1949 to carry out direct relief and works programmes for Palestine refugees, following the 1948 Israeli-Arab conflict." *http://www.unrwa.org/who-we-are*, accessed March 22, 2016.

[33] See John Traub, *The Best Intentions: Kofi Annan and the UN in the Era of American World Power*, (New York: Picador, 2007), xii-xiii. For more on these natural calamities see Emeka Christian Obiezu, *Towards a Politics of Compassion: Socio-Political Dimensions of Christian Responses to Suffering* (Bloomington, Indiana: AuthorHouse, 2008), 3-4.

celebrate the recent agreement signed with Iran for its nuclear power project.

Through its varied specialized agencies like the International Labor Organizations (ILO) and the NGOs, the UN raises concern over the scandalous contrasts of our time: the deep chasms between social development and human exploitation, between the outlandish wealth of the few and the dire poverty of the many, and between the dream of the common good and the reality of environmental degradation.

With its commitment to the Millennium Development Goals (MDGs) in the year 2000, the UN General Assembly charted the path toward world peace through sustainable and integral development. The eight goals referred to as "Millennium Development" were to cut the worst of poverty and hunger in half by 2015, to achieve universal primary education, to promote gender equality, to reduce by three-quarter the under-five child mortality rate, to reduce by three-quarters the maternal mortality rate, to halt and reverse the spread of HIV/AIDS and malaria, to ensure environmental sustainability and to develop a global partnership for development.

At the end of its fifteen-year timeline, the MDGs were replaced in September 2015 by another development program, the Sustainable Development Goals (SDGs). This program, with its seventeen goals and one hundred and sixty-nine targets, is a clear demonstration of the UN's renewed commitment to achieving peace through sustainable development. These and other economic and social agendas set by its ECOSOC as well as the International Criminal Court's prosecution of key actors in the most violent conflicts are evidence of the organization's dogged commitment to eliminate poverty and mass murder.

It is also to the credit of the UN that thus far none of the national or regional conflicts or wars has escalated into another world war. Contributing to this achievement is an array of multiple efforts. According to a UN information source, this world body provides food to one hundred eight million people in seventy-four countries, vaccinates forty percent of the world's children thereby saving two million lives a year, fights climate change, leads a campaign to plant a billion trees a year, helps three hundred million rural poor in the last thirty years to achieve better lives, mobilizes seven billion dollars in humanitarian aid to help people affected by emergencies, leads international efforts in clearing landmines in over thirty countries and promotes universal primary education reaching eighty-eight percent enrollment coverage in developing countries.[34]

As noted above, the UN system had also been engaged in the intense, rigorous process of drafting and negotiating further sets of sustainable development goals as replacement for the MDGs that expired in 2015. The process was built on the MDG successes and strengths while it learned from, and improved upon, their limitations. The outcome of this process known as Agenda 2030 with its robust ambition of "leaving no one behind" was adopted by the General Assembly on September 25, 2015. By stating in the first sentence of its preamble that it is a plan of action for people, planet and prosperity, Agenda 2030 expands the concept of development beyond economic growth to sustainable development and also incorporated social and environmental protection.[35]

On December 12, 2015, at the United Nations conference on climate change in Paris, the UN recorded another milestone for our generation and for later ones in keeping the world safe from the threat of climate change. The conference, 2015 COP21, also known as 2015 Paris Climate Conference, restructured the politics characterizing the over 20 years of UN negotiations on climate change to achieve a legally

---

[34] See UN card of its activities, *www.un.org.*

[35] *Transforming our world: the 2030 Agenda for Sustainable Development,* A/RES/70/1 Resolution adopted by the General Assembly on 25 September 2015, *http://www.un.org/ga/search/view_doc.asp?symbol=A/RES/70/1&Lang=E,* accessed March 22, 2016.

binding and universal agreement on climate so as to keep global warming below 2°C.[36]

Another monumental step taken by the UN to save lives and ensure people have the opportunity to realize the fullness of their potential is the September 19, 2016 UN Summit in New York on the Large Movement of Refugees and Migrants. Irrespective of the visible imperfections pointed out by many advocates on behalf of migrants and refugees, the Summit and its outcome document "The New York Declaration for Refugees and Migrants"[37]do demonstrate the desire of world leaders to save lives, protect rights and share responsibility on a global scale. Most important among its many suggestions is the call for a commitment and to "start negotiations leading to an international conference and the adoption of a global compact for safe, orderly and regular migration in 2018."[38] The Global Compact on Migration (GCM) has at this time of writing passed the last stages of the intergovernmental negotiation and undergoing the last processes leading to its adoption at the International Conference on Migration in Marrakesh, Morocco, December 10-11, 2018.

The 1948 Universal Declaration of Human Rights (UDHR) stands out as a stellar UN achievement and a most welcome turning point in the long history of human striving for global peace and security. Regardless of some noticeable weaknesses in its language that would signal a Western bias in its formulation, this foundational document affirms fundamental human rights, equal rights for men and women, and the dignity and worth of the human person. It lays down obligations of governments to take action and to refrain from interfering in critical specified areas of rights, freedoms, and obligations of individuals and groups. Some ways by which the UN enforces the promotion of

---

[36] *Paris Agreement, http://unfccc.int/files/meetings/paris_nov_2015/application/pdf/paris_agreement_english_.pdf.*

[37] "New York Declaration for Refugees and Migrants," September 19, 2016, *https://refugeesmigrants.un.org/sites/default/files/a_71_l1.pdf.*

[38] *https://refugeesmigrants.un.org/declaration.*

human rights, such as its "Right to Protect" (R2P) program, affectively abolishes Article 2(7) of the charter (non-interference in domestic affairs) and interferes in the internal affairs of oppressive regimes.

The continued relevance of the UN is obvious given the complex nature of global issues. World problems are simply too overwhelming for any one single government or country to handle. The UN offers the world the necessary space and opportunity for countries—irrespective of their size, wealth or might—to express their agreement or disagreement in a free environment promoting global collaboration to deal with threatening global issues day after day. Counter to claims that the UN limits sovereignty, activities among countries at the UN demonstrate and affirm sovereignty. Only a recognized sovereignty can belong to the UN as a member state. In fact, the UN is the instrument of the sovereign member states. They use the UN to achieve their intended purposes and so have created it and have given it support.

The UN acts only when its member states agree that it should and then determine the means they want it to act. Moreover, the mandate of all the UN system is to work with and serve governments. Though these parts of the UN system could and often do solicit the collaboration of other stakeholders such as the NGOs, neither their mandate nor their accountability are owed to these other collaborators. They are rather owed to the member states.

That the list of UN achievements is long and impressive is not in dispute. Nevertheless, not to acknowledge the limitations of UN activities is tantamount to denying obvious modern human realities. This is something both critics and supporters of the UN would agree upon. It is certainly a complaint having some truth that our world today has known unacceptable levels of fighting, less security and more terrorism, less unity and more disunity than before the UN was created. The UN was recently taunted by some people I encountered during my work there that it prefers the world the way it is because only a chaotic world justifies the UN's existence, especially with respect to its peacekeeping mission.[39] While the presence of one hundred sixteen thousand UN peacekeepers currently in seventeen operations on four continents is a real achievement, yet it may give credibility to such mocking as cited above.

Many people, especially critics of the UN, would observe that after saying "never again" to genocide at the end of World War II, the UN sat and watched helplessly as unspeakable carnage struck in Bosnia, Somalia, Rwanda, Darfur, and the Democratic Republic of Congo.[40] The Middle East crisis, exemplified by violence in Syria and the on-and-off Israeli-Palestinian confrontations, is still raging. The people of Central African Republic, South Sudan, and Ukraine have known little peace recently. Terrorism, increasing in sophistication and metamorphosing into different forms, continues to pose serious threats to global peace and development.

This is why for James Traub, journalist and contributor to New York Times Magazine, the famous sculpture of a gun with its barrel twisted into a knot is a symbol of UN powerlessness and incompetence in the face of human atrocities and natural disasters.[41] Top UN actors have expressed deep regret for not being able to do more. In his recent memoir, Kofi Annan named some situations he wished he could relive so as to do things differently, for example, the Sudan-Darfur conflict.[42]

The world has experienced more disparate economic development, more exploitation, more hunger, more suffering, and more death since 1945 than before.[43] Unfriendly border policies have resulted in the deaths of huge numbers of refugees and immigrants. Over one and a

---

[39] Author's interview in 2012 with a Haitian volunteer with the UN during the Haitian earthquake 2010.

[40] See Joshua Muravchik, *The Future of the United Nations*, 26-34.

[41] John Traub, *The Best Intentions*, xi.

[42] Kofi Annan, *Interventions: A Life in War and Peace* (New York: Penguin books, 2013).

[43] See Ida Urso, "The New World Order and the Work of the United Nations," A talk given at the World Goodwill Symposium. *Let the Future Stand Revealed: Envisioning the World We Choose*. New York City (October 28, 1995). 5.

third billion people live in abject poverty. Only ten percent of the world population participates fully in the civic institutions that determine their lives. Every year close to one and a half trillion dollars goes to military spending.

Accordingly, the Stockholm International Peace Research Institute's April 2014 Fact Sheet states that 2013 global military spending was one thousand seven hundred fourteen billion US dollars.[44] Though this represents a remarkable fall from the one trillion dollars in 2008 according to Anup Shah's study, yet the rate of this spending is actually on the rise in the most dangerous and vulnerable regions of the world. Moreover, an astonishing gap separates the fortune that countries spend on weapons and the pittance it would take for them to alleviate poverty and promote economic development. Most astonishing is the discovery that smaller countries struggling with economic crisis are among those that spend the largest sum in military and weapons, with a 5.9 percent increase among the top two small country spenders, Algeria and Angola.[45]

Considering all this, we can perhaps agree with Ida Urso "that our world is neither just nor at peace, and progress for all the peoples of the earth, as the UN Charter promises, is at best a remote dream."[46] Can we not then further ask why an international organization intended to be an international instrument for peace through non-violent means would allow under its watch more money to be squandered on military spending than for improving socioeconomic conditions of people across the globe? But conversely, perhaps we should more properly wonder why the UN is blamed for so much of this in the first place. Should there not be a redirection of the question. Maybe the real question should be how these sad realities come about

---

[44]"Recent trends in military expenditure,"http://www.sipri.org/research/armaments/milex/recent-trends (May 2014), retrieved July 26, 2014

[45] See Anup Shah, "World Military Spending," *Global Issues* (March 1, 2008), *http://www.globalissues.org/article/75/world-military-spending.*

[46] See Ida Urso, "Let Purpose Guide the Little Men," 3.

from the states themselves rather than from UN failure and negligence. How then can we accurately measure and justifiably assess the UN role in the pursuit of world peace and security? Our book explores these vital issues.

Many have blamed the UN's failures in preventing wars on its reluctance to employ coercive means in the pursuit of peace or to use any form of intimidation to enforce its laws. People like Dore Gold, former United States ambassador to the UN, identify this as the "UN's inability, or refusal, to recognize and boldly confront evil."[47] But by its very composition, the UN is not supposed to take arms or to encourage its use in resolving world issues. To act that way would self-negate a core component of its own *raison d'être*. The causes of perceived UN failures involve more than the claims alleged above. They rather lie in the very dynamics entrenched in the UN at its foundation. They are the politics governing UN operations. Appreciating these elements demands an understanding both of UN institutional dialectics and the challenges of continuous changes in the global governance environment.

Dynamics of the UN Structure & Operations: Their Strengths & Weaknesses

Seriously considering critics like Dore Gold, who claim that UN structural flaws date back to that organization's beginning, we can appreciate their viewpoints on inherent structural dialectics in the UN system despite those critics' political and ideological underpinnings. Even the most vocal UN supporters at least partially agree with them, for example, Thomas Weiss and his group of researchers, who make some relevant observations in their UN-sponsored publication

---

[47] Dore Gold, *Tower of Babble: How the United Nations has Fueled Global Chaos* (New York: Crown Forum, 2004), 8.

series.[48] They discuss a few items such as the role of member states in UN affairs, the structural imbalance of the organs of the UN system especially in that organ directly charged with the maintenance of peace and security. They also note the divergence between the way that the UN hopes to achieve peace and the expectations of people for this cause.

A prerequisite to approaching these issues is to keep clear the precise difference between government and governance and where the UN fits in. The UN is not a world government. It is in no way like a sovereign state government with ruling powers and privileges. It was not intended to be a world state nor would any of the world's states wish it to be. No nation is willing to support any external authority they could not control or significantly influence. This reality by far predates the UN, as state sovereignty was essential to any early attempt at global governance. Global governance is the collective management of global transnational issues without the trappings of formal government. Thus, the UN as an agency of international governance is a network of independent states exerting some global governance without in any way being itself a government. Following its constitution, the UN enjoys a defined level of autonomy, yet it never escapes the direct influence of its key stakeholders – the member states. Also, their collaboration is necessary for anything to get done.

---

[48]With support of some funding agencies and with UN sponsorship, some eminent scholars undertook academic research focused on the UN system. Their research was published in a collaborative series coordinated by Thomas Weiss, the distinguished scholar of international relations and global governance with special expertise in the politics of the United Nations. Outcomes of this research include: Thomas G. Weiss, David P Forsythe, Roger A. Coate and Kelly-Kate Pease, *UN and Changing World Politics* (Boulder, CO.: Westview Press, 2014); Richard Jolly, Louis Emmerij, and Thomas G. Weiss, *UN Ideas That Changed the World* (Indianapolis: Indiana University Press, 2009); Thomas G. Weiss, Tatiana Carayannis, Louis Emmerij, and Richard Jolly, *UN Voices: The Struggle for Development and Social Justice* (Indianapolis: Indiana University Press, 2005).

Global governance should also be distinguished from what has come to be known as international regime – "a set of shared principles, norms, rules, and procedures for governing or managing an issue."[49] Principles, norms and rules may be legal, diplomatic, informal or tacit. Procedures refer to the work of NGOs and States. The importance of this clarification is enormous as it conditions our expectations of the UN and our accurate evaluations of its competence, its successes and its failures, especially when we become more aware of the influence of the member states in the UN programs and agendas. In terms to be explained immediately below, the second UN can do only what the first UN wants, asks, supports, and funds it to do. As the old saying tells us, he who pays the piper calls the tune.

Without a clear understanding of the underpinning politics of the UN and global governance, it is inevitable to lay blame where there is no fault at all. This brings us to the issue of the states' role in UN life and activities. Weiss and colleagues propose that the UN be understood in a tripartite form, in what they call the "first, second and third UN." The first UN refers to the member states; the second UN refers to the Secretariat, and the third UN refers to the other actors such as civil society and the private sector.[50]

The face of the UN seen around the world is the second UN—the Secretariat. Yet the rights and responsibilities to make UN policies belong to the first UN—the states. But what of the third UN? The reference to "we the people of the united nations" in the UN Charter Preamble is interpreted from time to time to mean that the people own and thus should direct the UN. But according to UN scholar Leland M. Goodrich and Norwegian statesman and twenty-fifth President of UN General Assembly Edvard Hambro, the major purpose of this insertion was to "emphasize that the Charter is an expression of the will of the peoples of the world and is primarily concerned with their

---

[49] Weiss, et.al, *The United Nations and Changing World Politics*, lxi.
[50] Ibid.

welfare."[51] Even so it may still be overoptimistic to think that this insertion demonstrates a significant departure from previous international covenants, particularly that of the League of Nations, which recognized only states or their governments as parties to such instruments.[52]

Representing the will of the peoples of the world and being concerned about them does not necessarily imply that the world's people own or direct the UN. In fact, Weiss and his group note that this phrase of the Charter may not refer to the world's people at all. "The people" in the phrase could refer to the people who represent the states at the UN.[53] The preamble is very clear on this, as it concludes by acknowledging that it is governments alone that make the decisions at the UN though they do so through their representatives. This is a vital point needing to be thoroughly clear.

The will of the people which member states represent is often couched in the language of national interest and framed by those politicians who assume the responsibility of national leadership. The term "national interest" can be manipulated. It can mean the interest of the people of the nation. It can mean the interest of the state. It can mean the interest of the government in power. It can even really mean the personal interest of political leaders. In many instances, states have valued and pursued protection of their government to the neglect of the basic needs of their citizens, a tendency widespread in recovery models offered by many states in response to the current global economic crisis. The UN in all its magnificence is thus revealed as the interplay of different foreign policies and internal politics of member states and their representatives who call the tune and chart the

---

[51] Leland M. Goodrich and Edvard Hambro, *Charter of the United Nations: Commentary and Documents*, 55.

[52] Ibid.

[53] Weiss, et.al, *The United Nations and Changing World Politics*, lxi.

directions of the organization. This is how UN politics and policies are directed and unfold.

Countries exert their influence on the UN not only by their political maneuvers at negotiations but also by how they respond to the decisions, signings, ratifications and adoptions of resolutions, treaties, conventions and other UN decisions. Their responses depend on the nations' political leaders. Even the amendment of the UN Charter depends on these leaders. Conversely, another way that countries influence the UN is by whatever they do within or across their borders that then become a problem for the UN to deal with. This is the case even when countries act without a UN mandate—which is how they more frequently operate.

An additional way that state interest exerts influence on UN policies or its response in the face of a threat to peace and security comes from rights of sovereign states to intervene in the international community. An example of this is what is called the Right to Protect (R2P). This right is a basis for collective action in response to genocide, war crimes, ethnic cleansing and against humanity. Called for or permitted by the UN, it can override a state's right of nonintervention if that state is unwilling or unable to protect its citizens from mass atrocities or is itself their perpetrator.

It is true that sometimes some particular UN officials have a key role in decision-making. Yet in most cases these roles are either simply persuasive or they are the execution of a delegated responsibility such as the right given to the Secretary-General to recommend topics of state discussions through reports that form the work of the General Assembly per annum. Other examples would be the duties of some UN agency leaders to take on issues appropriately assigned to their department. Nevertheless, in general, the face of the UN seen around the world is that of civil servants of the UN—the Secretariat—"the second UN," implicitly employed by the states—the "first UN." Though the

UN Secretariat employs its staff, yet we can still say these are implicitly employees of the member states served by the Secretariat.

While states are represented at negotiations by diplomats, the power to act and the positions they maintain come from their capitals. Sometimes diplomats are even upstaged during negotiations by a capital representative, as revealed by the recently declassified UN Rwanda's cables. This must be understood within the complex interplay of sovereignty, national interest and territoriality. Thus included on the list of the diplomatic challenges of country delegates at the UN are: determining how to interpret instructions, when and how to revise them if need be and in very rare and extreme cases when to disobey such instructions.

The response to Rwanda by nations like the United States was influenced by an earlier experience in the region, when the United States lost helicopters and about eighteen soldiers in Somalia.[54] These losses made Congress and the White House far less willing to send and maintain forces in Rwanda. The recently declassified UN cables on the crisis published by the New York Times on June 24, 2014 showed the frustration of then-US UN Ambassador Madeleine K. Albright unsuccesfully trying to convince Washington that exiting Rwandan UN peacekeeping would put the US on the wrong side of history. In this following statement, she captured her reality and that of other delegates: "I was an instructed ambassador, not the secretary of state, but I do wish I had argued harder."[55] As we look back in history, people like Tom Blanton, director of the National Security

---

[54]Michael R. Gordon and Thomas L. Friedman, "Details of U.S. Raid in Somalia: Success So Near, a Loss So Deep," *New York Times* (October 25, 1993), *http://www.nytimes.com/1993/10/25/world/details-of-us-raid-in-somalia-success-so-near-a-loss-so-deep.html?pagewanted=all*, accessed March 23, 2016.

[55] Mark Lander, "Declassified U.N. Cables Reveal Turning Point in Rwanda Crisis of 1994," *New York Times* (June 24, 2014).

Archive at George Washington University, noted "the pull out of peacekeeping as the green light for the Rwandan genocide."[56]

A similar outcome was repeated in the situation in Syria and the Central African Republic, where United States allies, still recovering from their involvement in Libya, became unwilling to commit to force in Syria or the Central African Republic. Such events as these will continue to determine the politics within the UN and how it responds to issues. This analysis is why Weiss and his group recognize that politics outside the UN -- the first UN" – is utterly decisive for understanding "the second UN." It is likewise crucial that civil society organizations – "the third UN" – appreciate this in their advocacy directed to the UN policies.

The interplay and sometimes resulting gap between "the first" and "the second UN – the member states and the Secretariat – is exemplified in the enormous difference between Kofi Annan's document with recommendations for remaking the UN, i.e., his High Level Panel (HLP) report entitled "a more secure world: shared responsibility" and the far different outcome document of the 2005 San Francisco II Conference.[57] The HLP focused on known facts of the world's reality for its recommendations for a more secure world. Unfortunately, the Conference outcome document authored by the member states paid little attention to the facts but rather was determined by what these states considered politically right at the moment. "The first UN" trumped "the second UN."

Nevertheless, balancing of power between "the first UN" and "the second UN" still must take into account guarding solidarity against protectionism so that the global solidarity promoted by the UN does not slip into the "deterritorialization" and "reterritorialization" tendencies underlining current globalization. Antonio Negri and

---

[56] Ibid.

[57] Thomas G. Weiss, et.al, *The United Nations and Changing World Politics* (Philadelphia: Westview Press, 2010), 123

Michael Hardt use the terms "deterritorialization" and "reterritorialization" in their work *Empire* to refer to a historical imperial attitude now prevalent in supranational tendencies of multinational corporations where "the center is everywhere, and the circumference is nowhere." [58]

The UN might assume such an imperial paradigm if it is invested with unregulated power over all territories. When such is the case, we destroy a strong pillar of the UN — the identity of nation states. Necessary balance can be struck by taking seriously the insight of Pope Pius XII's warning against "the fatal drive of private interest and collective selfishness exclusively intent on the assertion of [nations'] own rights and ignoring those of others." [59] It is this drive that is responsible for some to consider UN resolutions tentative — merely provisional recommendations that nations can unilaterally rescind whenever these are no longer to their advantage. It is for "the third UN" — civil society — to see and to unmask the persistent imperial tendencies of the "big powers and economies." To confront these imperial manipulations is a proper role and a unique value of the NGOs. Neither the member states nor the UN staff can so properly live up to this challenge.

The immense power that the UN founders vested in the Security Council to deal with violations of peace has revealed a structural flaw in its responsibility to protect humanity from violence. The Charter states in Article 24, "In order to ensure prompt and effective action by the United Nations, its Members confer on the Security Council primary responsibility for the maintenance of international peace and security and agree that in carrying out its duties under this

---

[58] Antonio Negri and Michael Hardt, *Empire*, 5. This expression, "the center is everywhere and the circumference is nowhere," is courtesy of Mary Jo Leddy's representation of Negri and Hardt's thoughts.

[59] Pius XII, *Summi Pontificatus, 'On the Unity of Human Society,'* (1939), #76.

responsibility the Security Council acts on their behalf."[60] This is complemented by Article 25, which is meant to ensure the loyalty and compliance of all member states toward Security Council decisions. "The Members of the United Nations agree to accept and carry out the decisions of the Security Council in accordance with the present Charter."

The structural flaw is not an issue regarding the immense power of the Council as such but with its composition and procedural privileges contrary to equitable, universal participation in decision-making. This may limit the legitimacy and authority of the UN as well as its efficacy in attaining its stated goal of ensuring a stable world order free of violence, war, poverty, and oppression. The politics of self-interest and moral relativism that frequently underlie the Security Council's decision-making processes have resulted in a sometimes-pathetic response to global crises that have escalated into conflicts and other human rights violations. The root Security Council defect is the privilege of permanent membership and veto enjoyed by the five countries considered victors of World War II. That several states and regions as well as non-government agents are not properly represented in their various degrees compounds the problems. For instance, there is no representative of African, Latin American or Arab regions among the permanent members with veto power. In stark contrast to other UN organs, civil society presence or participation in Security Council meetings are very rare and restricted.

One of the greatest challenges the UN founders faced was how to balance national sovereignty with internationalism, especially in protecting the national egoism of the two emerging super powers at that time—the United States and the Soviet Union—while ensuring their commitment to the new world order. The drafters of the Charter provided a solution to this challenge by introducing the privilege of

---

[60] See UN Charter, Chapter 5, Article 24, in Leland M. Goodrich and Edvard Hambro, *Charter of the United Nations: Commentary and Documents*, 120.

permanent Security Council membership with veto power as the bait to lure the support and protection of the political, military and economic superiority of the World War II victors—the United States, the Soviet Union, the United Kingdom, China and France. These nations are the "P5" of the UN. The bait was costly indeed. It meant permanent membership in the most important UN organ with the right to forestall any decision that any one of the P5 felt would be against their interests.

The concessions and compromises that the UN founders made to the P5 would ripple in different ways throughout the entire Charter. For example, Chapter Seven, Article 51 of the UN Charter concedes that "Nothing in this present Charter shall impair the inherent right of individual or collective self-defense if an armed attack occurs against a Member of the United Nations, until the Security Council has taken measures necessary to maintain international peace and security."[61] While any member of the UN can invoke this article of the Charter, yet an understanding of this provision with its full consequences may reveal it as selectively granting the P5 a comprehensive privilege that removes any hint that the new organization would weaken their right to self-defense. This has resulted in the greater number of times those five nations have invoked this section as justification for waging war, as in the US invasion of Iraq in 2003 and the Russian invasions of Georgia in 2008 and Crimea, Ukraine in 2014.

These very privileges have become an anachronism in the present geopolitical scene. The recent agreement that restricts Iran from building a nuclear weapon was made between Iran and the five permanent members of the Security Council plus Germany with the help of the European Union showing that the present structure of the UN Security Council is or may not be sufficient today. These same privileges are also cited as one of the UN's greatest weaknesses. The General Assembly has the convening power involving all the member states and

---

[61] See UN Charter, ch.7, art. 51; also Paul Kennedy, *The Parliament of Man*, 39.

operates on the principles of one state one vote. Yet its decisions in most cases are not binding on members as is the case with those of the Security Council.

While UN membership is purportedly open to all "peace-loving" nations, the Charter in a later clause limits the right of admittance of any nation to the recommendation of the Security Council.[62] This constitutes one of the inherent contradictions in the UN system, allowing it to be easily manipulated by the P5. The prerogative of the veto makes it impossible for states perceived as threats to any of the super five to be admitted as a member state of the UN. The decision that a state is peace-loving may not depend on tangible evidence but on the opinion of any of the P5. It resumes prerogatives enjoyed by these nations in the nineteenth and early twentieth centuries that enabled them to delay or withhold the independence of their colonies. In order for entities like Palestine, Hong Kong, and Taiwan to be recognized as states and accepted as members of the UN, a change in this section of the Charter would first be necessary. For instance, United States of America has made clear its determination to veto Palestine's quest for UN membership.

Sometimes we encounter a school of thought holding that a critical look at the veto is often exaggerated and accords that privilege an unnecessary significance. It claims that the veto is only the ability to say 'No" with no capacity to control the UN or gain the positive endorsement of the veto-holders policy by the UN. Further, this position maintains that less attention should be paid to the significance of the veto since vetoes have timelines that demand of countries exercising a veto to rescind its position after a certain period. Moreover, this position cites several countries which subsequently became UN member states after being blocked from UN membership once or twice by veto. This argument is employed hoping that sooner or later the US would withdraw its opposition to Palestinian UN membership.

---

[62] UN Charter, Article 4 (2).

It could be further noted that no P5 member vetoed the 1966 Charter amendment that increased the Security Council to ten non-permanent members, allowing for African regional representation. Of course, one can rightly argue that the veto can be used as a threat to force a positive support, though this could rarely happen. Yet the fact that this privilege, exercised by a few and at times motivated by self-interest, has been used to slow down or prevent a UN response to particular issues still makes the veto problematic and warrants a sufficient and constructive criticism. As we maintain in this work, this legal right is both anachronistic and imperial in character. This is one reason we believe and demonstrate in this book that advocacy for the review and amendment of the UN Charter should be a necessary constituent of Christian UN apostolate. It is a policy change that those advocating for justice and peace should endorse.

Another way the power, structure and privileges of the Security Council have become an obstacle to UN goals is the exercise of the power of definition. Whatever the Security Council declares to be a threat to international peace and security is by that very fact a threat to international peace and security Whatever the Security Council does not so declare, is not such a threat. There is as yet no agreed upon definition of terrorism, nor is there any unified plan among Security Council members to combat it.

Darfur was a glaring example.[63] It is noteworthy that it was the threat of veto as well as politico-economic individualism that rendered the Security Council and the UN itself incapable of achieving consensus on the Darfur conflict and impotent to intervene swiftly and effectively. This was due to the economic interests in Sudan of two permanent members—China and Russia. China had interests in Sudan's oil

---

[63] Weiss et.al, *The United Nations and Changing World Politics,* 178

and both China and Russia were major merchants to Sudan of conventional weapons.[64]

While many civil societies, NGOs and independent representatives of other international communities pronounced the Darfur case "genocide," the UN did not recognize that conflict as such. In its January 31, 2005 report on the state of the Darfur conflict, the UN claimed that, while there were mass murders and rapes of Darfur civilians, they could not label the atrocities as "genocide" because "genocidal intent appears to be missing."[65] Yet later, on July 14, 2008 the UN, through the International Criminal Court (ICC), would indict Omar al-Bashir, the President of Sudan, on ten criminal charges, including three counts of "genocide."[66]

It is absurd that the five permanent members of the Security Council are among the top nine possessors of the over twenty-five thousand different kinds of the world's nuclear weapons. Thus, we may ask how we can continue to entrust the security of the world to the five nations that have the most weapons of terror. Because of situations like this, some, even dictators such as Muammar Al-Qadhafi, the erstwhile Leader of the Revolution of Libya, dubbed the Security Council "the terror council" or "security feudalism"[67] and saw it as a manipulation by the powers which use the UN to achieve separate or joint economic and socio-political interests. The privileges of permanent membership and the veto continue to demand that the weaknesses of the UN be evaluated. How can the only organ of the UN whose

---

[64]*China's Involvement in Sudan: Arms and Oil." Human Rights Watch.* 2007-12-23. *http://www.hrw.org/reports/2003/sudan1103/26.htm,* accessed, 12/11/09.

[65] Report of the International Commission of Inquiry on Darfur to the United Nations Secretary-General, United Nations, 25 January 2005.

[66] *"Darfur genocide charges for Sudanese president Omar al-Bashir". Guardian. http://www.guardian.co.uk/world/2008/jul/14/sudan.warcrimes1?gusrc=rss&feed=worldnews,* accessed, 12/11/09.

[67] See *The African Executive,* "64th UN General Assembly Speeches," *http://www.africanexecutive.com/modules/magazine/news.php?id_news=76&id_news_main=6&magazine=257,* published 09/24/2009, accessed, 12/11/09.

decisions are binding on all member states, the one with the sensitive and important responsibility of protecting world peace, be allowed to continue operating with these inherent structural deficiencies? These and other structural issues are treated in more detail in our last chapter. There we study them from the perspective of structural sin and how they should impact Christian UN participation viewed from the dialogical confrontation proposed in this book.

The question that bothers many Christians, especially Catholics as identified in the introduction of this book, is why with all its defects and structural deficiencies the UN still wins the admiration and support of a great religious community such as the Church. It is important for the sake of this work to seek an understanding of the Church's perspective on the UN. This is a prerequisite to exploring Catholic-inspired NGO UN participation.

The United Nations in the Catholic Church's Perspective: From Early Days of its Formation to Present

The point made earlier in this chapter that the search for an international commonwealth was not initiated by politicians is again validated by the remote role of the Church in the formation of the UN. In 1939, very early in World War II and well before a call for an international body occurred politically, Pope Pius XII referred to a new world order of international cooperation as a necessity for dealing with immediate and post-war issues. The Pontiff's experience as a trained diplomat with a comfortable knowledge of this world's power for better or for worse enhanced his appreciation of the tragedy of war and of the need to find a way forward to peace.

The American Jesuit, Joseph Rossi, wrote an insightful account of early roles played by the Church in the formation and operation of the UN. His work, entitled *Uncharted Territory: American Catholic Church at the United Nations, 1946-1972,* described the history of the American Catholic Church at the UN. Rossi appreciated the influence of Pius

XII on the formation of the UN and cited as influential for the UN's establishment his encyclical *Summi Pontificatus* (*On the Unity of Human Society*) and his Christmas messages of 1939, 1941 and 1942. These pronouncements influenced key UN players, both Catholic and secular.[68]

According to Rossi's evaluation, the Pope's contribution to the early formation of the UN came in two ways. First, he stated the need and called for universal support of a new world order; and secondly, he laid out principles upon which this order should be structured to ensure peace. *Summi Pontificatus* foresaw the impending World War II in apocalyptic and Christological terms as *"end-time."*

This same eschatological concept of *end-time* has also been employed by some Christian fundamentalist in their attack on the UN, calling for Christian disassociation from this world body. These fundamentalists consider the UN as the anti-Christ, the sign of the worldwide empire at the end time mentioned in the *Apocalypse (Revelation of John)*.

Theology will most likely have to contend with this interpretation from time to time. Indeed, it belongs to the very nature of theology that its themes and concepts will be ever open to varied interpretations and applications within the Church and among splinter groups such as sects and cults.

John Courtney Murray's interpretation of World War II follows the lead of Pius XII. He sees Jesus being crucified again and "a chill darkness [was] covering the face of the earth." This provided a Christological connection, linking Christ and his crucifixion with all human beings and with the whole of creation which was about to be "dehumanized in its spirit and its institutions"[69] by the unfolding calamitous event. Should she turn away from this reality, the Church

---

[68] See Joseph S. Rossi, *Uncharted Territory: American Catholic Church at the United Nations, 1946-1972* (Washington D.C.: Catholic University of America Press, 2006).
[69] See John Courtney Murray, *The Pattern for Peace and the Papal Peace Program*, 4-5, in Joseph Rossi, SJ, *Uncharted* Territory, 37.

would fail in her mission. It would be tantamount to abandoning Christ on the Mount of Calvary.[70] Therefore, all Christians were called to see the idea of an international order aimed at restoring peace to the world as a noble and necessary mission worthy of support.

In his November 10, 1939, response to Haiti's new minister, the Pope once again alluded to the urgency of a new world order, using the same argument based on the natural solidarity of our common humanity and universal love. "The human race is bound together by reciprocal ties, moral and juridical, into a great commonwealth directed by the good of all nations and ruled by special laws which protect its unity and promote its prosperity."[71]

Pius XIIs' Christmas Eve homilies, beginning with December 24, 1939, as well as his Pentecost message of 1941, enumerated five principles in support of a genuine peace in the new world order. These are known as the "papal peace program" and include

> the right of all nations to survival and independence that must respect national borders as inviolable; universal renunciation of violence as a solution to war and the search for peace; recognition of freedom of religion and the irreplaceable values of religious and moral principles; to redress the League of Nations' failure to meet the just demands and rights of nations and racial minorities; and the recognition that these principles and demands for peace are based on the natural order of justice and universal love.[72]

The importance of economic justice for all was also strongly emphasized in most of these messages. He denounced as evil the hoarding of natural resources that would deny some nations of the world equal and fair access to the world's wealth. By designating the weakness of the judicial system under the League of Nations as a reason for its

---

[70] Ibid.

[71] ACAIP/ANCWC, A Papal Peace Mosaic, "Response to the New Minister of Haiti, November 10, 1939," 35, Rossi, 49

[72] Rossi, *Uncharted Territory*, 30-33.

inability to forestall the wanton breaking of its treaties leading up to World War II, he expressed the need for a Security Council and provided support for it.[73]

Despite all this, many would still agree with the 1963 German playwright Rolf Hochhuth, who used his play *The Deputy* to accuse the Pontiff of doing little or nothing to stop the war.[74] They claimed that these interventions were expressed in a typical *vaticanesis* tone.[75] This expression suggests that these statements were broad and general, couched in a rather overly manner and elaborate style that was out of touch with reality--as some would still describe Vatican documents of even the recent past.

Without delving into a comprehensive assessment of the Pontificate of Pius XII, including the issues surrounding his response to the persecution of Jewish people during World War II, and concentrating on the scope of this book, we would argue that there is enough evidence provided by Rossi's interpretation and other sources to confirm Pius XII's influence on the formation of the UN and, even more so, his criticism of World War II and the trends and events that led to it.

The Pope's words had an important effect on the disposition of Catholics of his time toward the UN. The designs and strategies that his statements envisioned were an invaluable Christian model for peace. They also formed a systematic and substantive body of thought that encouraged the development of favorable Catholic positions toward the UN and a post-war order.[76] In the United States, they inspired the Peace Program of the nation's bishops and the establishment of their UN office, which Rossi refers to as a direct response to

---

[73] Ibid., 33.

[74] See Rolf Hochhuth, *The Deputy* (New York: Grove Press, Inc., 1964), in Kenneth D. Whitehead, "The Pope Pius XII Controversy," *The Political Science Reviewer*, Volume XXXI, (2002), 284 of 283-387.

[75] Kenneth Whitehead, "The Pope Pius XII Controversy," 284.

[76] Rossi, *Uncharted Territory*, 30-33.

the Pope's request for long-term Christian solutions to the perils of the world.[77]

In Europe, they engendered the UN support of Christian journalists like John Eppstein, who in 1946 wrote an article for a British journal that encouraged the Catholic hierarchy to accept the UN Charter. He called on the Church to adopt what he refers to as a *"politique de presence"* or "getting into the game," suggesting that a UN withdrawal was unworthy of the Church even if that world body did not conform to each and every norm of Catholic ethics. In fact, to withdraw would be tantamount to *"politique de bouderie"* or "a strategy of grumbling" that would be interpreted as turning a deaf ear to the cries of the children of the Church.[78] This is an explicit allusion to the Pope's apocalyptic and Christological reference to World War II and the need for a Christian response to the call for a new world.

Above all, as we shall later discuss, the Pope's words were the impetus for the activities of the early Catholic Church-inspired NGOs which took the Pope's message as an injunction to "Catholicize" the UN.

Pius XII also impressed some politicians of his time. This is evident in the language of the Atlantic Charter declaration and related correspondence of United States President Franklin D. Roosevelt. The 1941 *Atlantic Charter*, a joint declaration of war and peace between Great Britain's Winston Churchill and President Roosevelt, had a reflection of almost every issue the Pope had mentioned in his 1939 Christmas Eve allocution. This joint declaration even concluded with a religious tone. Apart from disarmament, the treaty acknowledged the importance of spiritual incentives for the pursuit of the end of the war and assurance of an enduring peace.

---

[77] Ibid.

[78] See John Eppstein, in Joseph Rossi, *The Uncharted Territory*, 17.

President Roosevelt's letter to Archbishop Edward Mooney of Detroit, on December 24, 1941, two weeks after the Japanese attack on Pearl Harbor, calling for support for the new world order, highlighted Christ as its basis, just as the Pope did. The President referred to "the establishment of an international order in which the spirit of Christ shall rule the heart of men and women."[79]

The impact of the Pope was not limited to religious audiences alone. The *New York Times* editorials on Christmas day 1941 and 1942 recognized the singular contribution of Pius XII particularly through his Christmas Eve messages towards ensuring a "real new order," one based on "liberty, justice and love." These editorials acknowledged the pontiff as "a lonely voice in the silence and darkness enveloping Europe" and described his "peace program" as richer than the *Atlantic Charter* in advocating an end to all national monopolies of economic wealth.[80]

In its 1941 Christmas day editorial, the *New York Times* wrote, "...as we realize that he is about the only ruler left on the Continent of Europe, who dares to raise his voice at all. The last tiny islands of neutrality are so hemmed in and overshadowed by war and fear that no one but the Pope is still able to speak aloud in the name of the Prince of Peace."

At this time, there were other voices that would agree with these contributions of the Church and support the Pope particularly in addressing World War II issues. In 1944, the great Jewish physicist Albert Einstein delivered the same message. "Being a lover of freedom, when the Nazi revolution came in Germany, I looked to the universities to defend it, but the universities were immediately silenced. Then I looked to the great editors of the newspapers, but they, like the

---

[79] See ANCWC, National Welfare Conference: United States Government: Department of State: 1941-1944, Roosevelt to Mooney, [Washington, D.C., December 24, 19941, Joseph Rossi, *The Uncharted Territory*, 34.

[80] See "The Christmas Editorials," *Catholic League for Religious and Civil Rights,* online edition, *http://www.catholicleague.org/pius/nyt_editorials.htm.*

universities were silenced in a few short weeks. Then I looked to individual writers ... they too were mute. Only the Church," Einstein concluded, "stood squarely across the path of Hitler's campaign for suppressing the truth ... I never had any special interest in the Church before, but now I feel great affection and admiration ... and am forced thus to confess that what I once despised, I now praise unreservedly."[81]

Apart from the influence his words exerted on the founders and principal actors in the formation of the UN, Pius XII made a direct attempt to register the Church as a member of the UN as well. In 1944, he reportedly inquired of United States Secretary of State Cordell Hull about the conditions and possibilities of the Holy See becoming a member state of the future UN. Hull apparently responded in the negative saying, "the Vatican would not be capable of fulfilling all the responsibilities of membership."[82] One such responsibility mentioned earlier in this chapter one is the obligation to contribute to the military security unit of the UN.

Other Roman Pontiffs followed Pius XII with their supportive statements on the UN. This began with his immediate successor Pope John XXIII, whose praise of the UN Universal Declaration of Human Rights is repeatedly echoed in later documents of Catholic social teaching. Not only did the Pope devote a significant section of his 1963 encyclical *Pacem in Terris* (*Peace on Earth*) to acknowledging the timeliness of the United Nations and its achievements,[83] he also recognized the Universal Declaration as reflecting Catholic principles and natural law theory.

---

[81] See Margherita Marchione, "The Truth About Pope Pius XII," *Catholic League for Religious and Civil Rights,* online edition.

[82] James Crawford, *The Creation of States in International Law* (Oxford: Clarendon Press, 1979), 152-161.

[83] See John XXIII, *Pacem in Terris,* (1963), 142-145.

MILLENNIUM DEVELOPMENT GOALS (MDGS)	CATHOLIC SOCIAL TEACHING (CST)
MDG 1—Cut the worst of poverty and hunger in half	Human dignity, solidarity, subsidiarity and universal destination of goods
MDG 2—Achieve universal primary education	Truth, Freedom and Human Dignity
MDG 3—Promote gender equality	Truth, human dignity and common good
MDG 4—reduce by three-quarter the under-five child mortality rate	Justice, love and solidarity
MDG5—Reduce by three-quarters the maternal mortality rate	Truth, love, human dignity and common good
MDG 6—Halt and reverse the spread of HIV/AIDS and malaria	Human dignity, freedom, and common good
MDG 7—Ensure environmental sustainability	Human dignity and common good
MDG 8—Develop a global partnership for development	Subsidiarity, human dignity, freedom and common good.[84]

Catholic UN participants recognized a similar harmony between the eight UN Millennium Development Goals and basic principles and concerns of Catholic social teaching. Brian Scarnecchia and Terrence McKeegan illustrated this parallelism in a chart that relates each Millennium Development Goal (MDG) to particular elements of Catholic social teaching (CST). Their schematic is briefly summarized in the preceding chart.

---

[84] See D. Brain Scarnecchia and Terrence McKeegan, "The Millennium Development Goals: In the Light of Catholic Social Teaching," *International Organizations Research Group: White Paper* no. 10 (September 04, 2009): 93 of v-95. *www.c-fan.org/docLib/20090904_IORG_W_Paper_Number10.pdf.*

John XXIII issued two great encyclicals on Catholic social teaching. The first was his 1961 *Mater et Magistra* (*Mother and Teacher*), a significant updating commemoration of Pope Leo XIII's 1891 *RerummNovarum*. The second, directed at unversal peace in truth, was his 1963 *Pacem in Terris* (*Peace on Earth*).

Both encyclicals encouraged a healthy Christian participation and dialogue with others in a neutral organization such as the UN. Writing on the possible relations between Catholics and non-Catholics in social and economic affairs, the Pope affirms their possibility and productivity and at the same time sets out cautions that must be observed. This hope is grounded upon natural law principles, the universality of reason and operative honesty. "On such occasions," the pontiff writes, "those who profess Catholicism must take special care to be consistent and not compromise in matters wherein the integrity of religion or morals would suffer harm. Likewise, in their conduct, they should weigh the opinions of others with fitting courtesy and not measure everything in the light of their own interests. They should be prepared to join sincerely in doing whatever is naturally good or conducive to good."[85]

Pacem in Terris sees this participation as a moment of discovering and adhering to the truth and cautions that such a venture not be abandoned on account of a history of past failure, stressing that "what was formerly deemed inopportune or unproductive, might now or in the future be considered opportune and useful."[86] This orientation differs from the nineteenth and early twentieth-century ecclesiology wherein the Church, conceived of as "holy and spotless," looked at the world disdainfully as sinful and incapable of solving its problems without looking up to the Church. Ascertaining its self-sufficiency and possession of all of the resources for the fulfillment of her mission, the

---

[85] *Pacem in Terris*, 157, and also in *Mater et Magistra*, (1961), 239.
[86] *Pacem in Terris*, 159, 160.

Church then did not consider such mutual and free participation in a secular institution necessary.

This particular teaching of the two encyclicals, *Mater et Magistra* and *Pacem in Terris*, is important for the theological reflection undertaken in the second part of this work. It provides the ground for the case made in our proposed alternative model of participation for Catholic-inspired NGOs at the UN, namely the dialogical confrontation. The model calls for a genuine collaboration of Catholic participants with colleagues of other faiths or of no faith at all. In such a way, theology intersects with contemporary social theories as they advance the common good of all, especially in empowering a constructive criticism of the UN systemic deficiencies in its structures.

On April 6, 1964, the Holy See took a bold step in the direction of this positive evaluation of the UN by establishing a Permanent Observer Mission to the UN in New York.[87] Before we proceed, some brief comments about the Holy See would be helpful. We take for granted that it is generally known that the Holy See is the authoritative and formal representative of the Church at the UN. *Holy See* refers to the supreme administrative body of the Catholic Church under the pope and his cabinet, known as the Roman Curia.[88] It has the responsibility of discharging the duties of the Vatican State as provided in the Lateran treaty of 1929, which recognized its sovereignty by granting it the geographical territory of Vatican City.[89] It is on the basis of this sovereignty that the Catholic Church enjoys in the UN the singular and unique privilege that no other religion has in its status of Permanent Observer State.

---

[87] See, *Path to Peace: A Contribution of the Holy See to the International Community* (New York: Path to Peace Foundation, 1987), 65.

[88] Canon 360, 361 of the 1983 *Codex Iuris Canonici – Code of Canon Law*. See *Code of Canon Law*, Latin-English Edition (Washington D.C.: Canon Law Society of America, 1983), 130, 131.

[89] Hyginus Eugene Cardinale, *The Holy See and the International Order* (Gerrads Cross, Buckinghamshire, England: Colin Symthe, 1976), 101, 124.

There is a divergence of opinion regarding this status and how the Church came to enjoy this favor. Some maintain that the Church was invited through the then Secretary-General, U Thant while others hold that the Church applied for acceptance. Considering UN Charter procedure for becoming a member state, it seems more plausible that the Church simply made application. Apart from the Holy See's Mission, there is no other source to confirm that the UN sought or offered the Holy See this relationship. Some people took John Paul II's remark that "Pope Paul VI initiated the formal participation of the Holy See in the United Nations Organization, offering the cooperation of the Church's spiritual and humanitarian expertise" to mean that the Holy See invited itself to the UN. This claim is equally supportable.[90]

As this issue is not a major concern of our book, it suffices to say that the historical controversy—whether the Holy See was invited by the UN or it invited itself to participate in the organization— is not of great importance to us nor does it merit the attention some critics have given it. The theological significance of this new development, the assumption of the permanent observer status in the UN, far outweighs the political or historical details. Considering that this took place barely a year and six months into the Second Vatican Council, it demonstrates the Church's acceptance of a renewed theological self-understanding that will reposition her to the world in service of the common good of global humanity for the cause of justice and peace.

As Pope Paul VI later declared, albeit not speaking of the UN specifically but of international relations in general, this relationship is sought "to solicit, encourage and promote the pursuit of the universal common good and the integral good of [humanity]."[91] This is based on the realization of the Church's interrelatedness and mutual responsibility with the world, within a "vision of a human family created and

---

[90] See "The Catholic Church at the United Nations: Church or State?" 3.
[91] See Paul VI, "Address to Holy See Representatives to International Organizations," (4 September 1974), Path to Peace, iv.

sustained by the love of its maker and called in Christ to a communion of lasting justice and peace."[92] For the same reason, Church officials do not consider this participation a privilege but a matter of duty which must be carried out respectfully and confidently.[93]

Subsequently, beginning with Paul VI, recent popes have made personal appearances at UN Headquarters and on occasions addressed the General Assembly. In many of these instances, the various pontiffs have lauded the mission and successes of the UN, though not without drawing attention to its deficiencies. Paul VI, in his address to the 20th Session of the General Assembly of the UN, praised the labor and sacrifice, even to the point of death, which illustrious men and women of the UN had endured for the cause of peace in the world.

More importantly, he singled out the promotion of human solidarity as the major achievement of the UN, describing it as a goal and mission that helps make the world one human family, a reflection of God's plan for humanity. "This is the finest aspect of the United Nations; it is its most truly human aspect; it is the ideal that mankind dreams of on its pilgrimage through time; it is the world's greatest hope; it is, we presume to say, the reflection of the loving and transcendent design of God for progress of the human family on earth a reflection in which we see the heavenly message of the Gospel."[94]

In a significant gesture that signaled the dawn of a new era in Church-world relations, Paul VI in the same address referred to the UN as a "great school of learning" in which all participants, implying even Church members, are students. He said, "…. The United Nations is the great school… and we are today in the Assembly Hall of the school. Everyone taking his place here becomes a pupil and also a teacher…"[95] This is another expression of the humble recognition by

---

[92] *Gaudium et Spes*, 2, 3.

[93] See Agostino Cardinal Casaroli, *Paths to Peace*, iii.

[94] See Pope Paul VI, "Address to the 20th Session of the General Assembly of the United Nations," (Oct. 4, 1965), 26, *Paths to Peace*, 5.

[95] Ibid., 9

Vatican II that the Church must not only teach but also learn from the world. This is based on the appreciation that the world has something to offer, for the spirit that inspires, permeates and blesses the Church with grace is also at work in the world (*Gaudium et Spes*: 11; 22).

We read the same in John Paul II's remarks on the UN and other documents of his papacy. He was fondly referred to as the "Pope of the UN" because of his several visits there and his open support for it. He often gave the UN credit for its promotion of human rights and for ensuring respect for the rights of nations, their cultures and particular models of development.[96] Pope Benedict XVI continued the same papal support, as is evident from his visit to the UN and his various interventions recognizing its many accomplishments. In his April 18, 2008 General Assembly speech, he recognized "the founding principles of the Organization – the desire for peace, the quest for justice, respect for the dignity of the person, humanitarian cooperation and assistance" as expressing both "the just aspirations of the human spirit, [and] the ideals which should underpin international relations."[97]

Pope Francis has taken the same line in reiterating the Holy See's esteem and appreciation for the United Nations as an indispensable means of building an authentic family of peoples. In a 2014 audience with Ban Ki-Moon, the UN Secretary-General, and some top UN officials, Pope Francis recognized the effort of the UN "to ensure world peace, respect for human dignity, the protection of persons, especially

---

[96] See John Paul II, "Address to the United Nations," (1979), 7, 9, 11; *Sollicitudo rei Socialis*, 26; "Address to the 50th General Assembly of the United Nations," (1995), 2; "Messages for the World Day of Prayer for Peace," (1980), 7; (1998), 1; (1999), 2; *Centesimus Annus*, (1999), 21. Most of these addresses can be found in the *Paths to Peace: A Contribution, Documents of the Holy See to the International Community*, (New York: Liturgical Publication in partnership with the Permanent Observer Mission of the Holy See to the United Nations, 1987).

[97] See Benedict XVI, "Address of His Holiness Pope Benedict XVI to the 62nd session of the United Nations General Assembly 95th plenary meeting New York, 18 April 2008," *http://www.holyseemission.org/Pope%20Benedict%20XVI%20GA%20English.html.*

the poorest and most vulnerable, and harmonious economic and social development." This same recognition was echoed by Pietro Cardinal Parolin, Secretary of State in his address to the 69th Session of the UN General Assembly September 29, 2014.

On September 25, 2015, Pope Francis addressed the 70th session of the UN General Assembly, recognizing the organization's enormous efforts towards the universal common good, global peace, development and wellbeing all. He echoed his predecessors' acknowledgment of the UN as "the appropriate juridical and political response to this present moment of history, marked by our technical ability to overcome distances and frontiers and apparently to overcome all natural limits to the exercise of power."[98] Building on that history, he remarked, "The history of this organized community of states is one of the important common achievements over a period of unusually fast-paced changes."[99] At the same time, he called for concrete actions on climate change, social justice and armed conflict.

Despite this positive view of the United Nations, the popes have made known and often reminded the organization that the noble aims for which it was founded remain yet to be achieved, and so they have challenged the UN to rise to its ideals. Paul VI pointed out many of the inhibiting factors: the lack of authority to carry out its goals, the growing tendency towards nationalism, states' non-compliance with UN policies, and the failure to consider the common good, especially of those most threatened by hunger and injustice.

To remedy these defects, the Pope recommended an increase in the authority of the organization, structural readjustments, a constructive reassessment by the total body, and a recommitment of individual member states. Addressing the UN General Assembly, he main-

---

[98] *Pope Francis, "Address of His Holiness Pope Francis to the General Assembly of the United Nations" (September 25, 2015) http://www.holyseemission.org/contents/statements/statements-56054736193b87.20279259.php, accessed March 27, 2016.*
[99] Ibid.

tained, "Your courage and your work impel you to study ways of guaranteeing the security of international life without recourse to arms. This is an aim worthy of your efforts; this is what the peoples of this world expect of you; this is what you must achieve. And for this, unanimous confidence in this institution must increase, its authority must increase; and this goal, one may hope, will be attained..."[100]

John Paul II believed the internal issues affecting the UN could be solved only if the organization readjusted its operational dynamics to rise from the merely functional to become a moral center where all nations truly feel welcomed and served so that they may then serve others. To this end, he suggested the use of "family" in its liberating qualities as an appropriate metaphor for the organization.

The family metaphor emphasizes virtues that counteract the present ills of self-interest, inappropriate use of power, lack of mutual trust, inequality and partiality. Addressing the 50th UN General Assembly in 1995, he said, "The United Nations Organization needs to rise more and more above the cold status of an administrative institution and to become a moral center where all the nations of the world feel at home and develop a shared awareness of being, as it were, a 'family of nations'. The idea of 'family' immediately evokes something more than simple functional relations or a mere convergence of interests. The family is by nature a community based on mutual trust, mutual support and sincere respect. In an authentic family, the strong do not dominate; instead, the weaker members, because of their very weakness, are all the more welcomed and served."[101]

The Pope also recommended greater cooperation of non-governmental organizations with the UN since the work is so enormous that no single institution can carry it out successfully and effectively. Pope Francis' address to the UN brought key elements that are seminal to

---

[100] See Paul VI, "Address to the United Nations General Assembly," 11.
[101] See John Paul II, "Address to the 50th UN General Assembly," 14.

the task we have undertaken in this work both in substance and process. In his words, "Beyond these achievements, the experience of the past 70 years has made it clear that reform and adaptation to the times is always necessary in the pursuit of the ultimate goal of granting all countries, without exception, a share in, and a genuine and equitable influence on, decision-making processes.

The need for greater equity is especially true in the case of those bodies with effective executive capability, such as the Security Council, the financial agencies and the groups or mechanisms specifically created to deal with economic crises. This will help limit every kind of abuse or usury, especially where developing countries are concerned."[102] Considering the place and importance of papal statements and magisterial teachings in the activities of Catholics including the UN project, these points are vital to our book. Together they lend a strong voice to a new form of relationship that awakens in the Roman Catholic participants the need to balance their support of UN activities with a compassionate challenge to the defects in the UN's structures.

It is the blending of these two aspects of UN participation that this book promotes in its call for dialogical confrontation as an alternative paradigm. Therein our unique project has its theological justification. The criticisms by these recent popes, especially regarding UN structure, will prove critical for the development of our position later in this work. We hold that Catholic NGOs must seek an alternative model of participation in the UN that would enable them to call the UN to the consciousness of these structural ills and take steps to redress them. Again, we find that alternative model in a dialogical confrontation that helps the Catholic participants hold together the two equally important aspects of their UN mission – collaborating with the UN in its programs and challenging its structural ills.

---

[102] Pope Francis, Address of His Holiness Pope Francis to The General Assembly of The United Nations."

The history and dynamics of the Holy See, the official representative of the Catholic Church in the UN, is not the focus of this work. Yet it is relevant to our project to mention that, from the very inception of the office of the Permanent Observer Mission in 1964 to the present, the Holy See has made a series of contributions through submissions that have left a lasting influence on the world's attempts to eradicate suffering and foster an enduring peace in the world. These contributions span areas as varied as environment and development, human rights, natural disaster reduction, population and development, social development, women, human settlements and food and disarmament. They have been documented in the various publications of Path to Peace Foundation.[103] Nevertheless, these achievements do not by any means deny that aspects of Holy See-UN relationship need improvement, especially in the light of the project of our work.

Conclusion

The story of the UN treated in this chapter is simply a story of the "human race groping towards a common end, a future of mutual dignity, prosperity, and tolerance through shared control of international instruments."[104] It represents the best humanity has attained in this regard. It remains as valid and relevant today as it was in 1945. Like every other human project, it is a product of evolutions, metamorphoses, and experiments, with tales of setbacks and advancements, failures and successes. It may sometimes be guilty of using a lot of words that have no meaning or, if they do, have no follow up. Yet at most

---

[103] See *Serving the Human Family: The Holy See at the Major United Nations Conferences* (New York: Path to Peace Foundation, 1997). Also for further readings on the Holy See and the Popes' addresses to UN and international organizations see André Dupuy, ed., *Pope John Paul II and the Challenges of Papal Diplomacy: Anthology (1978-2003)*, (New York: Path to Peace Foundation, 2004); *Path to Peace: A Contribution of the Holy See to the International Community* (New York: Path to Peace Foundation, 1987); André Dupuy, ed., *Words that Matter: The Holy See in Multilateral Diplomacy, Anthology (1970-2000)*, (New York: Path to Peace Foundation, 2003).

[104] Paul Kennedy, *The Parliament of Man*, xv.

times its words have helped shape the world positively and in many ways: conflict mediation, war prevention, and global mobilization to support the needy.

From the Augustinian socio-theological perspective, even with the best of government "to a greater or lesser degree, rulers no less than their subjects are fallen creatures driven by the lust for power."[105] We have seen from our brief survey, the UN too, though it sets out to minimize the power of conflict in society, is liable to be, and is in fact infected with the vices which it seeks to control. We recall the words of Kofi Annan.

> *While purposes should be firm and principles constant, practice and organization need to move with the times. If the United Nations is to be a useful instrument for its Member States and for the world's peoples in responding to the challenges [of our time], it must be fully adapted to the needs and circumstances of the twenty-first century... Its strength must be drawn from the breadth of its partnerships and from its ability to bring those partners into effective coalitions for change across the whole spectrum of issues on which action is required to advance the cause of larger freedom.*[106]

The Catholic Church recognizes the special role of the UN in global governance and in varied ways continues to accompany the organization in the quest for global peace and security through a common commitment to the protection of the common good of all human persons and the entire creation.

To make the UN viable and realistic is the responsibility of "the people" of the United Nations, indeed all of the people, seasoned believers as well as doubters whose will and concerns it is established to pursue. As Eleanor Roosevelt reminded the people of her day, "the United Nations is a piece of machinery, and the people of the world

---

[105]. R. A. Markus, *Saeculum: History and Society in the Theology of St. Augustine* (New York: Cambridge University Press, 1988), xx.
[106] See Kofi Annan, *In Larger Freedom,* 57.

must choose to make it work."[107] Again, the former Secretary-General of the UN, the late Boutros Boutros-Ghali once said, "We-all of us-are the United Nations. The UN is...what we choose to make it."[108] There are no groups more strategically poised to undertake this responsibility than those of civil society – "the third UN."

The call to make the UN work also makes the case for an alternative model of civil society participation, especially for participants that are inspired by the Catholic Church. The model proposed here is dialogical confrontation – enthusiastic support of the UN program while challenging the systemic structural issues hindering its goals.

---

[107] See Eleanor Roosevelt in Ida Urso, "Let Purpose Guide the Little Wills of Men," 3.
[108] See Boutros Boutros-Ghali's Message in the UN50 Press Kit, cited in Ida Urso, "Let Purpose Guide the Little Wills of Men, 3.

2

HISTORY & ACTIVITIES OF
CATHOLIC CHURCH-INSPIRED NGOS
IN THE UNITED NATIONS

A mong the pool of non-governmental organizations (NGOs) at the United Nations that identify themselves as religious, spiritual or faith-based are those of the Catholic tradition. We attempt in this chapter to explore the distinctive features of Catholic Church-inspired NGOs, especially in relation to their UN participation.

There are many studies on the nature and role of NGOs both in general and with respect to their UN relationship. Still our work will take special care to present selected aspects of well-known facts about NGOs, even though we may go somewhat beyond our scope and concerns. However, identifying the general nature and extent of NGO UN activities benefits those with little experience of UN NGOs, and it sets a useful framework for the exploration and assessment of the UN participation of specifically Catholic Church-inspired NGOs.

This chapter therefore begins with the nature and activities of the modern NGOs in general and in particular their UN role in ensuring global solidarity for the promotion of the common good, which is understood in UN terms as world peace, security and development. We will focus on how their UN participation advances an alternative identity of transparency and stewardship of the world that challenges the structural injustices, corruption and irresponsibility of governments and institutions—including the UN itself.

Nature & Role of Non-governmental Organizations in the UN

Due to their diverse purposes and approaches, NGOs are complex and seem ambiguous, particularly in relation to other aspects of the UN.

To their supporters, these NGOs are honored as the voice of the voiceless, "counterweights to authoritarian state power and exploitative multinationals."[1] To their detractors, they are distrusted as arrogant and overly judgmental groups, too quick to defend the cause of the "little guys" and to criticize authorities unfairly. Nevertheless, neutral observers would acknowledge that they give the UN confidence that its programs reach their desired targets—grass-roots communities, especially those of the world's poor and disadvantaged. Further, they keep the UN up to date with realities on the ground. However, they may be perceived, NGOs remain a vital force in the life of the UN and deserve attention.

Understanding the Concept NGOs

The term "NGO" encompasses a large group of organizations with diverse histories, values, ideologies, identities, objectives, and ways of acting.[2] Most broadly used, the term includes every private institution, both for-profit and nonprofit. In a narrower sense, the term refers

---

[1] Daniel Bell and Jean-Marc Coicaud, "The Ethical Challenges of International Human Rights NGOs," *Policy Brief* (a publication of the United Nations University), November 9, (2006) ,2.

[2] See Carolyn Stephenson, "Non-Governmental Organizations (NGOs)," *Beyond Intractability*, Guy Burgess and Heidi Burgess, eds. (Boulder, Colorado, Research Consortium, University of Colorado, January 2005), *http://www.beyondintractiblity.org/essay /role_ngo/*.

to any organization that is independent of government control, non-partisan, non-violent, nonprofit and which is not created by an international or intergovernmental agreement. This qualification derives from the first appearance of the expression "non-governmental organization" during the 1945 San Francisco Conference to distinguish between representatives to the UN and partners with the UN. The term thus distinguished private organizations from intergovernmental specialized agencies.

Article 70 of the UN Charter refers to "Specialized agencies established by intergovernmental organizations which can participate without a vote in the deliberations of the Economic and Social Council (ECOSOC)." Article 71 mentions "non-governmental organizations" which could have "suitable arrangements for consultations."[3] The distinction was based on the prevalent sociological stratification of societies and their institutions into private (both for-profit and nonprofit) and public or government institutions. Nevertheless, some opinions like that of Konrad Otto-Zimmerman maintain that "it was the World Bank which defined and classified NGOs in an Operational Directive of August 1989."[4]

The heterogeneity of NGOs has made it difficult for scholars to arrive at a common definition of this reality. For instance, categorization of NGOs as nonprofit is challenged by those who would rather refer to themselves as not-for-profit. They claim that, though profit making is not their goal, they nevertheless actively seek ways to raise funds for their projects. Thus, unlike profit-oriented corporations that share dividends with their shareholders, these NGOs put their surplus revenues into ongoing projects.[5]

---

[3] *United Nations Charter*, Articles 70 & 71.
[4] See Konrad Otto-Zimmermann, "NGO-the questionable charm of being defined by what you aren't: A Call for renaming an important group of actors," *ICLEI Paper 2011-2*, Bonn Germany, 2011
[5] John R. Seffrin, "Non-Governmental Organization," *Encyclopedia of Public Health*, Lester Breslow, ed. (Gale: Cengage, 2002), *eNotes.com*, (2006),

Given this complexity and ambiguity, several descriptors have been used interchangeably: e.g., interest groups, pressure groups, public interest groups, major groups, independent sector, volunteer sector, civil society, grassroots organizations, transnational actors, social movements, private voluntary organizations, lobbyists, self-help organizations, and non-state actors (NSAs).[6] In most cases, the use of such terminologies is an attempt at a more precise and constructive definition to clarify the group's own unique identity, instead of describing themselves by what they are not. This approach would thus avoid a general negative designation – a "non-group" — such as 'non-profit,' 'non-government,' etc.[7]

Scholars of international politics such as Peter Willetts, one of the earliest contributing researchers on the study of NGOs, have indicated the necessity of clarifying these terms in order to achieve a better understanding of the concept "NGO."[8] They consider this exercise a *via negativa* (a negative way) or a method by way of denial – a conscious attempt to describe the concept by rescuing it from what it is not, so that its true meaning may emerge. This clarification and sifting are necessary for us because of the implications that any definition we arrive at will have for Catholic groups. This would be especially vital for religious congregations or orders of men and women who have assumed this new identity of NGO.

Although there may be no substantial linguistic difference between "NGO" and these other terms, none of these can replace the term "NGO," which bears a more neutral connotation applicable to a

http://www.enotes.com/public-health-encyclopedia/nongovernmental-organizations-united-states.

[6] Ibid.

[7] See Mary Kaldor and Helmut Anheier et. al. eds., *Global Civil Society 2006/7* (London: Sage 2005); Drayton, W. "Words Matter," *Alliance Magazine* vol. 12, no. 2 (June 2007).

[8] Peter Willetts, "What is a Non-Governmental Organization?" 1-12; Idem, ed., *The Conscience of the World: The Influence of NON-Governmental Organizations in the UN System* (Washington D.C.: Brookings Institution Press, 1996), 1-6.

diverse and extremely wide range of political and humanitarian actors operating upon local and international terrain.

The other terms carry much more restrictive nuances. For example, interest groups tend to foster only narrow economic concerns, and pressure groups with all their political implications do not describe some groups devoted to charitable work. Likewise, "Private Voluntary Organizations" (PVOs) as used by United States Agency for International Development (USAID) place a heavy emphasis on charitable activities that would not properly describe the systemic approach of groups focused upon advocacy. Further, as many scholars have pointed out, much terminology is problematic since many NGOs are governmentally or corporately funded with projects managed by paid professional staff.[9]

Moreover today, a long list of acronyms are used to refer to NGOs, e.g. INGOs (International Non-Governmental Organizations), BINGOs (Business international NGOs), RINGOs (Religious international NGOs), ENGOs (Environmental NGOs), GONGOs (Government operated NGOs which may have been set up by governments to look like NGOs in order to qualify for foreign aid), and QUANGOs (Quasi-NGOs or those that are at least partially created or supported by states).[10] While these acronyms represent groups that are considered NGOs, the term "NGO" still embraces a much wider variety.

UN usage describes an NGO as "not-for-profit, voluntary citizens' group, which is organized on a local, national or international level to address issues in support of the public good."[11] This definition as well has come under severe criticism. Some note that the description of NGOs as voluntary is inaccurate since it does not take into account that many paid employees work in these groups. Even the claim that

<hr />

[9] Ibid.

[10] Carolyn Stephenson, "Non-Governmental Organizations (NGOs)."

[11] See "NGOs and the United Nations Department of Public Information," *DPI/NGO Section: Brochure* (New York: UN-Department of Public Information, 2005), 1.

they typically receive lower pay than do those in the commercial private sector has been put into question by the immense salary and expenses compensation of some top NGO executives. For instance, in Jem Bendell's *Debating NGO Accountability*, over thirty articles on ethical failures of NGOs published in leading US newspapers observed "the sky-high salaries of top executives, and expense for office, travel and other perks."[12]

In my interviews and surveys, a number of people supported this accusation. An investigation of the American Cancer Society conducted by Aaron Diamant of Channel 2 News, Buffalo, New York and posted on its website Monday Nov. 7, 2011 revealed that even in a year when the Cancer Society made wide-ranging program cuts, its CEO still received a more than two-million-two hundred-thousand-dollar compensation.[13]

Across the globe, in both developed and developing countries, NGO work is seen as one of the most lucrative forms of employment. Some international NGO workers, especially those who travel, boast of salaries and allowances their counterparts in commercial private sectors would never receive. Admittedly, some people volunteer to work in these organizations for altruistic purposes, yet a good many do for other varied non-altruistic reasons. Some do so with the hope that it will bring them immediate benefits such as experience, contacts, improvement of their skills and other forms of personal profit.

It was in accord with the UN NGO definition cited above that a good number of humanitarian organizations began referring to themselves as NGOs. This uncritical self-approbation led Peter Willetts to propose some basic features that must characterize any UN NGO. These include: independence from the direct control of any government,

---

[12] Jem Bendell, *Debating NGO Accountability* (New York: NGLS, 2006), ix.

[13] Aaron Diamant, "American Cancer Society: Where does your money go?" Monday, Nov. 7, 2011. *http://www.wsbtv.com/news/news/american-cancer-society-where-does-your-money-go/nFX4j/*.

absence of any ambition to seize political power by overthrow of a government, and a not-for-profit and non-violent approach to business. He defines an NGO as "an independent voluntary association of people acting together on a continuous basis, for some common purpose, other than achieving government office, making money or illegal activities."[14] Also, for Gerard Clarke, "NGOs are private, non-profit, professional organizations with a distinctive legal character, concerned with public welfare goals."[15]

Both definitions are somewhat limited. Willetts' definition does not describe the specific activities of the NGOs and fails to recognize the relativity of the concept "voluntary" in relation to NGOs, as indicated above. Clarke's view takes some basic issues for granted, such as the controversy between non-profit and not-for-profit and the ambiguity in the use of the term private.

For the purpose of this work and in response to the deficiencies discussed above, we will define NGOs as follows: NGOs are constituted not-for-profit organizations created by private persons or organizations which have no participation or representation by any government personnel in their official capacity as government agents and maintain no partisan political motives. Moreover, NGOs are non-violent in approach and are concerned primarily with the general good.[16] In cases where these organizations are government funded totally or partially, they maintain non-governmental status by ensuring that government representatives are excluded from participation in the organization.

We are aware that some may object to this definition, maintaining that no one has a monopoly on determining what the general good is. On

---

[14] Peter Willetts, "What is a Non-Governmental Organization?" 2.

[15] See Gerard Clarke, *The Politics of NGOs in South-East Asia: Participation and Protest in the Philippines* (London: Routledge, 1998), 1-3 in Raymond L. Bryant, *Nongovernmental organizations in Environmental Struggles: Politics and the Making of Moral Capital in the Philippines* (New Haven: Yale University Press, 2005), 1.

[16] See Peter Willetts, "What is an NGO," 2.

these grounds, they have contested and sometimes dismissed the notion of general or common good held by some NGOs as "unacceptable values, ideological extremism and special pleading." We may observe as relevant an example the divergence between pro-life and pro-choice group understandings of the common good, focusing on right to life of the preborn or personal freedom respectively. However, this does not deny that, above all, the pursuit of the general good of all is central to the activities of a majority of these groups.

The definition adopted in this work is suited to characterize Catholic Church-inspired groups, especially those of religious congregations or orders of men and women. Most of these are institutes with an enduring history of service to the needy and, with the desire to do more in this regard, which have come to adopt the activities and identities of NGOs at the UN. The rapid proliferation of NGOs and the sometimes-transient nature of their operations make it difficult to know the total number of these organizations. One account puts the number of internationally operating NGOs at 40,000. A greater number operates on the local level.[17]

Origin & Evolution of NGOs

Discussions are convoluted, and opinions are polarized, on the origin and evolution of the modern NGOs. That their origin dates before their modern form of existence and relationship with the UN is not in dispute. According to his essay, entitled "The Early History: From the Congress of Vienna to San Francisco," Bill Seary believes that a more accurate dating would place the origin of modern international NGOs in the nineteenth century. He dismisses attempts to trace their history

---

[17] See Anheier et. al., "Global Civil Society 2001" (2001); "U.S. on Russia N-G-O *Law Voice of America* January 27 (2006) *http://www.voanews.com/uspolicy/archive/2006-01-27-voa2.cfm*; "What is an NGO?" January 5 (2007*), http://www.indianngos.com/ngosection/newcomers/whatisanngo.htm*. See also *The Economist, 2000,* in Julia Berger, "Religious Nongovernmental Organizations: An Exploratory Analysis," *Voluntas: International Journal of Voluntary and Nonprofit Organizations,* vol. 14, no. 1 March (2003):19.

from the religious and academic networks of the middle ages because the activities of those groups then "were more cosmopolitan than international."[18] He does not explain the difference between cosmopolitan and international, nor does he outline how the activities of the religious and academic networks in the middle ages were more cosmopolitan than international. Nevertheless, he recognizes that there is no consensus as to when exactly in the nineteenth century they began.

While L. C. White suggests NGOs began with the world alliance of Young Men's Christian Association (YMCA) in 1855, F. S. L. Lyons thinks that there were four groups that existed in 1849, namely Royal Asiatic Society (1823), Society of St. Vincent de Paul (1833), British and Foreign Anti-slavery (1839) and World Evangelical Alliance (1846).[19] Seary believes this difference between White and Lyons is due to varied opinions as to what constitutes an international NGO.[20] Since his interest was with international NGOs, Seary's study may not offer us a true account of the origins of modern NGOs by excluding local, national, sub-regional and regional dimensions.

Nick Young, the founding editor of *China Development Brief*, developed a more systematic historical method in accounting for the origin of these modern NGOs. He classified this history under three distinct traditions: the faith-based tradition, the humanitarian tradition, and the philanthropic tradition.[21] His account does not deny that systematic organization of social welfare began in the nineteenth century, but it does recognize the long history of altruistic activities well before this

---

[18] Bill Seary, "The Early History: From the Congress of Vienna to San Francisco," *Conscience of the World*, 15.

[19] See L. C. White, *International Non-Governmental Organizations* (New Brunswick: Rutgers University Press, 1951), 4 in Ibid; F.S.L. Lyon, *Internationalism in Europe 1815-1914* (Leiden: A.W. Sijthoff, 1963), 13.

[20] Bill Seary, "The Early History: From the Congress of Vienna to San Francisco," 15.

[21] Nick Young, "NGOs: The Diverse Origins, Changing Nature and Growing Internationalization of the Species," *China Development Brief, online edition* Dec. 31(2004), 1, *http://www.chinadevelopmentbrief.com/node/297*.

period on behalf of those living in poverty. It also appreciates the significant trajectories in the development of these activities.

History witnesses to a visible progression from Church or state-based to private individual-initiated programs. From an account by Jos van Beurden based on the history of NGOs in Ethiopia, we discover another tradition beyond the three given by Young: the traditional self-help system. This is said to have existed in Ethiopia long before the advent of the modern form of NGOs. Referred to originally as "Debo" and "Afarsata," these systems provided mutual aid as well as support for reconciliation. They have metamorphosed into their modern forms as "Ekub" and "Edir", rotating savings and credit systems. In both their earlier and current forms, these Community Based Organizations (CBOs) still exist side by side with modern forms of NGOs. [22]

Nick Young claims that the faith-based tradition, especially in Christianity with its developed teachings and practices of charity and compassion, "remains a major catalyst of social services and motivates many individual donors, workers and organizations in [national and] international relief and development."[23] Throughout the development of European civilization, nation states, industrial capitalism and colonization, the churches provided centers for learning and arts and relief for the poor and the sick.

During the colonial period, various Christian churches brought European technologies, literacy, and medical knowledge to less developed areas. These church groups, as in the case of the Catholics groups studied here, still take the lead position in recent times. Like modern NGOs today, they defended the marginalized of society such as the outcasts of the Osus in Igboland in the eastern part of Nigeria, the Dalits of India, female prisoners and mentally-ill in nineteenth century Britain and the victims of racial discrimination in the new world. Further, they strove for the abolition of horrific inhuman acts such as the

---

[22] See Jos van Beurden, "Ethiopia – Country Profile 1998."
[23] Nick Young, "NGOs: The Diverse Origins...," 3.

98

killing of twins, which many of the local people in the then eastern Nigeria considered an abomination, the European witch-hunt and the slave trade.

In one of my interviews with an old man in this eastern part of Nigeria concerning his experience of NGOs, he cited the European churches with their community service. In his opinion, educational standards in Nigeria fell when the missionaries left, and the governments took over their schools. Standards of hospital care and of other social service institutions also declined.

One could refer to this stage of the faith-based group missionary activity as the beginning of social services internationalization or NGO activities with all the concurrent positive and negative side-effects. For instance, while they cared for the poor, the needy and the marginalized, they also promoted the interests of their major sponsors--the churches and the colonizing powers.

For this reason, many still despise the eighteenth and nineteenth century missionary enterprises, which are considered to be major players in that era's imperialism. There has been named an unholy trinity: "Gun, Gold and God," though this does not disparage the efforts of those who protected the locals from the worst effects of colonialism. This past history points out two of today's major challenges facing many NGOs, namely, the influence of donor interest in their work and the perception some people in the developing countries have of them.

Occasionally Church authorities criticized the state for failing to include in its policies and programs relief and protection for the people, especially the most disadvantaged. This criticism from the Church contrasts to the insufficient Church response to the horrible working and living conditions following the Industrial Revolution. This failure of Church response is due in large part to her ecclesiological self-understanding in that era that saw herself distantly apart from the world. Its corresponding articulated spirituality was dichotomized from lived Christianity, giving preference to private charity over socio-political activism. Given this history, the Church was unable to effect positive social change and so created a vacuum that was filled by the development of the humanitarian tradition.

Church leaders who remained silent in the face of state irresponsibility toward the needy sometimes came under attack for such negligence. This finds its early foreshadowing in writings of Church Fathers and is most systematically developed in today's Catholic social teaching. At times the writing of Church Fathers and other Church documents have influenced modern NGOs.

St. Augustine's reaction to what we refer to today as "a materialistic and consumerist society" has become a leitmotif among modern NGOs. In his words, "God made the world for all, but human pride seeks the accumulation of wealth. Although all have the same skin, all do not have the same dress. All were born naked, but now some swim in abundance while others do not have anything."[24]

Such ideas inspire the modern NGO fight for equity and fairness in the use of natural resources, a striving to redress the agonizing scarcity suffered by many in our world scarred by a culture of waste. Modern Catholic social teaching, with its basis in natural law, provides modern NGOs with the template for pursuing universal human rights and dignity as innate and inalienable, pertaining to every human person and realizable in every human context.

From these long-standing teachings and practices of Christian charity emerged Christian action groups, many of which have developed over time into NGOs and now have consultative status with the UN. A few examples are Caritas, Catholic Action, World Vision, Misereor, St. Vincent de Paul Society, Pax Christi and Pax Romana.[25] NGOs of religious congregations of men and women represent a noteworthy part of Church practice of charity evolving into a systematized

---

[24] See Augustine, *Sermon*, 39.4; 61.2; 177.6-7.
[25] See Nick Young, "NGOs: Diverse Origins…" 2.

structure of modern NGOs. It will be instructive to see how, in the light of contemporary challenges, these evolved NGOs hold together the dual legacy of their past—giving alms and chastising Church and state for irresponsibility toward the common good and the wellbeing of the most disadvantaged.

The two other traditions in Young's schema are the humanitarian and the philanthropist. The humanitarian tradition begins the dawn of a new era in charitable organizations. It underscores the nineteenth-century emergence of groups founded by private individuals independent of both Church and state beginning with the Red Cross movement. This organization, begun by the Swiss merchant banker Henri Durant in 1856, cared for wounded soldiers and other victims of war.

Other individuals and groups were found across Europe, and later those in the United States would follow. Foster Plan for War Children, or Plan as it is commonly called today, was formed in 1937 by a British journalist. Oxford Committee for Famine Relief (OXFAM) was established by British citizens in 1942 to supply relief to Greece during World War II.[26]

While most of the early organizations were concerned with the practical relief of their clients, some also engaged in advocacy for their cause. Examples of such groups include Save the Children Fund and Médecins Sans Frontiéres (MSF) or "Doctors without Borders."[27] There was evidence as well of environmental concern even at this initial stage. The Wildlife Conservation Society was started in 1895 along with the establishment of the New York Zoological Society to oversee public zoos in the American metropolis. Fauna and Flora International evolved from the Society for the Preservation of the Wild Fauna of the British Empire in 1903.[28]

---

[26] Ibid.
[27] Ibid.
[28] Ibid., 5.

The third tradition in Young's schema, the philanthropic, was associated with a few "nouveau riche industrialists" who, as beneficiaries of industrial capitalism, set aside some of their wealth for charitable trusts or foundations. This also began in the nineteenth century. Originating in Europe, it has since then developed most extensively in the United States, numbering about sixty-five private foundations with annual grants of nearly thirty billion dollars.

Included in this group are Carnegie Foundations (founded by Andrew Carnegie in 1901), Ford Foundations (founded in 1936 by Edsel Ford, son of Henry Ford of Ford Motors), the Rockefeller Foundation (founded in 1913 by John D. Rockefeller) and most recently, foundations established by William Kellogg, Bill Gates, Ted Turner and David Packard.[29]

Among this group, the Rockefeller Foundation has a remarkable history of UN relationship. John D. Rockefeller's donation to the UN of eight million five hundred thousand dollars towards the purchase of its permanent Manhattan site facilitated the relocation of UN headquarters from London to New York in 1947.[30] This foundation remains one of the prime sponsors of public relations for the UN.[31]

Young's schema reveals some organic relationships between these three traditions and modern NGOs, though these may not be symmetrical. Apart from that, his work makes us aware of some important aspects of NGO dynamics, such as the interrelationships of NGOs with different backgrounds and activities. NGOs of diverse traditions are not necessarily at odds with each other and may even share overlapping aspects. It is too quick an assumption to think there is something different in the activities of different traditions engaged in providing food for the hungry, homes for the homeless or advocacy

---

[29] Ibid.

[30] http://www.nationsencyclopedia.com/United-Nations/United-Nations-Headquarters-THE-HEADQUARTERS-BUILDINGS.html.

[31] "Partnership for Sustainable Development," https://sustainabledevelopment.un.org/partnership/partner/?id=2103.

for the voiceless. Divergence might be operative in motivation, inspiration, and work styles, as can be noticed among Catholic groups.

While consistent with their Christian roots, activities of many Christian NGOs are no longer strictly limited to faith issues. Though all Church NGOs are built within a Christian background and a spirit of service, the social issues they address are not always of a religious character. They also recruit members and staff from other faiths as well as people of no faith. This is why the first international conference of Catholic NGOs in Rome in 2007 preferred using the title "Catholic-inspired NGOs" instead of "Catholic NGOs."

A final common characteristic among these traditions is a commitment to the well-being of the entire world that is motivated by compassion. Compassion as their common denominator plays a key hermeneutical role in the theological assessment undertaken in this work on the activities of Catholic Church-inspired NGOs.

In conclusion, as Young suggests, it is "more helpful to think of these three historical traditions as distinct streams flowing into the headwaters of a single river."[32]

Globalization is another development of modern history that has increased the number and activities of NGOs both quantitatively and qualitatively.[33] As global economies, travel and communication began to unite the world's peoples, there also was stimulated a new kind of solidarity around human and environmental issues that have by now gone far beyond merely national boundaries. Though this development is of the modern world, it has much older historical foreshadowing.

---

[32] Ibid., 1.

[33] See C. Chatfield, "Intergovernmental and Nongovernmental Associations to 1945," J. Smith, et. al, eds., *Transnational Social Movements and Global Politics: Solidarity Beyond the State* (Syracuse, New York: Syracuse University Press, 1997), in Julia Berger, "Religious Nongovernmental Organizations: An Exploratory Analysis," 15.

The global dynamics of modern society with the solidarity they elicit in our day were addressed and reflected upon by St. Augustine in his own day. The saint spoke, wrote, and worked on three levels of community: his home, his state and his world.[34] Issues on any one level have their impact on the other levels, and issues become even more intertwined and more dangerous on the level of the world.

This modern analogy transposed from the time of Augustin e plays a central role in Catholic-inspired NGO self-understanding with respect to their UN presence, as we shall later see. We shall also learn to appreciate how issues on any level of community in any era of history make universal solidarity ever more necessary.

General Functions of NGOs

In their various forms, modern NGOs perform a variety of development, relief and other humanitarian functions. They bring citizen concerns to governments, monitor policy and program implementation, and encourage participation of stakeholders at the community level. They also provide analysis and expertise, give early warning signals of problems, and help monitor and implement international agreements. Some are organized around specific issues such as human rights, the environment or health.[35] These functions become clearer as we explore NGO - UN relations.

In principle, NGOs are fundamentally classified into two basic types: the operational, who are sometimes called "quiet operators," and those heavily involved in campaigning or advocacy. These latter are known as "activist lobbyists" or "campaign NGOs." These types as discrete entities bear definitions that are mutually exclusive, but most NGOs elude permanent, rigid classification since they often cross from one type to the other or engage in both areas. Generally, as Peter Willetts states, their classification "may be interpreted as the choice

---

[34] Augustine, *City of God,* 19.7; 18.2.
[35] See "NGOs and the United Nations Department of Public Information," 1.

between small-scale change achieved directly through projects and large-scale change promoted indirectly through influence on the political system."[36]

Their palpable difference in everyday reality is that operational NGOs tend toward fundraising for material relief and development projects while campaign groups tend toward organizing actions that address systemic issues that cause hardship to people and creation.[37] The activist lobbyists are like the Old Testament prophets, who tread ground where neither angels nor saints have trod. They act as gadflies, and do not withdraw from confrontation when challenged. Perhaps because obvious systemic injustice is today more popularly implicated in human suffering, the present time demands a constructive blending of the two types.

Beyond providing material relief, we would argue that NGOs should engage in advocacy that challenges systems that create and perpetuate suffering and oppression. In the face of injustice, none can afford to remain neutral. Blending that makes NGOs more responsive to current trends reshaping global poverty, inequality and insecurity demands that NGOs evolve new roles, relationships, and capacities.

In chapter four, this imperative is applied more explicitly to the role of Catholic-inspired UN NGOs, a role that should include constructive criticism of the defects inherent in UN structures and of the self-reflexive capacity of their own institutions. This commitment to effecting systemic institutional change provides us with a basis of judging their efficiency, of how they have succeeded in making the UN system adapt to structural change. And for Catholic Church-inspired NGOs, it would be important to see how they have internalized this role by challenging the structure of the Church herself to move toward positive change

---

[36] Peter Willetts, "What is a Non-Governmental organization?" 4.

[37] Paul Kennedy, *The Parliament of Man: The Past, Present, and Future of the United Nations* (New York: Vintage Books, 2006), 220.

The League of Nations made room for private organization presence and participation, including that of several women's international organizations represented by a liaison committee known as "the voice of women." Following the intervention of this group on the exclusion of women from provisions and decisions of intergovernmental bodies, the Inter-Allied Suffrage Conference (IASC) was formed and was granted the right to participate in certain peace conference commissions.[38] Article 25 of the Covenant of the League of Nations states specifically "the Members of the league agree to encourage and promote the establishment of and cooperation of duly authorized voluntary national Red Cross organizations..."

In 1921, the League considered it an undesirable risk to diminish the activity of these voluntary organizations. It thus began to invite these groups to some of the League Assemblies and even to the 1932 Disarmament Conference. Some of these organizations were given the same facilities as other participants. In those early days too, most of these NGOs had "assessors" on League committees, with rights and privileges of government representatives except for the vote. The International Labor Organization (ILO) of 1919 was another intergovernmental organization that had a close working relationship with NGOs. Its structure provided a model for the inclusion of NGOs in the UN.[39]

It is therefore surprising that none of the early UN conferences considered the inclusion of NGOs. There is no record of the participation of NGOs in the June 1941 London meeting for the *Atlantic Charter*, the 1942 *Declaration of the UN* or the 1944 Dumbarton Oaks Conference. Some individual delegates at the 1945 San Francisco UN international conference sought inclusion of NGOs in the UN charter as necessary

---

[38] Hilkka Pietilä, *The Unfinished Story of Women and the United Nations*, (New York: NGLS, 2007), 2, 3.
[39] See Bill Seary, "The Early History," 23-25.

partners of the Organization with particular reference to the Economic and Social Council (ECOSOC). Later reviews of the consultative right granted the NGOs at the San Francisco conference as included in Article 71 of the UN Charter specified the categories of this right, namely the general, special and roster status. The UN ECOSOC relationship with NGOs today is governed by the ECOSOC resolution of 1996.[40]

In the 2000 Millennium Declaration, member states agreed to give private sector NGOs and civil society in general greater opportunity to contribute to realizing UN goals and programs.[41] The two official channels through which NGOs participate in the UN project are the Department of Public Information (DPI) and the Economic and Social Council (ECOSOC).

Operative Mechanisms, Activities, &Achievements of NGOs at the UN

NGOs make their distinctive contributions to the UN decision-making process through "formal and informal, direct and indirect advocacy. They do not negotiate, vote, affirm or reject official UN agreements."[42]

The actual level of NGO UN participation depends on their official relationship with the organization, namely whether they are accredited to ECOSOC or affiliated with the DPI. These latter NGOs become DPI partners in its outreach. They act as liaisons with the UN, providing a range of information services to other partners including the academic community, various institutions and the wider society besides their parent organizations. They transmit information from the UN to grass-root communities and from these communities back to the UN.

---

[40] Resolutions and Decisions of the Economic and Social Council, E/1996/96, http://esango.un.org/civilsociety/documents/E_1996_31.pdf.
[41] See *Intergovernmental Negotiations and Decision Making at the United Nations: A Guide*, (New York: NGLS, 2003), ix.
[42] Ibid., 3.

Though this level of participation may seem limited, these NGOs make valuable contributions promoting UN initiatives and programs as well as mobilizing support for its specialized agencies through dissemination of vital UN information. Speaking to new NGOs and their representatives during the 2011 DPI-NGO orientation program at UN New York Headquarters, Under-Secretary General for Communications and Public Information, Kiyotaka Akasaka, credited the NGOs for the encouraging rating the UN receives in most countries of the world. This outcome is realized through the collaborative effort of the DPI with NGOs in addressing the UN audience, providing them with an accurate, objective and comprehensive report of UN activities and its programs.

ECOSOC-accredited NGOs are granted a consultative status classified as general, special or roster, depending on how they are evaluated by the NGO Committee of ECOSOC, its accreditation committee. The consultative status offers NGOs a greater level of participation and an avenue for influencing UN policy formation and implementation. These NGOs enjoy the privilege of participating in all formal ECOSOC meetings with the right to suggest agenda items and to submit oral or written statements. They may also be consulted by ECOSOC and other UN organizations on any issue if they have general status, on issues within their expertise if they have special status, and on occasion if they have roster status.

The NGO use of the right to submit proposals to ECOSOC did come under attack by some member state delegates allegedly both for lacking in coordination and for being hampered by unnecessary multiplicity. But these delegates were just hiding under the cover of this alleged dual tendency, in order to refuse NGO proposals as frivolous. It might have been true in the past that sometimes unhealthy competition could be found among NGOs as they strove to have their proposals appear on the ECOSOC agenda. These days, NGOs organize their thoughts and concerns through various NGO committees and subcommittees. They collaboratively sign on to each other's submissions.

This solidarity has offered them a unified voice in pushing for items that are important to them without losing the specifics of each group.

NGOs are eager to attain ECOSOC status because of its consultative privileges and the right to send representatives to each of the four major UN headquarters: New York, Geneva, Vienna, and Nairobi. The NGO Committee of ECOSOC might receive as many as six hundred new NGO applications seeking ECOSOC accreditation in one session every year. There are about four thousand ECOSOC-accredited NGOs among the three types of status, a sizeable number of them being Catholic-inspired.

Apart from the specific operation policies approved for NGOs within their respective kinds of UN affiliation, they can also participate in UN activities by organizing parallel events alongside General Assembly sessions or other UN conferences such as those of the Commission on the Status of Women (CSW) or the Commission on Social Development (CSOCD). These gatherings afford activists the world-over the venue to showcase the issues and activities they espouse.

These side-events, forums and conferences have had a significant impact on UN actions and decisions. Treating topics considered by the General Assembly or the Commissions, they attract thousands of people from around the world representing the UN system, member states, civil society organizations, grassroots constituencies, the media, academia, the private sector and other institutions as well as NGOs themselves.

Significantly, the very people with the most intimate first-hand experience of the particular issue in question have often been privileged to attend. They are of course the actual victims of the many instances of the world's neglect and cruelty. During the 2012 Commission on the Status of Women (CSW), VIVAT International facilitated the participation of a local woman leader from Papua New Guinea who presented the experiences of local widows in armed conflict. There is no doubt that their physical presence was more eloquent witnessing to even hardened hearts than any other language could possibly have been.

At the end of most of these events, a statement drawn up and signed by participating NGO representatives is forwarded to the appropriate UN organ or agency, such as the General Assembly. Some of these, like the 2009 Mexico DPI/NGO statement in particular, have made their way to becoming a General Assembly or even a Security Council document -- a very rare and privileged outcome.

The summary of the civil society declaration and proceedings of the civil society forum preceding the annual conference of Commission on Social Development is presented to the member states at the opening session of the conference. The same is true of other commissions and forums such as the Commission on the Status of Women and Global Forum on Migration and Development. On many occasions these documents are used as talking points during NGO visitations with member state missions such as the outcome document of the civil society forum at the 2014 Global Forum on Migration entitled *Stockholm Agenda* (SA) and its preceding document *Eight Point-Five Year Plan* leading to the *2013 High Level Dialogue on Migration and Development.*

NGOs also operate with great success in other informal and unofficial ways. Dinner or breakfast gatherings succeed in uniting diplomats, businessmen and women, ecclesiastics and literati as well as UN officials. Some of these individuals are often at odds on the floor of the General Assembly, but at these events they can discuss issues privately from an unbiased point of view.[43] This offers NGOs an interactive strategy of engaging with member state delegates before and after major UN events.

---

[43] See Patrick Bascio, *The U.N. was My Parish: Experiences of a Priest-Diplomat*, (Denville, New Jersey: Dimension Books, 1977), 95-106.

At times the open spaces at the UN—balconies, cafeteria, and hall-ways—provide NGOs informal opportunities to approach a diplomat. These chance encounters and visits to member state mission offices have become common effective ways of operating among NGO representatives. Sometimes an informal occasion becomes a crucial opportunity for an NGO to get a nation to commit to an action that the NGO supports. Success in this area can be the result of willingness of member states and UN agencies to co-host or cosponsor these events with NGOs. We are seeing an increase in number and substance of these opportunities and occasions.

Along with the numerous ways NGOs have affected UN decision-making and its approach to world issues, mention must be made of the moral and ethical dimension they propose to the UN. It is this above all that has widened the UN's vision to recognize and respond to world crises. We saw that on the road to the second UN Conference on Sustainable Development known as Rio+20. NGO pressure introduced ethical and moral phrasing of the conference outcome document within a human rights framework.

This ethical and moral framework brought governments to negotiate with the political will and financial commitment that would ensure the implementation of the mandate. NGOs call this moving the UN system from the head to the heart, in other words from the overly political and theoretical to an awareness of persons and what can be achieved for them.

NGOs have also labored to secure a religious space in the UN. In 1952 inspired by the vision of the then Secretary General, Dag Hammar-skjöld, a meditation room was dedicated to world peace for people of all faiths and religions. It is on the west side of the visitors' lobby of the General Assembly building. Yet the mention of the word "religion" was for long time seriously regarded within the UN as a taboo. With the gradual, friendly lobbying of the Committee of Religious NGOs at the UN, religion is celebrated in the UN in what is today known as World Interfaith Harmony Week. This event, celebrated the first week of February, was adopted by UN General Assembly resolution of October 20, 2010.[44]

Also, through the leadership of United Nations Population Fund (UN-FPA), there has been an ongoing interaction series among UN agencies, the academic community and faith-based organizations (FBOs) on the intersection between the UN and religion in development. The series aims to strengthen the relationship between the UN and various faith-based organizations where one exists or to create a relationship where one has not yet existed. Special focus is given to mainstreaming this relationship into the operational systems of the UN in such way that faith-based contributions are recognized not only in delivering services but also in formulating policies of development programs.

Another ready example of NGO success at the UN is in helping to reframe the UN language, definition and scope of certain issues. Effort of the NGO Committee on Social Development (CSocD) was instrumental in the UN redefinition of poverty beyond its traditional meaning, so as to appreciate its multidimensional nature and to identify access -- or lack thereof -- as key to understanding it.

The Committee insisted that it is no longer acceptable "that persons living in poverty be called 'the poor,' which takes away the humanity of the individuals by identifying them with their situation. These people are richly endowed human beings who have much to contribute to society" but lack access to the opportunities to do so.

We should refrain from classifying these people as "the poor" and rather describe them as "people living in poverty...." "Their poverty is a limiting social condition often imposed from sources beyond their control." Governments and civil society must promote attitudes of

---

[44] http://daccess-dds-ny.un.org/doc/UNDOC/GEN/N10/512/84/PDF/N1051284.pdf?OpenElement.

social inclusion and ensure that public services are made accessible to all while respecting culture and diversity.[45]

This new understanding of poverty shifts the focus of social development towards a more people-oriented approach rather than keeping it upon the mere increase of capital or material resources. Today, UN development discourse deals with every citizen across the whole course of life and acknowledges development as a moral imperative for all governments to protect.

Some people may see these efforts as superficial rhetoric, but the power of words can make enormous changes for good or for ill. Sr. Joan F. Burke, SND de Namur (SNDdeN) UN representative and former chair of CSocD, credits this language change on poverty for making an unprecedented impact on UN policies and actions. With appreciation of the language of exclusion and its role in describing world poverty as expressed above, several diverse issues were introduced into social development discourse.

Social development can now be seen from the perspective of human rights principles. In this view, employment promotion is recognized as not only a response to social needs but also as an integrative dynamism positively contributing to the well-being of the person, the family and the community. More widely, social development must also accommodate social justice by requiring that principles of equity, participation, mutuality and reciprocity be among its necessary components.

This perspective also injects the interplay of systemic social development into the discourse, as it claims that economic, social and political structures which sustain poverty and unjust relationships must be

---

[45] See "Gleaning from *CSocD* Statement," a working draft to track origins of value statement of the submissions for *SG* report.

transformed in order to balance abject poverty against surplus wealth.[46]

One can easily discern in this discourse an echo of Pope Paul VI's *Populorum Progressio* and other documents in its tradition. Social justice principles of equity, participation, mutuality, solidarity, and family/societal orientation of labor were core elements enunciated in these Catholic social teaching documents as well as the right to work. These vocabulary shifts point to how much, even though a seemingly inconsequential intervention, the participation of Catholic-inspired groups help in shaping these dialogues and their outcomes. Consequently, we can clearly see from this example a particular contribution of Catholic tradition NGOs in these UN-NGO committees.

The General Assembly resolution on the Arms Trade Treaty was adopted in April 2013 after years of frustrating delay and obstruction from super powers and major arms producing member states. Much credit for this achievement belongs to the unwavering persistence, expertise and lobbying skill of NGOs. They have also succeeded in "addressing plenary meetings of UN member states, contributing alternative reports and strategic information to treaty bodies, briefing the members of the Security Council on occasion and increasingly sitting on government delegations at UN sessions."[47]

To quote Joe Donnelly, who heads the Caritas International delegation in the UN, "The General Assembly and the Security Council don't have any windows, so we provide them with a window on the world. We're a grass-roots global organization and so can give the diplomats and UN staff a sense of the reality on the ground. We act as a bridge between governance and policy to members of our network in local communities everywhere."[48]

---

[46] Ibid.

[47] *Intergovernmental Negotiations and Decision Making at the United Nations*, vii.

[48] See Joe Donnelly, in Patrick Nicholson, "Window on the World," *The Tablet,* 12 April (2008): 4.

In addition to influencing UN decision-making and collaborating in project management, the NGOs also assist in the implementation of UN decisions. This entails ensuring that member states execute UN policies. For example, in the ratification of the convention on the rights of migrants, NGOs achieved government compliance through publicity, an effective means of pressure. In other instances, because people in grassroots communities often trust NGO members more than governments or the UN and its agencies, NGOs have become effective agents for implementing policies on such issues as "sex education, family planning, development projects, disaster relief and work with refugees."[49]

Depending on issue and circumstance, NGOs, by reason of their expertise or experience, may be directly commissioned by the UN as operational agents to implement policy. Most ECOSOC general status NGOs have been commissioned by the UN to conduct research and collect data on various issues within their competence.

The International Catholic Migration Commission (ICMC) has ever since 2011 been commissioned by the Migration-related Intergovernmental Forum as its major link and coordinator with civil society relations on migration and development issues. For example, ICMC coordinates the participation of civil societies at the Global Forum on Migration and Development (GFMD) — "an initiative of the United Nations Member States to address the migration and development interconnections in practical and action-oriented ways, in an informal non-binding process, outside the UN system."

The one area in the UN/NGO relationship where, in my estimation, the NGOs have failed is in addressing the structural imbalances of the UN with the inconsistencies of the Charter. That the UN structure inhibits in some ways its progress and negates what it stands for is acknowledged by almost every participant.

---

[49] Peter Willetts, "Consultative Status for NGOs at the United Nations," 48, 49.

A unique privilege that NGOs enjoy at the UN is the liberty to say what UN diplomats and staff dare not say because of their jobs. One would expect therefore that the issues of UN operations and internal dynamics are areas where NGOs would readily exercise this privilege. However, the call to accept the challenge of seeing to it that the UN seriously reviews its structures and Charter has typically been ignored by NGOs.

For reasons like this, the alternative mode of presence we propose for NGO UN participation demands their accountability, fidelity to their foundational goals and reflection upon what expectations people have of them. It behooves them, especially those of Catholic inspiration, to demand that the UN live up to its goals and commitments to justice and fairness both in principle and in its own practice.

History & Activities of
Catholic-Church-inspired NGOs in the UN

We reiterate the need to set aside any quick presumption that social activity by Christians or, in this case, Catholic Church-inspired NGOs, is substantially different from those that are secular. Indeed, they are not. On the whole, religious and non-religious NGOs share in common the history of the modern NGO. They both represent the emergence of an alternative model for ordering the world that openly challenges the exclusive monopoly of military might and capital in the post-enlightenment era.

Church-inspired NGOs, together with other religious, faith-based, or ethical groups, bring an alternative voice to the UN seeking a civilization of love and dialogue against the prevalent "clash of civilizations." What may be the real difference between these Catholic-inspired and non-Catholic-related NGOs, both religious and non-religious, is that the former draw on the spiritual traditions of their Catholic Church — its practices and teachings — as the inspiration for their explicitly public missions.

We may recall here in Young's study on the evolution of modern NGOs his observation about the influence of gospel values and Christian teachings and virtues in this evolution especially on those who are Christian. Kevin Ahern, former president of IMCS-Pax Romana, uses the same normative description for Catholic NGOs. All their activities, whatever their divergent focus or charism, are based on the witness and call of Jesus Christ and the social teaching of the Church: "At the heart of these concerns is our common desire to protect the sacredness of human life and to promote the common good."[50] He relates how Catholic groups are both related to and distinct from those without a Catholic influence.

It is quite difficult to identify organizations that are representative of this field. Until recently, all NGOs of Catholic background were, without qualification, referred to as Catholic NGOs. However, it seems that there might have been evidence of the distinction (though tacit) between Catholic NGOs and Catholic-inspired NGOs in the early days of the UN.

Joseph Rossi included in his account of the first groups of Catholic UN NGOs the effort of Catherine Schaefer in facilitating the admission and participation in ECOSOC of a Catholic-inspired organization and those with predominantly Catholic membership.[51] Even with this evidence, the fact that this distinction was rarely mentioned by any other account suggests that many of those early NGOs that were Catholic-related would have come under the general umbrella of the Catholic NGO. The first Catholic Church-related NGOs accredited to the UN, especially the very few present at the San Francisco conference, did not seem to have any problem with this identity.

---

[50] Kevin Ahern, "Catholic NGOs Working Closely with the Holy See," an address to a forum on Catholic Non-Governmental Organizations at the Vatican, (Vatican City, November 30 – December 2, 2007).

[51] See Joseph Rossi, *Uncharted Territory*, 11.

Upon the arrival of later groups with their varied dynamics, the question became both complex and polarizing. Some have difficulty determining whether they can consider themselves "Roman Catholic" or simply "Catholic." This difficulty revolves around issues such as funding, the source of authority, legitimacy of Catholic groups that include non-Catholics, adherence to other charisms and sources of inspiration as well as compliance with the institutional structure of the Church. Organizations that are not directly funded by the Church or any of its institutions and which do not take directives from them but believe their activities draw from the principles of Catholic teachings seem to have more difficulty in deciding their identity.

Also, there are other groups of Catholic origin that have over time expanded to include more interfaith and secular actors, e.g. Project Orbis and Franciscans International. Those which have real trouble identifying themselves as Catholic are those who have problems relating with the institutional Church, such as Catholics For Free Choice. Of course, NGOs of various religious orders or congregations pursue their goals based on the distinctive charism of their founders and/or institutes. They do have no issue with being identified as Catholic. This situation of confusion in identity may not be new to many Catholics as it also parallels a prevalent pew conversation going on in many churches today concerning the relationship of true faith and loyalty to an institutional church with spirituality and religiosity.

Another factor at work in this convolution that is worth mentioning is the fear among these Catholic groups of being confused with the official voice of the Church at the UN. They quickly assert that they do not speak for the Church. A question of interest this tendency poses for us is the assumed restriction of the official voice of the Church to the hierarchy even considering the emphasis on collaborative ministry underlining the ecclesiology of Vatican II. In other words, are adherence to the gospel teachings of the Church and expertise not enough for baptized Church members to speak as the voice of the Church without being accused and denounced as usurping a power they do not possess? How may their Catholicity then be defined? Such questions as these go to the heart of the task undertaken in this work.

The extent of this NGO diversity was highlighted by Pope Benedict XVI in his opening address to the conference of all Catholic-related NGOs in December 2007. The pontiff noted: "Also present are groups mainly committed to advocacy, and others chiefly concerned with the concrete management of cooperative projects promoting development. Some of your organizations are recognized by the Church as public and private associations of the lay faithful, others share in the charism of certain institutes of consecrated life, while still others enjoy only civil recognition and include non-Catholics and non-Christians among their members. All of you, however, have in common a passion for promoting human dignity. This same passion has constantly inspired the activity of the Holy See in the international community."

The designation *Roman Catholic Church-inspired NGOs,* also used in this book, is of coinage that came into currency at the first international conference of all Catholic-related NGOs — *Forum of Catholic-inspired NGOs* in Rome 2007 referred to above.[52] This conference, convoked at the initiative of the Vatican, was one of the many activities slated by the Church to commemorate the fortieth anniversary of *Populorum Progressio.* It is an adaptable phrase, given the various characteristics of these groups. Nevertheless, all these designations--Catholic NGOs, Catholic-inspired NGOs, Catholic Church-inspired NGOs—are used interchangeable in this work to refer to groups inspired by the spiritual traditions of the Catholic Church.

Apart from the issues of terminology, there is also the difficulty of determining the exact number of these Catholic Church-inspired NGOs

---

[52] The term "Catholic" refers to all of the *sui-juris* Catholic Churches in communion with Rome, yet this term is preferred in this book even though specific groups studied are mainly from the Roman Catholic Church. We use the term "Roman Catholic" when it is absolutely necessary.

in the UN. This is because many of them do not use identities that suggest their relation to the Catholic Church. For instance, the NGO of the Congregation of the Handmaids of the Holy Child Jesus is simply called *Center for Women Studies and Interventions*. Without prior knowledge, there is no way one can identify this as a Christian and much less a Catholic group. Frustration is evident in the recent survey conducted by the organizers of the *Forum*.[53]

In order to capture the dynamics of the Catholic Church-inspired NGO participation in the UN — their history and activities, their relationship with the Holy See UN Mission and their achievements and challenges—this section of this chapter is structured using three sets of pairings that compare and contrast different NGO groups. These three pairings are NGOs from the early days of the UN and later arrivals, those of religious communities and lay associations, and those in accord with official Church teaching as opposed to those that dissent from Church positions.

Catholic-Church-inspired NGOs from the Beginning of the UN to Later Arrivals

A comparative study of Catholic Church-inspired NGOs with respect to their earlier or later arrival at the UN clearly captures some distinctive elements of the history and activities of these two groups. The distinction between these two NGO groups can be based both on the calendar date when they began UN association and the particular epochs during which they began it. If both ways of characterizing their beginnings are simultaneously taken into account, the significant trajectories their history has taken are held together.

Thus, we are evaluating history by looking at two timelines. Concerning actual dates, we note whether the NGO UN association began during the years 1945 to1980s or from the 1990s-onward. Concerning the

---

[53] See *Results of the Mapping-Questionnaire* (Rome: Catholic-inspired NGOs Forum, Forum des ONG d'inspiration Catholique, March 2009).

different epochs during which the NGO UN association began, we note the different global realities, both secular and ecclesiastical, that were salient then.

Like many of the secular NGOs and those from other faith traditions, Catholic Church-inspired NGOs were present in the League of Nations. Pax Romana was one of them.[54] Some members of these Church-inspired NGOs took part in the assembly in Dumbarton Oaks, Washington, D.C. meeting in 1944 and the San Francisco UN International Conference, albeit mostly as part of the representation of their various countries.[55]

Once again, we recall Catherine Schaefer of the United States, a representative of the Catholic Association for International Peace (CAIP) and a member of United States delegation. She succeeded in ensuring the inclusion of article 71 of the UN charter that provided for NGO consultation by the Economic and Social Council, ECOSOC.

By the time the UN admitted its first group of NGO collaborators in 1947, two Catholic NGOs made the list: the International Union of Catholic Women's League (IUCWL) and the Catholic International Union for Social Service.[56] These were joined in 1949 by Pax Romana – an amalgamation of the International Catholic Movement for Intellectual and Cultural Affairs and the International Movement of Catholic Students (ICMICA-IMCS).[57] In 1951, two others added to the Catholic voice, namely the International Catholic Union of the Press and the International Young Christian Workers.[58]

---

[54] See *A Brief History of IMCS-Pax Romana (1887-2006)*, online edition, *www.cccm.ca/stage/files/uploads/docs/ABriefHistoryofIMC.pdf*,

[55] See Arthur Jones, "Catholics Were There at the Start," *National Catholic Reporter*, 1 October (1999), 1.

[56] Jean Gartlan, *At the United Nations*, 14.

[57] See *A Brief History of IMCS-Pax Romana (1887-2006)*, online edition, *www.cccm.ca/stage/files/uploads/docs/ABriefHistoryofIMC.pdf*, 4.

[58] See Kevin Ahern, "The Role of International Catholic Organizations in Promoting the Gospel in the 'Community of Nations,'" 2.

The 1990s witnessed an increase in the number of Catholic Church-inspired NGOs present at the UN. Examples of these later arrivals include International Catholic Association for Girls (ACISJF) and Partnership for Global Justice. They were accompanied by several religious congregations of women and men.[59] Researchers have attributed this rise to the change in the requirements for NGO registration with the UN and the influence of globalization which demanded a wider scope for charity and the globalization of solidarity as outlined previously in this chapter.

The effect of globalization is graphically illustrated in the words of Dominican Sr. Eileen Gannon. "The best and worst part of all this work is that there's nothing that does not connect to something else. I'm working on the Campaign to Eliminate the Child Solider. That connects to Human Rights and the rights of children – the Convention on the Rights of the Child. And that connects to the Eradication of Poverty group, and that connects you to the world debt, World Bank."[60]

Other reasons for this increase in Catholic Church-inspired NGOs, and perhaps the most significant, is the effects of the reception of Vatican II that increased significantly in the 1990s and the call by John Paul II to all humanitarian agencies, especially the NGOs, to engage seriously in UN activities. Speaking to groups of NGOs during one of his visits to the UN headquarters, the Pontiff advised:

> No organization however, not even the United Nations or any of its agencies, can alone solve the global problems which are constantly brought to its attention, if its concerns are not shared by all the people. It is then the privileged task of the non-governmental organizations to help bring these concerns into the communities and the homes of the people, and to bring back to the established agencies the

---

[59] See *Results of the Mapping-Questionnaire.*
[60] See Sr. Eileen Gannon, in Arthur Jones, "Catholics Were there at the Start," *National Catholic Reporter,* (October 1, 1999): 1.

priorities and aspirations of the people, so that all solutions and pro-
jects which are envisaged be truly geared to the needs of the human
person.[61]

Some of these socio-economic, political and ecclesiastical factors also had their influence on the first groups of Catholic Church-inspired UN NGOs. As we saw in chapter one, the Papal Peace Program of Pope Pius XII provided both the inspiration and the language for Catholic UN participation. It influenced not only delegates of Catholic countries but also the representatives of civil society for whom the document was taken as a mandate. For groups such as Pax Romana and Caritas Internationalis, globalization, Vatican II renewal and Church social documents contributed to the gradual inclusion of ad-vocacy in their operational dynamics.

With the arrival of the later groups, the generic use of the term "Cath-olic NGO" became more complex and unclear due to their varied dy-namics and their differing views on the mission proper for Catholics in the UN. For many of the later groups, their major reason for coming to the UN was to collaborate with it in its mission of pursuing the common good for all. They are comfortable with simply promoting UN policies and influencing from time to time policy formation as their level of accreditation would allow. Their Catholic inspiration re-mains quietly in the background, providing spiritual encouragement for their participation. They do not usually recognize this participa-tion as a particularly opportune means of promoting Catholic princi-ples per se.

In that light, it might be more appropriate to reserve the name "Cath-olic NGOs" to the first groups because they were never in doubt about their relationship with the Church. In fact, they thought, as Joseph Rossi pointed out, that one of their major roles was to "catholicize"

---

[61] John Paul II, "Address to the NGOs gathered as the UN Headquarters, New York, (1979)," in *Serving the Human Family*, 200.

the UN. They went to the extent of impeding UN accreditation for NGOs whose ideology seemed opposed to Catholic Church teaching.

Rossi records that in 1947 Catherine Schaefer recommended to the UN/NGO committee not to admit two Communist organizations—*the World Federation of Democratic Youth* (WFDY) and *the Women's International Democratic Federation* (WIDF).[62] There is no proof as to whether the earlier groups were in agreement with this decision or understanding. Specifically, we are not sure if groups like *Pax Romana* and *Caritas Internationalis* held the same view as Schaefer did. Today's experience makes it clear that Caritas, for instance, favors the more inclusive attitudes brought in by the newer NGOs of participation without compromising allegiance to the Church.

As mentioned above, statements of Pius XII played a great role in influencing the attitude of these initial Catholic participants, particularly those present at the earliest beginnings of the UN. Apart from representing their various countries, they considered it their responsibility to ensure that the Papal Peace Program was fully integrated into the framework of the UN Charter and into the Universal Declaration of Human Rights. Rossi speculated that one of the reasons why the National Catholic Welfare Conference (NCWC) was reluctant to endorse the UN was the perceived failure of the San Francisco conference "to mold the UN in the spirit of Pius XII and his predecessor Benedict XV."[63]

Though an increasingly shared acceptance of willingness to accommodate has narrowed the differences between these two groups – the earlier and later Catholic NGOs—a silent anxiety still lurks among some of them. This situation highlights some of the remaining issues unresolved in the transition from a Neo-scholastic theology and a pre-

---

[62] See Joseph Rossi, *Uncharted Territory*, 12.
[63] Ibid., xii. Even though this was the official representative of the Catholic Bishops of the United States, yet we recall that its mouthpiece was a group of lay people. It also did not have the status of a state at the UN.

Vatican II triumphalist ecclesiology to the more pluralistic, humble, and collaborative ecclesiology of Vatican II itself.

Despite appreciating the refreshingly inclusive attitudes that later NGOs brought to the Catholic UN presence, we admit that earlier groups grasped more clearly UN internal dynamics and so could be prompter and more effective in responding to them than the later groups were and are today. This readiness has yet to attract its deserved attention and is at the heart of our book. Indeed, the early Catholic NGO initial recognition of the inconsistency between UN structure and its ideals prompted the inclusion of NGO admission and full participation into the UN Charter and UN structures in the first place.

Pioneers like Catherine Schaeffer and Alma Zizzamia were quick to criticize a totally government-constituted UN as a contradiction to the organization's ideals. It went against the opening words of the Charter Preamble – "We the people of the United Nations." This raises the question whether the UN is genuinely concerned with the peoples of the world or serves only the economic and military security of the nations that won World War II. Also, these first Catholic-Church-inspired NGOs were part of the movement that first addressed the gender inequality ingrained in the UN administrative structure. Their initiatives began the inclusion of women in UN Secretariat administrative roles.[64]

The contributions of these earlier groups of Catholic-inspired NGOs to the language and text of the UN Universal Declaration of Human Rights (UDHR) and the inclusion of women in the administrative stream of the UN Secretariat have been gratefully recognized. As we read in Jean Gartlan's *At the United Nations*, the Catholic participants at the UN San Francisco conference and subsequent meetings on the drafting process of the UDHR drew on "Catholic doctrine and social teaching" in their contribution to the draft of the declaration.

---

[64] See Joseph S. Rossi, "The Status of Women: Two American Catholic Women at the UN, 1947-1972)," 310-15.

Moreover, they powerfully influenced Eleanor Roosevelt, who often created opportunities for these NGOs to speak during key stages of deliberation.

An original document prepared by the National Catholic Welfare Conference (NCWC) became useful to the UN Human Rights drafting committee for both formal and informal discussions. The NCWC document contained a general preamble and sections on the Rights of the Human Person, Rights Pertaining to the Family, the Domestic Rights of States and Rights of States in the International Community. Though the NCWC document made no explicit reference to God the Creator as source of rights, the final text of the Declaration insisted on the right of parental choice in their children's education and on the right of free choice of employment.[65]

To the credit of these early Catholic NGOs, the improvement of the status of women in the Third World grew into a burning issue quite early in UN history. The NGOs achieved this awareness by advocating the ratification of the International Convention on the Suppression of the Exploitation of Prostitution of Others and its inclusion in the agenda of the 1960 London World Congress on Prevention of Crime. They also saw to it that the Third Committee of the General Assembly's 1962 Draft Convention on Free Consent, Minimum Age and Registration of Marriages incorporated the "linking of child betrothal, child marriage, and the abuse of the bride price — to the general status of women."[66]

The legacy of these earlier achievements can be sensed in the activities of the later NGOs as they champion causes on the status of women, social protections, minimum health, education and employment standards and universal human rights as well as in the passing of the Arms Trade Treaty. However, taking on the UN system with

---

[65] Jean Gartlan, *At the United Nations*, 67-77.
[66] Joseph Rossi, *Uncharted Territory*, 189, 193, 194.

126

impressive zest and bravery as did the earlier Catholic NGOs has not been passed on from them to the later arrivals.

It is clear that the earlier NGOs knew that their prophetic responsibilities demanded not merely UN participation but also criticisms of the inconsistencies and normative deficiencies in the UN system. In other words, they saw the UN as Augustine saw every human institution — a combination of grace and sin, of the city of God and the earthly city, of compassion and lust for domination.

The later groups are in no way oblivious of this reality. Today's Catholic Church-inspired NGOs certainly realize there are shortcomings imbedded in the UN structure inhibiting the full realization of its goal. The difference between the earlier and the later groups is that the earlier followed (though implicitly it may seem) what we take to be a key Augustinian precept: the role of a Christian participating in such institutions includes working to diminish the opportunities for sin and lust for domination and to expand the space for the expression of love. This they did by holding the UN accountable for its structural and operative dynamics that privilege some at the expense of others. This dimension of the prophetic in the UN participation of the newer Catholic Church-inspired NGOs seems to have diminished.

The task for us therefore is to discern the most effective way of returning to the tradition of the earlier groups without losing the newness of spirit and genuine solidarity provided by the newcomers. This would at the same time demand challenging the subtle, outdated triumphalist attitude of the earlier group shaped by the ecclesiology of their time. This effective way is what is proposed here as dialogical confrontation. It is discussed in chapter four.

Catholic-Church-inspired NGOs: Religious Institute NGOs versus Lay NGOs

This paired-set comparison helps to capture distinct historical trajectories in the development of Catholic-inspired NGO UN participation.

It also illustrates the great variety these two groups bring to UN discourse and the ecclesiological implications of their activities.

Among the later groups of Catholic-inspired NGOs at the United Nation are those of religious institutes of men and women. Like other organizations, these religious institutes have an enduring tradition of concern for those living in poverty, demonstrated by commitment to the immediate needs of the people they serve in various missions worldwide. Concomitantly, the enormity and complexity of contemporary societal sufferings and their links to systemic causes in social structures demand more effort in challenging the sources that cause and perpetuate the evils bedeviling humanity and creation. This in turn demands from religious a profound paradigm shift, seen in Vatican II as renewal based on the spirit of their founder and a reading of the signs of time.[67]

Bearing the marks of the hopes and anxieties of people today in their own experiences, men and women religious are ever more determined to take up the concerns of our changing modern world. They are less and less satisfied being mere spectators. Their responsibility as bearers of God's dream especially for the downtrodden implies both providing for immediate needs of the marginalized and committing themselves to the promotion of justice in the society in which they live and work. Because this demands involvement in the formulation of social policies promoting structural changes as a matter of justice, religious at the UN thereby give the virtue of justice a tone of charity. This in turn makes justice itself more effective in the modern world. Undertaking a UN apostolate is a bold step in this direction, with its opportunity of participating in universal solidarity on behalf of those they serve.

---

[67]*Decree on the Up-to-Date Renewal of Religious Life: Perfectae Caritatis,* #2 in Austin Flannery, ed., *Vatican Council II: The Conciliar and Post Conciliar Documents,* vol. 1, New Revised Edition (Northport, New York: Costello Publishing Company, 5th reprint, 2004), 612.

Today there are over thirty religious institute NGOs with varying ECOSOC status and DPI affiliation present at New York UN headquarters, and many more such institutes operate on grassroots levels. As indicated in the introduction, we draw on the Order of St. Augustine's NGO in exploring the experience of religious institute UN NGOs.

Community is a central element of Augustinian spirituality. It also provides a compelling impetus for their UN mission. In his three levels of communities—the home, the state and the whole world—mentioned above, Augustine recognizes both the connectedness of societal reality and its complexity. What is local may and does have a global impact, the converse being true as well. Policies made in the UN are lived out locally and on state levels, just as questions raised in local situations generate UN policies. Thus, responses to today's social questions demand that agents of social change be involved in each of the three levels of community in which we live. Augustine realized that issues become more extensive and dangerous at the larger level, i.e., the whole world, and they beg for universal solidarity. "... And, of course, as with the perils of the ocean, the bigger the community, the fuller it is of misfortunes."[68]

Thus inspired, Augustinians, like other Catholic NGOs, sought UN participation as their response to calls for universal solidarity before the world's complex social questions. The Augustinian NGO, 'Curia Generalizia Agostiniana' was affiliated with the DPI in April of 1997 and accredited with ECOSOC with special consultative status in May of 2014. In typical style, all NGOs of religious institutes of men and women bear the various identities, theological self-understandings, spirituality orientations and charisms of their specific groups. These characteristics condition who they are, when they got here, their activities, their achievements, lessons learned, challenges, prospects and

---

[68]*City of God*, 19.7.

how their UN NGO mission is a religious apostolate and not merely social activism.

Ever since making their entrance upon the UN scene, religious institute NGOs' continue to increase in number more than Catholic lay groups do, at least at the New York UN headquarters. According to Joan F. Burke, SNDdeN, former UN representative of Sisters of Notre Dame de Namur, this flourishing may be due to the finances and personnel needed to maintain an active UN office in New York. Her observation is reinforced by success of the few lay groups that can maintain such presence.

Indeed, physical presence at UN headquarters in New York and other strategic places matters, since it greatly increases the ability to contribute directly to the UN. It promotes a healthy interplay between local outlets of organizational activities and the global needs discussed in the UN. By that fact, it ensures the opportunity of bringing the voice of the periphery to the center where the decisions that impact those on the periphery are made.

The presence of many worldwide religious institutes and the wide range of experiences available from them add to their advantage over lay groups, especially in localization and internationalization of NGO projects. Their community activities place them at the grassroots with communities of those whose general interest the UN is meant to serve. According to Sr. Eileen Gannon of the Dominican Leadership Conference at the UN, "justice, poverty, fair trade and sustainability are global. They are local issues as well, and our work at the UN complements the good work done by our sisters and brothers where they live. Global policies are lived locally, and we make the connection."[69]

Gannon's point is expressed another way by Michael Edwards et al, authors of *New Roles and Relevance: Development NGOs and the*

---

[69] See Sr. Eileen Gannon in Patrick Nicholson, "Window on the World," *Tablet*, 12 April (2008), 4.

Challenge of Change. They maintain that "NGOs cannot succeed through stand-alone projects at the local level. They must build from concrete innovations at the grassroots level to connect with the factors that influence patterns of poverty, prejudice, and violence." We appreciate the efforts of those NGOs that have started already to think and act in this manner: integrating micro- and macro-level action into their project and advocacy activities. The global reality demands that they make this a natural way of working and not an optional extra. [70]

Hands-on local experiences equip these religious institute NGOs with varied competencies that significantly aid UN policy formation. Being present in fifty of the world's countries and involved in the everyday lives of numerous people, particularly those on the margins of history, a religious institute like the Order of St. Augustine is most likely better placed than most lay groups for informing and executing UN policies.

An example of how the international nature of religious institutes has supported their UN NGO activities can be taken from the experience of Sr. Clare Nolan of the Good Shepherd Sisters. In an interview with Arthur Jones of *National Catholic Reporter*, Sr. Clare confessed that her experiences drawn from six thousand. Good Shepherd Sisters working with girls and young women in sixty-seven countries equipped her more than any of her co-discussants in the UN panel set up following the 1995 Conference on Women to discuss the plight of girls.[71]

For instance, she alone had an accurate account of the current condition and numbers of uneducated, ethnic minority girls in Thailand. She also was familiar with facts on female genital mutilation in places like Ghana and Egypt. The international justice and peace commis-

---

[70] See Michael Edwards, et. al., David Lewis and Tina Wallace, eds., *New Roles and Relevance: Development NGOs and the Challenge of Change* (Bloomfield, Connecticut: Kumarian Press, 2000), 10.

[71] See Arthur Jones, "Nuns at the U.N." in *National Catholic Reporter*, online edition (October 1, 1999): 1, *http://www.natcath.com/NCR_Online/archives/100199/100199d.htm*, visited February 04, 2009.

sions of these religious institutes are valuable assets to their UN representatives.

The competence on UN issues enjoyed by religious institutes, especially those of women, was once powerfully affirmed by Leister Wilson, Professor of UN Studies at Long Island University, New York. Talking about religious women participants in the UN he said that they are so good at the work that you cannot afford not to grant them their needs.

Concurrently, the presence of these religious NGOs at the center has yielded equally positive results for their local constituencies. Several programs and projects based on the UN policies have been formulated and executed by the Augustinians. An example is the Hunger Awareness Program and the Jubilee project in Baba Dogo, Kenya for the needs of HIV/AIDS patients. Also, Augustinian students in the Province of Cebu, Philippines partnered in a collaborative program with students at St. John Paul II High School in Canada on healthcare outreach to the poor as a context for human rights education.

The extent to which Catholic-inspired religious institute NGOs are integrated into UN activities is evident from the number of their members in leadership positions in various UN-NGO committees. Joan Kirby of the Religious of the Sacred Heart (RSCJ) was past president of the DPI/NGO Executive committee. Thomas Brennan of Salesian Mission served on the Board of Directors of the DPI/NGO Executive Committee. Ignatius Harding of Franciscan International was the pioneer vice-chair of the ECOSOC/NGO Committee on Social Development. Joan F. Burke of the Sisters of Notre Dame de Namur, Winfred Doherty of the Good Shepherd Sisters and Margaret Mayce of the Dominican Leadership Conference all served as chairperson of the same committee. Mary Jo Toll, SND and Emeka Obiezu, OSA were the chair and vice chair of the NGO Committee on Migration respectively.

In Geneva too, Religious NGOs have held and continue to hold leadership roles. Franciscan International headed the Committee on

Development as well as the Committee on Freedom of Religion and Belief.[72] Franciscans International was behind the establishment of the NGO Values Caucus that provided for the inclusion of ethical questions in UN proposals through NGOs. According to Sr. Kaithe Uhler, co-chair of Franciscan International, before 1993, words like, "values, ethics, spirituality and religion were almost taboo."[73]

However, it is fair to observe that this visibility of religious institute NGOs may be variously interpreted. On the one hand, it positively witnesses to the level of their integration in the system and commitment to service. On the other hand, observers with contrary opinions have seen it as a demonstration of the domination of the religious groups within the NGO forum. Such was the insinuation of some representatives of a few Catholic lay group NGOs, particularly as they reflected on the rise and fall of the International Catholic Organization (ICO). We shall return to the ICO later in this chapter.

Religious institute NGOs have also progressed more than the lay groups in the area of collaboration among their groups. Some individual institutes have entered into organizational partnerships with each other to form an NGO or a coalition of NGOs at the international level. While UNANIMA International presents a good example of the former, Vivat and Franciscan International — a combination of Franciscan sisters, brothers, priests, lay associates and Dominicans -- represent the latter. UNANIMA is a coalition formed in 2002 of 16 congregations of women religious committed to work in harmony with the UN Charter for justice at the international level for the economic and social advancement of all peoples. It envisioned united action that can make a difference.[74]

---

[72] See Kevin Ahern, "The Role of International Catholic Organizations in Promoting the Gospel in the Community of Nations," 6; also *www.ngocongo.org*.
[73] See Arthur Jones, "Nuns at the U.N.," 2.
[74] *http://www.unanima-international.org/english/index.htm*. *http://www.vivatinternational.org/*.

VIVAT International is a faith-based NGO founded jointly by the Society of the Divine Word (SVD) and the Missionary Sisters Servants of the Holy Spirit (SSpS), whose work, expertise, and experience have direct bearing on issues related to social justice, development, peace and ecology. Collaborators include those directly associated with these congregations in their apostolate and activities related to these issues. The VIVAT family has increased in recent times with the admittance of twelve associate members. There is also a formal network of all religious congregations and orders in the UN known as Religious at the UN (RUN) with twenty-two registered members.

UNANIMA and VIVAT present enormous lessons in this UN apostolate. They both hold the hope for the continuation of the UN presence for those groups which may not always have the resources, personnel and finances to continue on their own. They boldly witness to a great spirit of collaboration emerging among different religious groups, where individual identities are not a barrier to unity or collaborative ministry.

Like their religious counterparts, their UN presence helps lay groups originally focused only on material relief to add advocacy to their program. Following its 1949 UN accreditation with ECOSOC at special consultative status, Pax Romana added advocacy to its projects. It is represented in five UN headquarters – New York, Geneva, Paris, Vienna and Nairobi. It is present also in UN specialized agencies such as the International Labor Organization (ILO), the United Nations Educational, Scientific and Cultural Organization (UNESCO) and the World Bank as well as other international establishments like the Council of Europe.

In its early history, Pax Romana was initially committed to practical aid on behalf of persons, primarily students, victimized by various disasters. During and after World War II, it helped to organize war relief efforts on behalf of those adversely affected. It was instrumental in the founding of the European Fund for Aids to Students and the

134

later 1943 World Fund for Aids to Students. This fund first helped refugees and students who were prisoners of war and then afterwards students suffering from tuberculosis. Pax Romana worked at various centers in Leysin, France, Rocca di Papa, Italy, and Ashton Hayes, Great Britain. They arranged funding to establish university hostels in China and India and to provide pharmaceutical products and laboratory equipment in other countries. In 1946, Pax Romana, through the auspices of the Swiss Catholic Mission, sent six hundred thousand books to student prisoners.[75]

Since its partnership with the UN, Pax Romana played significant advocacy roles in areas such as "human rights, conscientious objection, social development, sustainable development, youth, education, religious freedom, women's rights and disarmament."[76] Conscientious objection refers to refusal to participate as a combatant in war, or in some cases to undertake any role supporting a combatant organization or armed forces.

Pax Romana was among Catholic Church-inspired NGOs led by Pax Christi and represented by Mike Hovey and Eileen Egan that partnered with many other NGOs and interest groups to seek UN recognition of conscientious objection as a human right. In 1998, through the United Nations Commission on Human Rights resolution 1998/77, the United Nations Office of the High Commissioner for Human Rights officially recognized that "persons [already] performing military service may develop conscientious objections."[77] Together with Franciscan International, Pax Romana contributed eight of the forty oral interventions made by seventeen Catholic Church-inspired

---

[75] See *A Brief History of IMCS-Pax Romana (1887-2006)*.

[76] Kevin Ahern, "The Role of International Catholic Organizations in Promoting the Gospel in the 'Community of Nations,'" 4.

[77] See CHR 54th 4/22/1998E/CN.4/RES/1998/77" (United Nations Human Rights, Office of the High Commissioner for Human Rights, 1998), *http://ap.ohchr.org/documents/sdpage_e.aspx?b=1&se=10&t=11*.

NGOs during the 60th Session of the Human Rights Commission (2004).[78]

Connecting the Local & the International

One of the noteworthy advantages of religious groups over their lay counterparts is the worldwide reach of their international communities. Through that structuring they can make the priceless connection between local issues and international policies. However, some international lay groups share this characteristic—sometimes surpassing their religious colleagues. *Pax Romana*, a confederation for all Catholic students and all legitimate Catholic groups in universities all over the world, has a constituency most likely larger than any religious institute. It has active representation at five UN headquarters, New York, Geneva, Paris, Vienna, and Nairobi as noted above, where it focuses on the primary program of each of these five. For example, its Geneva representatives deal with human rights, while Pax Romana brings to Paris a youth perspective on education, culture and other areas of UNESCO competence.[79]

Pax Romana also gives a good example of connecting the local with the international. Its representatives in the international arena maintain a healthy relationship with their local base by organizing programs that bring UN projects close to other members of the organization. Kevin Ahern, former president of the organization, notes that since 1999, Pax Romana has brought the UN agenda on human rights to both its members and diocesan promoters of justice and peace through its two annual internship programs. This has provided the occasion for on-going formation of these activists in Catholic social doctrine.[80] Ahern notes that Pax Romana holds an annual study session at UN New York Headquarters on various themes of Catholic

---

[78] Kevin Ahern, "The Role of International Catholic Organizations in Promoting the Gospel in the 'Community of Nations,'" 5.
[79] Ibid., 8.
[80] Ibid., 6, 8, 9.

social teaching. Theologians are often invited to these on-going formation events to interact with UN representatives. Participants assume responsibility for organizing similar events at their local campuses. This process of interlinking local and international levels represents a symbiotic relationship. It ensures the interpenetration of ideas and programs to realize the organization's mission of caring for the youth within a globalized world.

Caritas International shares this same goal of connecting the local with the international, proving that this linkage is not simply a religious institute NGO advantage. This NGO also represents the seamless transition from sole focus on relief to inclusion of advocacy, which either came from their UN relationship or was strengthened by it—or both. Caritas International, a confederation of one hundred sixty-two Catholic organizations present in over two hundred countries and territories, guarantees a global dimension with an outreach equal to or surpassing most religious institutes. It enjoys a privileged place within Church circles like no other Catholic-inspired NGO, originally defining itself as a relief, development and social service organization. With 1947 Vatican Curia approval, *Caritas* was endorsed as the official representative of all Catholic Church welfare organizations of an international level, particularly at the United Nations. It is one of the very few NGOs directly funded by the Church and used by governments to reach the needy at the grassroots.

With the tsunami of events from recent global crises, Caritas added advocacy to its activities, getting deeply involved with systemic problems leading to poverty, exclusion, intolerance, and discrimination against people based on race, religion, culture, age or gender. Its UN relationship with ECOSOC status opens opportunities for it to pursue these goals, and it is one of the few Catholic NGOs, in fact one of the few NGOs of any kind, that can afford to maintain representation at the several UN headquarters.

In 2005, *Caritas International* opened an office at the UN High Commission for Refugees and the Commission for Human Rights headquarters in Geneva with Maddalena Occhetta as delegate.[81] Its current UN representative at New York, Joseph Cornelius Donnelly, works in collaboration with the UN and other NGOs as one of the very few Catholic organizations having significant input relating to Palestine and Israel, to peace in Colombia, Northern Uganda and Sudan as well as to the Millennium Development Goals (MDGs) and now to the Post-2015 Development Agenda.

Another of its UN mission achievements is its joint sponsorship with the International Cooperation for Development and Solidarity of *Putting Life Before Debt*, published by the International Catholic Organization in 1998. This publication called for the cancellation of the "unpayable debt" at Jubilee 2000, and it was used by the UN Department of Economic and Social Affairs (DESA) to aid in its examination, recommendation and promotion of the process known as the program "Financing for Development."[82]

In 2006 Caritas provided the opportunity for Ugandan Archbishop John Baptist Odama to visit New York UN headquarters to present the horrifying story of the twenty year brutal unreported Ugandan war resulting in the abduction of over 20,000 children recruited as child soldiers, into forced labor or for sexual exploitation.[83] It also facilitated the New York meeting of the religious leaders forum of Sudan with Secretary General Ban Ki-moon and various member states that expedited the 2012 referendum establishing South Sudan as a state. This exemplifies its effort in connecting the local and the

---

[81] *Globalisation of Solidarity*, 17, 18.

[82] "Financing for Development," was the outcome of the UN International Conference on Development in Mexico otherwise known as "Monterrey Consensus of the International Conference on Financing for Development." See *Presence*, vol. 7, issue 1, Fall (2008), 3. *Presence* is a publication of International Catholic Organizations Information Center, New York.

[83] See Patrick Nicholson, "Window on the World," *Tablet*, 12 April (2008), 4 of 4-5.

international so that the voices of the people impact international level decisions.

Lay groups have also played a leading role in the UN NGOs community. Kevin Ahern of Pax Romana was vice-president of the Conference of Non-governmental organizations in consultative status with the ECOSOC (CONGO). Joseph Donnelly of *Caritas* was chosen chair of the NGO Committee on the Security Council. He also chaired the 58th DPI-NGO Annual Conference.

Many lay groups have an advantage over religious institutes in dealing with institutionalism and inflexible bureaucratic structures. While there are other instances of lay group advantage, this one in particular is singled out for its significance to our project. As their more flexible structures may generally allow lay NGO adaptation to be easier, adaptation for religious NGOs can be all the more difficult for having to see every change pass through cumbersome stages of religious institute decision-making.

An example is the Augustinians' intention to progress to ECOSOC status, proposed by its NGO ten years ago and just recently approved by the Order. It is characteristic of orthodox ways of thinking and of bureaucratic structural systems to limit opportunities for a participative decision-making-processes. This limitation can inhibit putting into practice NGO rhetoric promoting equity and participatory management. Not only do these orthodox administrative patterns and high bureaucratic structures delay effective NGO action, they also hinder NGO ability to foster reform and to promote justice, equity, democracy and accountability in the world.[84]

John A. Coleman, S.J. identifies this high bureaucratic structure as a general weakness of Catholicism as well. Its hierarchical inflexibility remains an obstacle for NGOs and other organizations under its guidance. These cannot function effectively in global civil society as

---

[84] Michael Edwards, et. al., "Increasing Leverage for Development," 13.

modern NGOs should be able to do. He claims, without specifying names, that groups that are "semi-autonomous," with little dependence on the Church or any of its organized institutions, are more likely to be the major Catholic actors adaptable and flexible in activist global networks.[85]

One illustrative problem is a difficulty that religious-institute NGO representatives endure every day if they have a specific mandate. Because they have no authority or freedom to modify their mandates, they become frustrated, cut off from the fluidity of UN procedures. Such a situation may be compared, albeit in varied degrees, to those of the member states delegates as discussed in chapter one. An example of this can be cited in those Catholic religious NGOs whose headquarters have identified specific issues their representatives can follow and the extent they can participate in the advocacy. These representatives have to confer with their headquarters before signing on to any collaborative advocacy statements. This may take a back and forth communication before the authorization is obtained. Often times, such authorization may arrive too late for the deadline to endorse the statement in question.

Despite advantages of the one group over the other, lay and religious institute NGOs have learned that it is better to work in collaboration with each other. Some groups of religious institutes now include lay associates in their UN NGO apostolate. But the rise and fall of the International Catholic Organizations (ICO) casts a shadow on this acclaimed collaboration between lay and religious groups of Catholic-inspired NGOs. Further, its impact has significant theological implications.

From its 1927 beginnings with eleven of the Catholic NGO representatives at the League of Nations, ICO was formed mainly by lay

---

[85] See John A. Coleman, "Making the Connections: Globalization and Catholic Social Thought," in John A. Coleman and William F. Ryan, eds., *Globalization and Catholic Social Thought: Present Crisis* (Ottawa: Novalis, 2005), 25 of 9-27.

groups. Created to ensure greater harmony among Catholic voices,[86] it always operated in loose structures aimed at facilitating information exchange, mobilization of support and co-ordination of strategies to ensure effectiveness and efficiency. The arrival of male and female religious institute NGOs effected a dramatic change in the dynamics of the organization, especially in its leadership.

Some lay groups feared that increased religious presence in the organization would lead to them dominating it. For these lay groups, this would be tantamount to religious usurping an apostolate that is not theirs. The notion as we will later see in chapter three, under the theological self-understanding of communion ecclesiology and the dilemma of divided ministry is that witness in secular plane is a prerogative of the laity. This above sentiment, the main issue among several others, led to the call by the 2007 Rome Forum for Catholic-inspired NGOs' Conference for the dissolution and restructuring of the ICO. This eventually led to the closure of its Information Offices in Paris and in New York June 19, 2008 and summer 2012 respectively.

It is moreover obvious that many lay groups do not appreciate that their religious counterparts exclude them from participation in Religious at the UN (RUN). As mentioned earlier, RUN is an association in which representatives of religious institutes of women and men may informally interact. RUN members believe lay and religious groups have ideas about the UN apostolate so divergent that lay admittance into RUN should be discouraged. Moreover, lay – religious Catholic UN collaboration is thought to be most difficult. Even lay representatives of religious institutes are not allowed to participate in RUN. These are serious concerns for a theological assessment of a UN apostolate.

---

[86] See Rosemary Goldie, *From a Roman Window, Five Decades: The World, the Church and the Catholic Laity* (Blackburn: HarperCollins 1998), 47, in Kevin Ahern, "The Role of International Catholic Organizations in Promoting the Gospel in the 'Community of Nations,'" A Research Paper, 2.

These considerations highlight one of the problems raised by Yves Congar's ecclesiology mentioned in the general introduction to this Part One: the "distinction of planes" between "ecclesial-clerical and lay-secular action." If socio-political activities are reserved only for the laity, as this distinction implies, it would be right for lay NGOs to object that religious NGOs are intruding into areas inappropriate to their vocations. Or they may see these organizations as another avenue of clerical domination. More of the theological questions raised by this situation are taken up in the part two of this work. The importance of this ICO dynamics to this work merits a close look at the organization capturing especially the various opinions and events leading to its closure.

The International Catholic Organizations (ICO): Its Rise and Fall

As mentioned above, the history of the International Catholic Organization goes back the 1927 initiative of eleven of the Catholic NGO representatives at the League of Nations, mainly lay groups, known as the Conference of Presidents of International Catholic Organizations. The intention was to ensure greater cooperation among the Catholic voices.[87] This idea was resurrected at the San Francisco UN International Conference in 1945, with the same aim of ensuring a greater coordination among Catholics, especially the NGOs. In their first meeting in Brussels, the association was renamed *Conference des Organizations Internationales Catholiques* – the Conference of International Catholic Organizations (CICO). International Catholic Organization (ICO), as it would become commonly known, opened centers in Paris (1947), Geneva (1950) and New York (1977).

---

[87] See Rosemary Goldie, *From a Roman Window, Five Decades: The World, the Church and the Catholic Laity* (Blackburn: HarperCollins 1998), 47, in Kevin Ahern, "The Role of International Catholic Organizations in Promoting the Gospel in the 'Community of Nations,'" A Research Paper, 2.

The New York office of the International Catholic Organizations was from 1946 until 1972 run concurrently by the National Catholic Welfare Conference, staffed by Catherine Schaefer, the main contact person for the Conference's UN office and the president of the ICO. It was upon the closing of the NCWC-UN office in 1972 by the US bishops Conference, that the ICO sought its own office. Until its demise in 2012, the ICO office was on the premises of Holy Family Parish, the Catholic Parish Church of the UN, New York, as it is called. By 1953 it received the Holy See's official recognition.

It is important to note that some members of this group were invited to the Second Vatican Council as resource persons. One of them made a major contribution to the final draft of *Gaudium et Spes*. Others were appointed auditors to the Council by the November 1963 request of Paul VI: "We felt that a few qualified representatives of the laity could and should be associated, as Auditors, with this great 'review of life,' and be admitted to attend the Council. And we turned in the first towards the movement which represented the laity in the most authoritative and ample fashion: the Catholic International Organizations."[88]

As discussed earlier in this chapter, the ICO represents an example of the Network groups, one of the three coalition mechanisms through which NGOs operate, especially in relation to the UN. This mechanism of a very loose structure was aimed at facilitating exchange of information, mobilization of support and co-ordination of strategies that help to ensure their effectiveness and efficiency. It provided Catholic groups at the UN with UN logistics, including accreditation details, other administrative protocols and the latest news in the UN. To be able to deliver in these areas, its staff attended daily briefing sessions of the DPI/NGO and ECOSOC sections. The center also served as a meeting place for some groups of Catholic NGOs who came to New York for business. It also organized the annual wine and cheese event, an informal forum that followed the prayer service held by the

---

[88] Ibid., 3.to see the request of Paul VI.

Holy See at the Holy Family Church for all the participant member state delegates at the opening session of the General Assembly.

In its later years the organization's membership and leadership shifted towards more presence of religious both male and female. Of the forty-two registered members of the ICO, twenty-four were of religious congregations. As was alluded to above this shift in presence did not seem to go down well with some members of the lay organizations who felt overwhelmed, dominated, and edged out. They would seek for a restructuring or complete dissolution of the organization as was later recommended by the Forum for Catholic-inspired NGOs' Conference (Rome, 2007). There was polarity of opinions on this alleged domination and its contribution to the later demise of the organization.

One opinion linked the death of the organization to the negative reception of some of its members to the organization's relationship with the Holy See Mission. This was the position of the Dominican Sr. Dorothy Farley, the last director of the ICO Information Center, concerning the closure of the organization. In my interview with her, she claimed that many members of ICO viewed the center's relationship with the Holy See as too close, and they claimed that the center had become a "stooge" of the Holy See. This perspective led such groups not only to withdraw from the ICO but, through the spread of such propaganda, they also discouraged others from associating with the center.

Interestingly, Sr. Farley noted that as members accused it of a too-close-for-comfort relationship with the Holy See, ICO also often came under criticism by the Holy See, which in most cases considered the association too "liberal" to be called Catholic. She believed that it was such controversies as these more than anything else that led to the convocation of the 2007 Rome conference, which aimed to strengthen the collaboration among NGOs, and to develop a greater and healthier relationship with the Holy See.[89] This conference was itself another heated controversy in the Holy See-NGOs relationship, as many religious NGOs, particularly the women's groups, who were not invited to the conference, were critical of the criterion for the selection of participants.

Following the injunction of the Rome Forum, the Paris Chapter of the association voted on June 19, 2008 with more than two-thirds majority of its members to dissolve the organization. Nevertheless the New York ICO center undertook a series of attempts to keep the organization alive. First a committee was set up by some concerned members of the organization to see what could be done to revive it, considering its importance in the life of the Catholic NGOs at the UN.

A "transition committee" headed by the Dominican Sr. Eileen Gannon worked on the modalities of the center's future operations. Among the committee's main challenges were the constitution of the board of directors of the center and the financial responsibility for the maintenance of the present office in the premises of Holy Family parish in New York City. Two different regimes of board of directors would serve the organization before its final closure. These different regimes organized series of educational, advocacy and outreach events.

The last board, in which I was privileged to serve as vice chair, following the impossibility of maintaining the ICO's information center experimented on a rebranding of the organization. What came forth was the International Catholic Organization Network (ICON), described as ICO without border. This would be a metamorphosis from a physical to a virtual center utilizing the advantages of the free information technology age. The Communication department of Franciscan College New York agreed to help coordinate this new form of existence.

---

[89] See John Ketelers, Secretary General, International Catholic Migration Commission, "A Synthesis of the Discussion," *Forum of Catholic-inspired NGOs*, Rome November 30 – December 2 (2007): 1-8.

Included in the ICON model is periodic public educational event to showcase the Catholic presence in the UN.

To test their hopes in this new venture the board in December 2011, organized a lecture event on the state of Christians in Palestine. Though it received massive participation and good commendation from participants, it still could not come up with the result the committee needed — the commitment of the members to the association.

The efforts to save the ICON proved too late, as even other issues emerged. These included lack of sufficient understanding of the role of ICON apart from provision of meeting space as well as member disinterest in maintaining anther structural organization. It seems the ICON role and values were taken over by other realities.

It might be significant to consider the impact of the creation of Religious at the UN (RUN) on ICON and its demise. As we noted, religious congregations and orders of men and women had the highest number of NGOs on the member list of ICON. They were also the highest supporters of the center in recent times. With many of them securing office spaces within New York, it became financially difficult for them to continue to support the funding of ICO to pay its rent and maintain its staff. RUN also provided for them the opportunity of informal interaction more appropriate for themselves as religious than what ICON might offer if it were to do so. I still believe there is a need for a space for the wider Catholic NGOs at the UN. There is a whisper that the Catholic NGOs in Geneva are mulling over the thought of re-inventing the ICO.

Following an evaluative process and voting of its membership, the board of directors voted six-to-one to finally close the organization in summer of 2012. The record of the Organization, a 21.25 linear-feet of 17 boxes is archived at the "American Catholic History Research Center and University Archives of Catholic University of America.

Relations between Catholic Church-inspired NGOs
& the Holy See UN Mission

Many would assume that the catholicity of Catholic-inspired NGOs may be judged by their relationship with the Holy See, the official representative of the Catholic Church at the UN. This assumption leads us to take a look at this relationship. Official Church UN participation does encourage many Catholic-inspired NGOs, especially those of religious institutes, to participate in the UN themselves. The Augustinians are among the groups that openly allude to their affinity with the Church as their main reason for seeking UN relationship.

In its Constitution #39, the Order of St Augustine pledges its unreserved loyalty to the Church and its unflinching cooperation in all the Church's missions. "We are, moreover, sons of the Church brought into being for her service, and we cannot give a better witness of this service than by taking up the work that Mother Church desires of us." This particular text references Augustine's *Letter*, 48.2; 243.6-8. Also, by quoting Augustine *Ps.* 132 and *Ep.* 243, the 2011 General Chapter of the Order acknowledges its commitment to the Church and her needs as it declares: "We have not been called to community life in order to find security, but rather to aid the Church in giving birth to new children of God, reborn in Christ's image." This conviction is enunciated in the Chapter document supporting the Order's UN apostolate: "this association provides us with the opportunity to make our voice one with that of the Church..." [90]

Nevertheless, following the regulations of NGO UN accreditation and affiliation as earlier discussed, Catholic Church-inspired NGOs do not need the encouragement of, or direct association with, the Holy See to become UN partners. Even though some of them may have received direct funding from the Church, these NGOs, like their secular

---

[90] See *Rule and Constitution of the Order of Saint Augustine*, #39 (Villanova, PA: Augustinian Press, 1991), 48; *Document of the Ordinary General Chapter* of the Order of St. Augustine, (B-9, CGO, '01).

counterparts, generally and officially relate with the Holy See in an unattached manner as separate bodies with different rights and responsibilities in the UN.

Unlike secular NGOs that at times publicly criticize their nations on general attitudes or particular stands on issues, Catholic Church-inspired NGOs tend not to criticize the Holy See. This does not mean that they necessarily agree with the Holy See on all issues. Church-inspired NGOs have been known to differ from the Holy See on many issues. Yet these NGOs still derive their inspiration from the wisdom of the social teachings of the Church. Without taking public positions on problems the Holy See would invest interest in such as abortion, contraception and the response to the HIV/AIDS pandemic, most Church-inspired NGOs turn attention to the root causes of these problems. They might discuss such public and socio-economic factors as women in marriage, poverty and welfare to the extent these may be connected to abortion, birth control, and HIV/AIDS problems.

In most cases the relationship between the Holy See and the Catholic-inspired NGOs echoes the internal dynamics of the Church's life marked by the line between left and right wings and also of the neutral group. A Catholic Church-inspired NGO that has engaged the Holy See in public criticism is Catholics for a Free Choice (CFC), which might be dubbed a leftist group. It holds the Holy See partly responsible for the over six hundred thousand women who die each year during pregnancy and childbirth, for the five million eight hundred thousand people living with HIV and the two and one half million who die from AIDS each year. According to this group, the Holy See's culpability comes from its objections to women's rights to control their sexuality and fertility as well as its condemnation of artificial means of family planning as morally unacceptable. Its members hold that, in frustrating the majority consensus by its strong opposition, the Holy See weakens the power of resolutions that would work to reduce these horrors. It accuses the Holy See of providing support for nations like Libya, Sudan and Afghanistan among others that refuse to grant full human rights to women—a continued violation of the dignity of womanhood. For these and other reason, the CFC has named the Holy See one of the obstacles to UN effectiveness and called on the UN to revoke the Holy See's membership and privileges. The CFC further insist that the Church should not have a special UN platform but rather be restricted to NGO status.[91]

There is little substance to the allegations behind their demand, as the Holy See has not likely influenced UN resolutions on these issues in any way irrespective of its stand on them, and in the ways that it may have used its diplomatic privilege to lobby the voting members. There are strong indications that the Holy See exercised the power of such privilege in lobbying the outcome documents of the Cairo Conference on Population, 1994, the Beijing Conference on Women, 1995; the General Assembly Special Session on HIV/AIDS, 2001 and many more in recent time. In all, it does not seem that the CFC understands the consequences of the Holy See's voting option in the UN. Its choice of neutrality means it has no direct effect on UN policy since it is the UN understanding that the Holy See has chosen not to vote in any matter. This accusation only serves to blur the dynamics of the Holy See relationship with the range of NGOs purported to be Catholic-inspired.

Conversely, there are NGOs like Catholic Center for Family and Human Rights (C-FAM), seen as an army defending and promoting the Holy See pro-life agendas in various UN debates. The Holy See on its part has not shied away from identifying with the group and defending it when need be. Holy See representatives have lobbied other state delegates on behalf of C-FAM during the organization's ECOSOC status application. Such help was considered to have yielded a positive result as the organization, after many years of attempts, finally

---

[91] See, "International Campaign Calls into Question Vatican's Seat at the UN," *Catholic For A Free Choice: News Release,* March 24, (2000):1; "The Catholic Church at the United Nations," and "Catholic Church Abuses its Position at the UN," *National Secular Society,* February 4, (2004):1-8.

obtained consultative status from the ECOSOC NGO Committee January 2014 Session.

In general, the Holy See respects the rights and freedom of Catholic Church-inspired NGOs and does not wish to control them. However, it does contend that some Catholic NGO activity lacks focus. It also charges many with a lack of sound knowledge of Church teachings and principles, thus needing guidance by Church authorities. That being said, a Catholic-inspired NGO UN presence is a rare opportunity. A healthy relationship between the Holy See and the NGOs would enable the Church to keep concerns close to her heart in the forefront of UN deliberations.

As with other member states, Holy See delegates are limited in what they can say and do on topics easier for NGOs to deal with because of their place in the UN. This type of relationship is already perceivable between the Holy See and some Catholic NGOs. We recall that long before the establishment of its UN New York office, the Holy See collaborated with Catholic groups already at the UN. For instance, the United State Catholic Conference (USCC) Office for United Nations Affairs provided the visible face of the Church at the UN and helped to ensure the achievement of Holy See goals in certain areas of interest.

Jean Gartlan writes, "It was at the instance of the Holy See that Alba Zizzamia, a staff member of the USCC UN office, and a member of the first Catholic NGOs at the UN, was sent to Geneva in 1950 to monitor the UN Trusteeship Council deliberations on the status of Jerusalem."[92] This manner of representation has continued in recent times. Olivier Poquillon, O.P, the Dominican Order UN representative, attended a European Union event in 2011 representing both his Order and the Holy See. Co-sponsorship of side events at UN conferences is another way the Holy See maintains its outreach to and collaboration with Catholic NGOs. Most recently, during the 49th session of the

---

[92]See Jean Gartlan, *At the United Nations*, 54.

Commission on Population and Development, April 12, 2016, the Holy See sponsored and co-hosted a side event on "Migration, Population and Agenda 2030," with four Catholic NGOs, namely, Curia Generalizia Agostiniana; Congregations of St. Joseph; Passionists International and Congregation of the Mission.[93]

These considerations may not prove that Catholic-inspired NGOs have a functional relationship with the Holy See UN Mission. But through their different charisms and missions within the Church they do prove their catholicity. Yet the question remains unanswered as to whether or not the catholicity of an NGO may ultimately be evaluated by its relationship with the Holy See.

General Observations

At this point we reiterate that while these NGOs are not the official voice of the Catholic Church at the UN, they nevertheless represent a valuable UN presence of the Church, each in their own special ways. Beyond any doubt they have made significant contributions to the UN. With fascinating variety, these Church-inspired NGOs bring insight to issues affecting the world, and together they have contributed enormously to a language shift in many UN issues. They have joined other advocates seeking the transposition of security discourse from an exclusive stress on national security to a greater emphasis on peoples' security, from security of armaments to security through human development, from territorial security to food, employment and environmental security. This shift does not undermine the traditional attention to provide for military and territorial security but instead

---

[93] During the last UN Conference on Sustainable Development in Brazil (June 2012), the Holy See with Franciscans International, Caritas International, Catholic Relief Services will be co-organizing a side event titled "Agriculture and Sustainable Societies: Food Security, Land and Solidarity." Most recently, during the 49th session of the Commission on Population and Development, April 12, 2016, the Holy See sponsored and co-hosted a side event on "Migration, Population and Agenda 2030," with four Catholic NGOs, namely, Curia Generalizia Agostiniana; Congregations of St. Joseph, Passionists International and Congregation of the Mission.

seeks to balance the situation "where bread and bombs intersect," to employ Douglas Roche's imagery.[94] By this expression, the former Canadian Ambassador to the UN insists that human security is possible only by the "extension of social and economic development throughout the world and the elimination of nuclear weapons from military arsenals."[95]

The UN recognizes this and more especially the NGO role in organizing advocacy initiatives, immediate material relief and development internationally, nationally and regionally. A few examples can witness to the contributions of Church-inspired NGOs at the UN, especially in policy formulation and implementation. They provided effective information and advocacy that addressed issues of illicit armament trafficking in the Democratic Republic of Congo and of violations by the guerilla movement in Uganda. They also cooperated with UN agencies to initiate and sustain the reconciliation process in Burundi. The UN and its members looked to these NGOs for support and expertise on how to fulfill the Millennium Development Goals (MDGs) and still look to them now in the formulation and delivery of the post-2015 development agenda.

According to Isolda Oca, information officer of the UN Department of Public Information (DPI), "Catholic NGOs at the UN have been active advocates for the alleviation of poverty, access to primary education, empowerment of women and climate change."[96] These successes, as Patrick Nicholson, a regular contributor to the *Tablet*, observes, came about because many of these NGOs shunned any identification with Catholic ghetto ideology and instead embraced partnerships with NGOs of diverse backgrounds.[97] Various Catholic-inspired groups,

---

[94] Douglas Roche, *Bread not Bombs: A Political Agenda for Social Justice* (Edmonton: University of Calgary Press, 1999), 33.
[95] Ibid.
[96] See Isolda Oca, in Patrick Nicholson, "Window on the World," *Tablet* 12 April (2008), 4.
[97] Patrick Nicholson, "Window on the World," 4.

irrespective of their ideological stance, know well the value of partnership with other groups and regularly, effectively seek it. This is something that conservative groups would hardly ordinarily do. At the UN they liaise with evangelicals, Muslims and secular institutions that pursue their similar agendas and at times share resources with them — be they human, informational or financial. Some evangelicals hold key positions in Catholic Center for Family and Human Rights, and in turn this NGO provides training and lobbying resources for some evangelicals in gaining admission into the UN system.

From a Church perspective, the UN presence and activities of Catholic-inspired NGOs are of great value. These are distinct manifestations of the Church's commitment to solidarity with the human family for the pursuit of the common good for all, as we continue to claim. Through their unbiased collaboration and by integrating people of other faiths into their networks, they continue in a very practical way to progress in inter-faith and ecumenical dialogue, a privileged Church activity since Vatican II. In fact, the Church recognizes their work not only as an implementation but also as a source of her social teaching. As we read in John Paul II's *Centesimus Annus* (Hundredth Year) "social Catholicism is found not just in social doctrine but in [the Church's] concrete commitment and material assistance in the struggle against marginalization and suffering.'"[98]

Catholic UN NGOs of both women and men religious have enhanced their relationship with the UN by promoting uplifting spiritual celebrations of key UN events. Several NGOs have developed liturgical formats such as the Marianist Lenten Program featuring 40 days and 40 Least Developed Countries. "This program presents a rich opportunity to learn about people living in poverty and the health challenges they face in various countries around the world." Also, we

---

[98] See John Paul II, *Centesimus Annus*, #26, in John Coleman, "Making the Connection," 15.

recall that seven UN observances have been adopted into the liturgical calendar of the Augustinian Order.

The collaborative arrangements taking place among religious UN NGOs identified in this work and the important lessons they hold for the future of religious life deserve reflective emphasis. Are we seeing the beginning of a new era of religious life and identity that collapses institutional ideals into core issues of gospel values and witnessing? We saw that some such arrangements are developing between various groups of the same tradition, sometimes bringing in men's and women's groups into a harmonious focus on their common heritage and its implication for living in today's world. Examples include Dominicans, Franciscan and Passionists. This is also taking place among groups of varied traditions that are coming together under the common gospel imperative interpreted in the context of service to humanity and creation.

In this group are UNANIMA and VIVAT. Some also depute lay people, their third order or associates as sole representatives of their groups, such as the Loreto Community and the Little Sisters of the Assumption. As religious groups continue to struggle with membership crises especially in the global north, many are forced to merge into federations of their groups or the gradual introduction of lay people into strategic administrative positions of their apostolates. UN collaborative identity is a welcome experimentation in this direction.

There remain several problems that Catholic Church-inspired NGOs encounter in their UN relationship. Even considering tendencies still visible in international organizations like the UN to reject anything of religion, we must admit that the real challenges that Church-inspired NGOs must confront are attacks from within. Lack of unity and coordination pose a great threat to the riches of the plurality of these groups and their collective effect on the whole UN system.

Examples might fall into two categories. First, there is an ideological tendency that has given rise to apathy or indifference among some people of religion who oppose the UN and are therefore against any Church UN involvement. Exclusive focus on particular issues (often among pro-life partisans) arouses criticism of any Church collaboration with a group like the UN that is not absolutely pure--no matter how morally acceptable from the viewpoint of Catholic theology this collaboration may be.

Examples of UN faults that could arouse a call for a "litmus test" condemning the entire UN system are the tolerance of abortion among some in the UN population fund and the acceptance of condoms in UNICEF. Within this first category, some Christian fundamentalists, including Catholics, see the UN as the anti-Christ, a sign of worldwide empire at the end times as imaged in the book of Revelation. They see the UN as an enemy advancing programs and issues contrary to gospel values, particularly in reproductive rights and rights of people of various sexual orientations and expressions. They may even interpret the emergence of such anti-gospel values as signs of the end time, the world coming to an end.

The second category would be the tension between the earlier and later arrivals of Catholic NGOs at the UN, already discussed above. We refer on one hand to the apologetic tendency of the earlier groups who thought their work was above all else to promote and ensure the enthronement of Catholic Church principles at the UN by any means possible. In contrast, the later groups adopted a liberal attitude that acknowledges and works with UN programs even if they may not conform to basic Catholic principles or positions. In other words, while the earlier may insist on maintaining the perfect ecclesial mentality without whose help the world cannot rightfully think, the later work from a new mentality of a humble Church which realizes that the spirit of God is present in and gently leads even secular institutions with or without Church interference or blessing.

Many Catholics, including members of religious institutes, still cannot make the connection between private charity and socio-political dimensions of compassion. This situation results in what Richard A. McCormick refers to as the dichotomy between articulated Christianity and lived Christianity.[99] It leads to a pathology otherwise known as a socially dormant conscience, with its various symptoms such as ignorance, inadequacy and apathy. A socially dormant conscience is a type of social attitude associated with seriously questionable ideas about compassion held by some Christians that contribute to the multiplication and continuation of societal evil. "Such ignorance suffices in separatism or dualism – that continues the belief of discontinuity between this life and the life after, church attendance and domestic virtues." It also gives rise to "individualism that conceives social responsibility in terms of one-on-one relationships."

The combination of the two—separatism and individualism— McCormick says leads to "inadequacy – a sense of hopelessness and powerlessness and ultimate apathy."[100] With this kind of mindset, these groups of Catholics not only feel content with their one-on-one acts of charity but view socio-political activities like a UN apostolate as an unnecessary distraction for religious persons. These groups of Catholics fail to understand that charity, as Benedict XVI writes, "is the principle not only of micro-relationships…but also of macro-relationships (social, economic and political ones)."[101]

Indeed, charity that does not attend to social realities is a contradiction in terms, for charity is never without cares. This deadly confusion also reflects a failure to appreciate that the social question has taken on a truly worldwide character as stated in modern Catholic social teaching. Because of this confusion, many religious men and women have not understood the implications of the new identity their communities

---

[99] Richard A. McCormick, "The Social Responsibility of the Christian," *Blueprint for Social Justice*, Vol. LII, No. 3 (November 1998): 1.

[100] Ibid., 1-3.

[101] See Benedict XVI, *Caritas in Veritate*, #2.

have undertaken in adopting the status of an NGO and in turn associating with the UN. Some religious institute members would blame the situation on the failure of their UN representatives to find effective language and means of communicating this new reality to their membership.

Appreciation of the Catholic-inspired NGO UN mission is hindered by yet another factor: the various ideologies and attitudes toward the UN. It is important to underscore that, more than a theological concern, a principal drive behind various Christian attitudes toward the UN apostolate is perceptions of the UN held by people for various reasons. In many cases these reasons may bear national, regional or ideological undertones. They may even be media propagandized.

For instance, some developing counties may see the UN as part of their problems, as they observe the artificial economic inflation that some UN staff introduced into their countries by their lifestyles. Their people wonder why their Catholic representatives would want to be associated with such an organization and its stigma. On the other hand, other developing countries may experience benefits from the organization and see their Catholic brethren's presence there as necessary and hopeful.

Europeans, be they Catholics or not, have more faith in and allegiance to the European Union than to the UN which they treat with an attitude of reserve. Even when they do acknowledge the UN, they are more comfortable associating it with the Geneva than with the New York headquarters.

In North America, especially in the United States, the attitude toward the UN divides along party lines. Democrats tend to be more open to the UN apostolate than Republicans would be. Thus, as Joseph Rossi puts it, the Church outlook on the UN depends on overall national attitudes. It is important that we are aware of this reality as we aim toward theological reception of this apostolate.

This again calls to mind the role of acceptance of the global social question and the pursuit of faith life as a fundamental personal option. Some NGOs are already doing things to reverse ideologies and attitudes hostile to the UN. We recall the commendation cited above that was given to these NGOs by Kiyotaka Akasaka, Under-Secretary General for Communications and Public Information, for helping in re-branding the UN through their dissemination of helpful, accurate and objective information about the UN and its activities around the world.

Above all this, while we celebrate the success of Catholic Church-inspired NGOs in the areas of advancing UN developmental projects and language change, we regret that the integration of compassionate criticism of unjust UN structures into this participation has not been considered as a necessary constituent element. Indeed a few earlier attempts by Catholic Church-inspired NGOs did successfully challenge UN structures. These brought into the UN Charter NGO participation in UN organs and admission of women into key UN positions. But no other similar attempts have been recently recorded. Today there are few Catholic voices among the NGOs calling the UN to a more democratic and transparent governance. Indeed, such proactive advocacy may in the short-term demand of NGOs a self-sacrifice that might imply reevaluation of their mandate, mission and strategies. Nevertheless, in the long term it might become a stronger force for liberation.

Our study reveals some possible reasons why this important aspect of NGO participation is neglected. One is the internal deficiencies or conflicts that NGOs experience. Another reason may be inadequate assimilation of the theological principles that underlie these practical activities and implications for Catholic-inspired participants. There is also the lack of sufficient critical social analytical and relational skills that would enable the NGOs to identify and critically respond to UN structural inadequacies. As Ronald Nash states, "Few Christians, whatever their political persuasion, have made the effort to study the foundational issues that underlie the problems of social justice. It is not enough to feel compassion for the poor and oppressed. Compassion and love must be coupled with a careful grounding in the relevant philosophical, economic, political and social issues."[102] This situation makes more urgent the aim of this work for relevant theological reflection on these practical activities in order that they may bear desired fruits.

With this chapter, we come to the conclusion of Part One of this book, in which we have undertaken the practical description and analysis of the relationship between the Catholic Church and the United Nations. Even though this exercise has been more of an historical and socio-political analytical exposition, it does hope to evoke concerns that in themselves are theological. How do we interpret these activities so that they may legitimately belong to the soteriological mission of the church? How do theological categories help to sustain and improve such practical activities? These questions lead us to the second part of this project where we seek to make NGO UN participation an expression of the Church's solidarity with all humanity — an act to be interpreted theologically as within the graced economy of salvation.

---

[102] Ronald H. Nash, *Social Justice and the Christian Church* (Michigan: Mott Media, 1984), 2.

PART TWO

A Theological Interpretation & Assessment
of Catholic-Inspired NGOs at the UN

W hen we attempt a theological interpretation of Catholic-inspired NGOs at the UN, we are met by an age-old question that has always troubled Christianity: how do we confront a social concern of this world so that our response is more than a merely secular exercise and is seen as specifically Christian. This question remains open-ended because it relates to a wide variety of situations and issues. How can we claim an authentic, active Christian participation in our world's affairs within the economy of salvation, especially when it concerns social transformation of the human person? If we leave this question unanswered, analysis of such activities as we have been considering up to now would never rise above the level of an historical, political, or sociological study.

One reason why it is difficult to develop a theological interpretation of Christian activities in an utterly secular establishment such as the UN is that many Christians are still fixated on childhood notions that the Christian life is solely related to Church attendance and the reception of sacraments. It is still not easy for many to grasp the connection between faith and social activism.

"[T]he implicit theology that Christians live out in their daily lives," which Howard W. Stone and James O. Duke refer to as *"embedded theology* or *first-order theology,"* is at the root of Christian skepticism or indifference toward the real-world. "It is embedded theology that rushes to the front line in every battle over social issues of the day. Christians rise up to defend their theological convictions or express outrage when those convictions are threatened."[1] Many Catholics whom I have encountered on various occasions in the course of my work barraged me with questions rooted in this theological attitude that could be summarized by "what has Jerusalem to do with Athens." Yet, social-life situations and activities as are abundant at the UN remain significant occasions and means by which Christians can serve God and their neighbor. This is a fundamental claim of our work.

A further source of difficulty already mentioned in chapter two is that most of the social activities of Christians responding to the world's suffering, in this case Church-inspired NGOs, are not observably different from those of secular groups. To claim otherwise would seem to deny experience. Relief workers responding to victims of war may bring food to the hungry, provide shelter to the displaced, seek asylum for refugees and advocate for the rights of the most disadvantaged victims. These are common activities that cannot be readily labeled either Christian or secular.

Though there might appear to be no immediately observable factor that distinguishes such activities performed by Christians, there is a definite qualitative difference based on interpreting these activities in the light of one's own particular viewpoint—Christian faith—distinct from the viewpoints or perspectives of others such as non-Christian politicians, social activists, historians, economists etc. This interpretation influences activities of Christians so that even non-Christians may notice a hint of the extraordinary in the way these acts are performed.

---

[1] See Howard W. Stone and James O. Duke, *How to Think Theologically,* second edition (Minneapolis: Fortress Press, 2006), 13, 14, 15.

We may recall among many other examples the words of the elderly Muslim woman among beneficiaries of Caritas International experiencing the difference of how Caritas agents attended them asking, "I want to see what inspires you people to love us so much and to treat us with so much respect [more than others do]."[2]

Sensitive to these difficulties and concerns of many Catholics, we can surely grasp why the theological interpretation undertaken in this work is both necessary and urgent. Further, it is important that our theological interpretation be made within the broad project of theology "making faith connections," that is, bringing a faith perspective to the realities which lay before us. This also means that we do not exclusively corner for ourselves the prerogative of theological reflection. In reality, this activity belongs to all Christians, who are called in all circumstances to relate their faith to everyday experience and to discern what actions they are called upon to take. Rather, in our overall approach theological reflection assumes the task of appreciating and assessing the various interpretations of these Catholic, Christian actors.

Consequently, in this work we aim at a theological reflection relevant to Catholic Church-inspired NGOs involved in seemingly secular activities. Thus, the second part of this book seeks an interpretation and assessment that would specify the activities of these Catholic Church-inspired participants in the United Nations as valid Christian activities belonging to the economy of salvation—the Church's mission to continue the saving word and work of the risen Lord in space and time.

We do not intend to construct a new theology of Christian social encounter or an inflexible application of formula, let alone a conceptual framework itself etched in stone. Our process is rather a theological

---

[2] See Denis Viénot, "Message from the President and Secretary General of Caritas Internationalis," *Globalising Solidarity: 2005 Activities Report, Caritas Internationalis* (Vatican City, Rome: Caritas Internationalis, 2005), 5.

critique recognizing signs of hope uncovered by an attentive but cautious examination of these seemingly secular activities in the light of faith. We first analyze the distinctively Christian reasons given by NGO representatives for their activities, linking them to major theological principles while expecting that our analysis would inform and improve these activities as well as show them as duties incumbent upon us as Christ's witnesses in the world. Thus, we attempt to identify, interpret, correlate and assess the reasons for these NGO activities in relation to faith in the message of God and the mission of the Church. Through theological reflection, we hope to establish the Christian rationale and trustworthiness of these activities, i.e., their Christian appropriateness, intelligibility, moral integrity and validity. Our aim is to gain a deeper and fuller understanding of issues and uncover a theological motivation for improved action.

We will use two related and interactive approaches to achieve our goal. The first analyzes the movements of the spirit identified by these Catholic-inspired NGOs as inspiring their activities. The second seeks an interactive and critical engagement that clarifies these movements by subjecting them to principles of Catholic social action drawn from the scriptures and Catholic social teaching. For this interactive engagement, we draw on the insights of prominent Catholic theologians and others whose approach to theology offers salient insights. Our methodology consists of both deductive and inductive components consistent with a practical theology within which we classify this work.

We also hope that our approach will enable us to respond to some of the theological issues emerging from our analysis in preceding chapters. One theological issue is the intersection of political activism and evangelism—the urge to change people's spiritual conviction and the urge to change people's material condition.[3] This issue is tacit in the

---

[3] Erica Bornstein, *The Spirit of Development: Protestant NGOs, Morality, and Economics in Zimbabwe* (New York: Routledge, 2003), 27.

Christian fundamentalist criticism of the UN in apocalyptic terms as the anti-Christ, as well as their claim that the salvation of the human soul and mind separate from embodied, social activities is the only sure step towards salvaging humanity.

A second theological issue is divergence of opinions between earlier and later Catholic Church-inspired NGOs on the position the Church should take in their UN relationship—a serious ecclesiological concern. An earlier aim of NGO-UN relationship was solely to propagate Catholic principles; a later aim is to participate in programs the UN itself initiated. A third theological issue is the legitimacy of the presence of Roman Catholic clergy and religious congregations or orders in the UN.

In summary, this second part of our project is structured to achieve four goals: first, to articulate the various theological self-understandings that enable Catholic-inspired NGOs to engage in socio-political undertakings; second, to provide an assessment of their activities in the light of these various theological self-understandings and their articulated visions; third, to propose revisions to theological positions that would respond to what is being neglected in the works of these Church-inspired NGOs, i.e. a form of participation that would respond to the structural injustices inherent in the UN system; fourth, to inquire how this relationship would enable these NGOs to deal with their own decision-making on related issues such as respecting and acknowledging divergent voices.

3

THE CATHOLIC-INSPIRED NGO/UN RELATIONSHIP
& THEOLOGICAL-PASTORAL PRINCIPLES FOR
CATHOLIC SOCIAL ACTION

T his chapter examines the various theological self-understandings that enable the Catholic Church-inspired NGOs to engage
in their UN undertaking. It correlates these self-understandings with
principles of Catholic social action to validate their authenticity. Finally it assesses the activities of these NGOs enumerated in chapter
two in the light of their various theological self-understandings, their
articulated visions and principles of Catholic social action.

Theological Self-Understandings of
Catholic-Inspired NGOs Participating in the UN

The term "theological self-understandings," as used here, includes not
only the way in which Catholic Church-inspired NGOs understand
themselves but also the theological bases or principles they identify as
inspiring and sustaining their activities. Both aspects are inextricably
bound up with each other and in the final analysis never operate sep-
arately. For instance, those who follow in the footsteps of Augustine
ask themselves how they are to be witnesses to his life and legacy built
on the gospel in such an earthly establishment as the UN. This question cannot be resolved by proof text reaches into Augustine and his

spirituality. It must be approached by asking what he would say to them and what he would demand that they do if he were alive and with them.

This is how each of these NGOs returns to its heritage and varying traditions to find theological thread to weave their story of UN presence for the larger Catholic Church. This section depends mostly on my interviews with representatives of several of these Church-inspired NGOs.

These interviews were held with six representatives of different Catholic Church-inspired NGOs and were structured taking their diverse natures into account. Interviewees were drawn from representatives of the laity, religious men and women, and those in leadership positions on UN-NGO committees. Both DPI and ECOSOC status NGOs were chosen. Each interview location was chosen for the convenience of both the interviewer and the interviewees. Interviewees were asked similar questions with only slight modifications: "What in your Christian faith makes you consider your activities, especially participating in the UN, a Christian duty?" and "How could you interpret these activities in a way that would differ from interpretations by non-Catholic or Christian actors?"

In general, during the interviews I observed exceptional receptivity, honesty and openness to new information and to the illumination of the Spirit that would counteract complacency or satisfaction with old preconceptions. Again, the legitimacy of this approach is consistent with the characteristic of practical theology that takes seriously every Christian's interpretation of their faith encounter as a lived experience. Consistent with the thought of Karl Rahner, theology exists first in an unthematic horizon which must be respected as an irreplaceable component of doing theology itself. Without necessarily assessing the theological implications, I could see that these Catholic actors were always at least somewhat conscious that their actions were driven by their love of God and his call to them.

From the results of these interviews with Church-inspired NGO representatives as well as from the insights of other sources, it is clear that these groups primarily define the reason for their UN participation in terms of their identification with the Church whatever their particular focus or charism may be. Nevertheless, some wanted to be sure their expressed understanding of Church was not misconstrued as limited to its hierarchical structure. In this way they fully affirm their catholicity and assert their link with the Church, which answers one of the major concerns bothering some people about the UN apostolate.

The Augustinian Order—specifically directed in its activity toward the service of the universal Church—states emphatically "We are there because the Church is there."[1] While specifically declaring that they went to the UN to help promote the Holy See's agenda there, the Augustinians went further, tracing this bond with the church and its implications as far back as the Acts of the Apostles' first Christian community on which they are modeled.[2] They understand the formation and subsequent movement of the early Church from Jerusalem to Rome from the outlook of a theological geography.

Of course, there are varied interpretations of this movement of the early Church to Rome. The Augustinian perspective referred to here arises from the Order's search of its traditions for a normative impetus for its new apostolate of denouncing acts committed against social justice now at a time when the "social question" has become worldwide. This movement to Rome, recounted in the last two chapters of the Acts of the Apostles, shows a Church committed to the salvation of the entire world. This community of the early Christians knew that this task entailed permeating society with its founding principles and qualities. Rome symbolized, and in reality was, the center of power and the personification of empire. Their task is therefore described in terms of

---

[1] Guidelines for the OSA-UN/NGO Apostolate.

[2] See "Rule #4", *Rule and Constitutions: Order of St. Augustine* (Rome: Pubblicazioni Agostiniane, 2008), 9.

community versus empire, an encounter aimed at overcoming such imperial tendencies as accumulation, domination and self-centeredness and replacing them with fellowship, service and witness. As people of the Acts of the Apostles, Augustinians see their relationship with the United Nations as an authentic manifestation of their heritage regarding witness, service and fellowship. We cannot assert our identity with the structure of the first Christian community without identifying with its movement to Rome, exactly where empire is confronted with this new structure.[3]

Of particular significance is this Augustinian NGOs' reference to developments in theology and interpretation of scriptures encouraged by the Second Vatican Council. Later incoming NGOs describe these developments as the indispensable foundation for their UN apostolate. As "our Gospel understanding changes," says a Maryknoll sister, "our work changes also..."[4] A representative of the School Sisters of Notre Dame, in an interview with Kevin Ahern, succinctly captured this binding relationship with the Church in its new theological outlook on the world: "With the Church we are immersed in the modern world; interpreting the 'signs of the times' in the light of the Gospel, committed to the work of building the kingdom of God by transforming unjust structures and establishing justice and peace."[5] Finally they see the post-conciliar unification of evangelization with work for justice in the world as a providential result of these theological and scriptural developments coming from the Second Vatican Council that provide impetus for their activities.

A few excerpts from our interviews illustrate the various interpretations of this new theological understanding in relation to the NGO

---

[3] See John Szura, O.S.A, "The Augustinians: Promoters of Justice and Peace," in John Paul Szura, O.S.A. and Robert Dodaro, O.S.A., *Augustine: Promoter of Justice and Peace* (Rome: Augustinian Secretariat of Justice and Peace, 2003), 35.

[4] See Kevin Ahern, "The Role of International Catholic Organizations in Promoting the Gospel in the Community of Nations," 13.

[5] Ibid.

actions in and with the UN. Kevin Dance, CP of the Passionists International, referenced John 10:10 "… I have come that they may have life, life in abundance" as one typical scriptural example shaping their identity as a religious group and supporting their active participation in the United Nations, the community of nations committed to the human goal of "life in abundance and quality."

He goes further by linking such projects with the Cross, thus challenging NGOs to put faces on the tragic statistics of contemporary suffering. "In people's struggles that find a voice in the UN, we hear an echo of Jesus wrestling with evil – hunger, poverty, filthy water, others' greed, disease."[6] This he illustrates in a graphic parallel between the UN Millennium Development Goals and the messages of Christ.

- People surviving on less than a dollar a day… if you did it to one of the least you did it to me!
- People who suffer hunger … Don't send them away, feed them yourself!
- People with no access to safe drinking water … I thirst!
- The mortality rate of children under five … Let the little children come to me!
- Halt and reverse the spread of HIV/AIDS … Of course, I want to be healed!

Joan Kirby of the Sisters of St. Joseph also recognized this link, maintaining that "the Millennium Development Goals, an integral part of the UN's Mission in the world, are consistent in many ways with Catholic social teaching. Catholics around the world are working to achieve many of the same goals. It becomes far more effective to work together world-wide." It is hard not to appreciate the efforts of these Catholic actors in making a faith connection of their activities with

---

[6] Kevin Dance, "The Mystery of the Cross and the Work of the United Nations," *http://www.cptryon.org/compassion/75/un.html*, in Kevin Ahern, The Role of International Catholic Organizations in Promoting the Gospel in the Community of Nations," 13.

scripture and the social teachings of the Church that validates the Christian way of life as one that is practical and effective. In this manner they bequeath to the church the privilege of retaining and transmitting the faith through visible actions directly impacting the lives of the world.

We should recall that Pius XII in 1939 had warned that not to identify with the new world order in the search for the solutions to the many problems threatening humanity was to crucify Christ a second time. The Passionists' share in Christ's mission of giving people life in abundance demands participation both in UN activities that provide direct material aid to the needy and in forming UN policies on behalf of the whole world through advocacy.

Christopher Malano of International Movement of Catholic Students (IMCS), a subsidiary of Pax Romana, understands their work in the light of the mission mandate in Matthew 28:19, "go and make ye disciples of all nations...." Identifying their UN presence as a missiological task, Malano demonstrates his organization's connection of preaching the gospel with the imperative of renewing the earth by tangible actions that enhance the wellbeing of the world's people.

In this perspective, evangelization legitimately includes working to achieve Christ's injunction in Luke 10:27 "love your neighbor as yourself," which, as Matthew 25: 35-40 specifies, is to feed the hungry, clothe the naked, shelter the homeless, and visit the sick and imprisoned. As existential social realities come to bear on this imperative, it becomes evident that there are some demands of love of neighbor that cannot be met effectively on a private, one-on-one basis. Within this context we acknowledge that there are aspects of our responsibility for neighbor that can be approached and dealt with only through socio-political activities.

As an international NGO working within the UN to improve the quality of life of students, especially those less privileged, and advocating change in the social structures that marginalize students, IMCS-

Pax Romana considers itself no less vital an evangelizer than those engaged in primary evangelization. This is the whole meaning of "new evangelization" initiated by *Evangelii Nuntiandi*, which adds the concern for justice and material wellbeing of the most disadvantaged of the world as necessary constituent of proclaiming the gospel. So even before *Evangelii Nuntiandi*, this group of Catholic youth has connected their faith profession with practical action for justice, with transformation of the world and with promotion of the common good.

Clearly, these activities understood from the perspective of the several interpretations of NGO representatives are a demonstration of spirituality in action, a spirituality that does justice. Such activities help to illustrate to NGO members and to Catholics in general the necessary interlink between faith and actions so that their spirituality becomes discernible not only in church attendance and sacramentality but also in the ordering of their daily actions toward their neighbors.

These considerations provide a response to one of chapter two's challenges against participation of Christians in social action: the dichotomy between church attendance and domestic virtue or between private charity and socio-political approaches to compassion. Reference to the Second Vatican Council again stands out clearly in most of these group attempts to describe their activities theologically. Thus a close reading of council documents, especially regarding their theological principles for Christian social action, provides another way of undertaking a theological assessment of these activities as truly legitimate Catholic actions.

Catholic-Inspired NGO/UN Relationships
& the Reception of Vatican II

Vatican II has provided the ground for doing and endorsing practical theology. Put another way, the council provides the needed leverage for every Christian to seek answers to theological questions without having to pay allegiance to a formal theological enterprise. This is what the representatives of the various Catholic-inspired NGOs interviewed for this work alluded to in their claim that Vatican II gave them the impetus for their active UN presence and participation. We certainly can evaluate their interpretations as theologically valid.

Gaudium et Spes &
Catholic-Inspired NGO/UN Relationships

When NGO representatives refer to Vatican II as empowering their UN presence and activities, it is *Gaudium et Spes* (*The Church in the Modern World*,) to which they most frequently and readily point. This should not surprise anyone, for the document in its nature and subject is not only a leitmotif for Christian social action but also is rightly believed to offer proof of the Holy Spirit's presence and intervention in the Council. Since comprehensive study of this document is beyond our scope, we will narrow our examination to those elements specifically pertaining to our subject of inquiry. We will focus on how *Gaudium et Spes* interrogates, or validates as the case may be, various theological self-understandings evidenced by Catholic-inspired NGO representatives as supporting their UN presence. We also will investigate the document itself to see how it could provide further assessment for this unique presence, especially in line with the claim made here to an alternative model of their presence.

Consequent upon the historically unique circumstances of the 1960s pressing upon it, the Church in *Gaudium et Spes* saw in a new light the dynamism of human history and the significance of wide ranging emergent global challenges. It was in this light that the Church abandoned its previous attitude of opposition to the world. Reacting to the Enlightenment and Marxist critiques of religion, the Church had previously adopted unconstructive responses that pushed theology to withdraw from the sociopolitical arena. It retreated to the inner world of the individual, leading to further privatization of religion and propagation of a kind of "ghetto spirituality," a sectarian tendency describing "a group of individuals who are inadequate to meet the demands of life; people who glorify a ghetto-like way of life as lived in the protected places of history."[7] This tendency created an illusion of "an apolitical theology and an apolitical Church," that is a "Church and theology totally independent of social and political considerations."[8]

However, the experience of World War II taught the Church bitter lessons about non-participation in public life. If it withdraws completely from politics or fails to respond to emerging new realities such as the rise of an educated middle class or advances in technology with its problems, the Church cannot raise an ethical voice against injustices. Vatican II led the Church away from this former sectarianism and toward seeking neither to dominate the world nor to flee from it. The Church now, in its irrevocable commitment to the service of humanity, is determined to enter into dialogue with the world, and to participate in its developing history including modern currents of culture and science.[9] As William French writes, "It clearly notes emerging problems and sources of brooding anxiety, like the injustice of vast social inequity and the scourge of the destructiveness of war with greatly enhanced modern weaponry, but it generally affirms the world, its cultures, and modern history as a genuine sphere of Christian engagement, learning, and responsibility."[10]

---

[7] Karl Rahner, "Diaspora Community," *Theological Investigations*, vol., x (New York: Seabury, 1977), 97-8.

[8] See John Shelley, "Introduction," Dorothee Sölle, *Political Theology* (Philadelphia: Fortress Press, 1974), xii, xiv.

[9] See Karl Rahner, "The Abiding Significance of the Second Vatican Council," *Concern for the Church: Theological Investigation*, vol. 20, trans. Edward Quinn (New York: Crossroad, 1981); 93-4; "Basic Theological Interpretation of Vatican II," ibid, 81. For some examples of the Church's affirmation of secular efforts, especially the international organizations towards human fulfillment see *GS*: 84.

[10] William French, "Greening Gaudium et Spes," in William Madges, *Vatican II*, 196.

Following this new sense of dynamism of humanity and its history was a new and serious appreciation that our fellow Church members, those whom we are to love as our neighbors, are at one and the same time social beings affected by the world outside the Church. Thus, in the opening words of *Gaudium et Spes* the Council declared: "The joy and hope, the grief and anguish of our time, especially of those who are poor or afflicted in any way, are the joy and hope, the grief and the anguish of the followers of Christ as well. Nothing that is genuinely human fails to find an echo in their hearts" (*Gaudium et Spes* 1).

In order not to drift aimlessly with the tide and flow of circumstances, the Council observes that the Church "can find no more eloquent expression of its solidarity and respectful affection for the whole human family ... than to enter into dialogue with it about all these problems" (*Gaudium et Spes* 3). Further, in the following words of *Gaudium et Spes* 89 the Church concludes: "Accordingly, the Church ought to be present in the community of peoples...motivated by the sole desire of serving all men, it contributes both by means of its official channels and through the full and sincere collaboration of all Christians."

The Holy See's admission into the UN family and the establishment of its New York office in April 1964 was of a huge theological significance, as we mentioned in chapter one. That it happened barely a year and half into the council spoke volumes about the seriousness with which the Church has taken its new self-understanding, especially in its relationship with the secular world.

The UN presence of the Holy See and the explicit words of the Council with the theological and pastoral principles issuing from them offer the fundamental impulse that today provides the theological principles for Christian participation in civil and political projects, just as Catholic-inspired NGOs at the UN have witnessed to. Some important theological categories and the new understandings that they assumed in *Gaudium et Spes*, namely anthropology, Christology, Pneumatology, ecclesiology, soteriology, and solidarity, corroborate the claim of these Catholic-inspired NGOs.

Each of these theological categories involves a more universal, limit-breaking approach than do previous theological perspectives. Anthropology is considered in terms of the whole person, his or her relatedness and historical context. Christ is understood to be beyond all institutional constraints, as is the Spirit and the Church. Salvation is understood to be open to all people and a hope for all people. Solidarity is considered between and among the unorganized masses of the poor and not limited to specific organized social groups.

Anthropology

A prime sign of the new perspective in theological formulation discernible in Vatican II is seen in the Council's initial insistence that it is the human person considered whole and entire, with body and soul, heart and conscience, mind and will, that is at the center of its new disposition to the world (*Gaudium et Spes* 3). The emphasis here on the human person as a totality clearly shows that the Church harbored no intention of continuing the "regional anthropologies" which compartmentalized the human person into empirically and clearly separate units--matter and body or spirit and soul.[11] Instead, Vatican II saw and treated the human person as a substantial unity, "a corporeal person with an absolute and ultimately irresolvable unity of matter and spirit."[12]

The absoluteness and insolubility of this unity between matter and spirit also avoids any hierarchical tendency in the human composite

---

[11] Karl Rahner, *Foundations of Christian Faith: An Introduction to The Idea of Christianity*, tr. William V. Dych, (New York: Crossroad, 1978, reprinted 2007), 27. According to Michael W. Petty, "Nondualistic emphasis is a thread which is woven through the fabric of [Rahner's] entire theology." See Michael W. Petty, *A Faith That Loves the Earth: The Ecological Theology of Karl Rahner*, (New York: University Press of America, 1996), 172.

[12] Karl Rahner, *Foundations of Christian Faith*, 434

that would place the spiritual as a substance and unduly above the material. It was the dualistic and hierarchical tendency of the former anthropology that gave rise to the "socially dormant conscience" we referred to in chapter two, which unfortunately still dominates the consciousness of some Christians today. This consciousness is built on misleading ideas of compassion as something of mere individual concern and of private charity. This is further promoted by a social doctrine perspective categorizing all efforts for the material good and improvement of the earthily conditions of the human person into "corporal works of mercy." These in turn are placed lower than the "spiritual works of mercy" as concerns of the soul with its heavenly aspirations. With such a disposition, Christian actions in the public realm towards issues of suffering and their causes would at least sometimes be limited to sentimentalism, masochism and apathy.

The Council also advanced another characteristic of the human person that has great significance for Christian mission in the public forum, namely the ontological relatedness of the individual—or better, particular--human person. Every human person is a person in relation, a creature made for communion with the creator and with other creatures (*Gaudium et Spes* 17, 24-25). "From this," says Kenneth Himes, "flow a number of consequences, including the right of persons to express themselves freely in social existence so as to become more truly human."[13] This notion of ontological relatedness of all human beings is critical to the development of solidarity for the poor, as well as collaboration for the common good.

The scope of this anthropology in its nuanced relationality extends beyond the former exclusively anthropocentric perspective that treated humanity in isolation from its history. Though the Council still maintained a hierarchy of creation wherein the human person ranks first, yet it clearly saw this human person as, for good or ill, utterly wedded to the world in such a way that it could be said that the human person

---

[13] Kenneth Himes *Woodstock Report*, 3-8.

and his or her world are but one flesh. As Karl Rahner would say, "our existence in the world is not a mere coincidence; it is not an aspect foreign to who we are."[14] Our "with the world" is an integral relationship from which we cannot distance or withdraw ourselves.

There is a further claim of this new anthropology that our knowledge of God and salvation is tied to this relationship with the world, for the salvific acts of God—God's self-communication of himself to humanity—are mediated through our human world history.[15] This resonates with the psalmist's verse "The earth is the Lord's and everything in it" (Psalm 24: 1). Against the early modern view that claims belief in God alienates one from the world and its historical contingencies, this later and indeed conciliar anthropology holds that the Christian, who by faith affirms God, equally affirms the world and human history. "It is in history that the subject must work out his salvation by finding it there as offered to him and accepting it."[16]

The language and scope of this Vatican II anthropology pervades the entire theological conception of Catholic-inspired NGOs at the UN available to us through their self-understandings and the assessment of their activities. From their concern for the development of human persons which they concretize by actions for material relief and advocacy for structural change, we see as obvious that their foundational conception of the human person reaches beyond a narrow concentration with the soul.

Just as importantly, their involvement in activities affirming the integrity of all creation witnesses to the cosmological expanse of their anthropology. In this cosmic anthropology these NGOs see themselves as bearers of the creator's dream for every living being, for the fertile earth and for the mysterious universe. The responsibility and privilege of bonding humanity to the earth and to the universe is readily

---

[14] Karl Rahner, *Foundations of Christian Faith,* 28, 40, 41.
[15] Ibid., 142, 143.
[16] Ibid., 41.

perceived as participating in the ongoing creation of the universe. We see this openly visible in their UN work that advances development in its three dimensions: economic, social and environmental--otherwise known as sustainable development.

Christology

Christology is another area in which the Council's reconsideration of former teaching provides a solid ground for the Christians' solidarity with one another and with the whole world. This is of paramount importance to the Catholic-inspired NGO self-understanding and their presence at the UN besides other commitments for the common good. It is especially significant for those NGOs of vowed religious men and women who question the religious significance of such witnessing with respect to their call to follow Christ in chastity, poverty and obedience.

In that regard, the Council acknowledges the importance of Christology in the fundamental understanding of the human person and his or her contingencies. In *Gaudium et Spes* 24 we read, "In reality it is only in the mystery of the Word made flesh that the mystery of humanity truly becomes clear." To this, *Gaudium et Spes* 45 would also add "the goal of history and civilization, the centre of human race, the joy of every heart and the answer of all yearnings." The earlier approval by the Church of the use of scientific methods and of modern historical and critical approaches to scripture study was useful to the Council reconsidering Christology as it sought to restore the ancient truths about the Jesus of history in such a way that he would become relevant to the modern person to whom the Council addressed itself. With the application of a narrative method to the Jesus story as recounted by the synoptic gospels, it was possible to recover the concrete memories of him and his impact on society.

With the recovered story of Jesus there was a wide rediscovery with deeper appreciation of the genuine humanity of the Word made flesh, bringing theologians to correlate Christology with the contemporary situation of believing people discerning the dignity and value of every human being. This demanded a shift in the *status quaestionis* (the state of the question) of traditional Christological propositions. The greater emphasis therefore shifted from a classic concentration on the correctness of abstract axioms to the desire to articulate a Christian faith in Christ that responds to practical issues from human experiences. Consequently, while we must re-affirm the Nicean formulation — *Qui propter nos homines et propter nostram salutem descendit de caelis. Et incarnatus est..., et homo factus est"* (for our sake and salvation, he became human), yet the scope of this salvation must include all that is our experience.

Aware of the nuanced new anthropological outlook and the Christological perspective that does not limit itself to human beings but embraces all creation, we must therefore include all other species, non-sentient beings and our environment on the list of those for whose sake and salvation Christ became human. As St. Paul teaches, it is all creation that groans and yearns for redemption (Rom. 8: 19-22). Thus, Christological questions, even with their soteriological implications, must deal with contemporary issues such as the ecological crisis, global injustice, poverty, war and the relationship between genders.[17] These are issues at the center of the UN project and of heartfelt concern of those who participate in it, including the Catholic-inspired groups advancing the common good of all.

Another important Christological advance of Vatican II which plays a significant role in Christian participation in social institutions dedicated to the common good such as the UN is the Council's pronouncement that the discovery of the mystery of Christ "holds true not for Christians only but also for all [people] of good will in whose hearts

---

[17] For further reading on the development and major tenets of this new Christology see Elizabeth Johnson, *Consider Jesus: Waves of Renewal in Christology* (New York: Crossroad, 1999).

grace is active invisibly" (*Gaudium et Spes* 22; *Lumen Gentium*, ch. 2, #16).

From a missiological perspective, this unseen action of grace can yield what is termed "mutual evangelization." These words describe a dynamic in which missionaries discover that, though they make Jesus present in a new, explicit way through their gospel witness, yet the Lord has preceded them, in fact having always been present to the people to whom the missionaries were sent. By mutual evangelization, Catholic-inspired NGOs coming to the UN often discover that many Christian values they have always held sacred are also held so by the people they serve and by the UN itself. Jesus has preceded his missionaries. It also echoes Pope Paul VI's assertion, earlier mentioned, that the UN is a great school in which everyone who participates, including the Church, is a student. By these words he acknowledges the superb mutual educational opportunities the UN provides for the wide range of world issues today.

Within this overarching Christological understanding, Catholic-inspired NGOs see themselves as imitators of Christ, as Christ's people, with a mandate to be luminal people of deep prayer and integrity. They are to be a courageous voice for those whose voices are not heard at all. They are to be yeast in the bread of life that it might enrich the world by its nurturing presence. This aspect of their UN presence is visible in the Passionists International's constructing their UN mission within the Christological image of the cross by which Christ is present in every way humanity and creation today suffer and call out for our solidarity.

David Hollenbach tells us how powerful the central Christian symbol of the cross of Jesus Christ is for gaining a deepened awareness of human suffering. The cross reveals the interplay of personal behavior, self-interest and an oppressive status quo as underlying causes of suffering that leaves the major part of the world's population powerless, marginalized and alienated. In our world of these sorrows, the Cross of Christ is reason for hoping that the advance of solidarity may render our human efforts in this area fruitful.

At the same time the cross holds the fate of those who heed this call to solidarity in the face of the "idolatrous power that is the antithesis of solidarity." [18] Thus in the image of the cross, Passionists International draws its call for solidarity. "In a world where increasing numbers of poor people are being 'crucified' by unjust political and economic structures, our sense of solidarity calls us to proclaim the Gospel of Justice and Peace. Justice is an essential part of the Gospel." And in a manner that synthesizes the various nuances of the conciliar anthropological and Christological understanding within their cosmological context, the Passionists conclude, "A proper sense of solidarity also requires us to take a stand alongside those who defend the integrity of creation, for we know that 'all creation groans in birth pangs' (Rm 8, 22). It calls us to promote a holistic view of life, aware of the interdependence of its many elements: spiritual, political, social, economic and environmental. We hold a passion for life in all its richness, diversity, plurality and fragility."[19]

For the Augustinians as well, the UN apostolate is of immense Christological significance vividly appropriating the *Totus Christus* Christology of Augustine, which is all-encompassing anthropologically and cosmologically. *Totus Christus* (Total Christ) is Augustine's conception of Christ in his all-embracing scope including all human beings and all other parts of creation, together with which we form the one common body of God's gift; for that is the only way he can exist. Thus, commenting on Matt. 25, "whatsoever you do to the least of these [brothers and sisters] of mine you do to me," Augustine in *Sermon*, 25.8.8, writes, "Each of you expects to receive Christ seated in heaven. Turn your attention to Him lying in the street. Direct your

---

[18] See David Hollenbach, *The Global Face of Public Faith: Politics, Human Rights, and Christian Ethics* (Washington D.C.: Georgetown University Press, 2003), xiii, 64-6.
[19] Congregation of the Passion of Jesus Christ, 44th General Chapter, Itaici, SP, Brasil 2000, No. 4.6

attention to Christ who is hungry and suffering from the cold, Christ in need and a stranger."

In this very illustration, Augustine's Christology also establishes an eschatological theology that connects the two worlds and their respective realities and scope--this-world and other-world, as seen in the unity of the heavenly Christ with the poor of this earth. This insight plays a prominent role in the UN activity of these Catholic-inspired NGOs, endowing them with a theology of activity that links genuine concern for the individual and for creation with the Christian's personal relationship with Christ. Thus, we can say for the religious men and women who are called in evangelical vows to live for Christ, their UN participation demonstrates their understanding of this wider scope of relationship with Christ as including concern for all that is created. We saw earlier how this understanding is now shaping the various institutions' understandings of their mission and the range of the evangelical vows they are called to live.

Soteriology

Anthropology and Christology are both closely related to soteriology. They are so treated in Church teaching in general and even more so in Vatican II, especially regarding their connection with the social reality. The Christian life as understood in UN activity is often dealt with in these teachings by linking belief and hope in the life hereafter to the reality of life here and now. With this understanding of soteriology forming the basis of encounter between Christian *mythos* and state *mythos*, we can say that salvation is the overarching notion underlying the UN language of peace. As Archbishop Renato R. Martino, president of the Pontifical Council for Justice and Peace, writes, the salvation the Son of Man came to bring translates to the restoration of every human person's full dignity. "That human dignity is also the reason for the work of the United Nations, whether in the fields of security, peace building, social welfare, economic development or the protection of the environment."[20]

By understanding their UN activities as pertaining to salvation, Catholic-inspired NGOs help us realize that salvation is not liberation *from* the body or *from* the world. It is rather freedom and liberation *in* the body and *in* the world from all that threatens integral human fulfillment. Jesus redeemed us and the physical world in which we live, and so salvation must not be understood apart from this world. On the contrary, salvation is fulfilled in this world, which will be taken up into glory at the end of time as total gift to God the Father by the Son in the Holy Spirit.

This perspective holds together the two dimensions of salvation: *immanent* and *eschatological.* In other words, the mission of the Church to participate in the Christocentric-events of salvation must be freed from all forms of bifurcated existence. Then we can more readily bring compassion to the human person in its wholeness and care for the integrity and identity of human existence and all creation comprising both the immediate and the not-yet of their existence.

These perspectives correct the fundamentalist claim mentioned at the beginning of this project: that the salvation of the human soul and mind apart from material-socio-historical contexts is the only sure step towards salvaging both humanity and secular society. Because of this claim, fundamentalists see no need for any Christian UN participation except to rescue humanity from strangulation of soul enforced by the UN universal human rights agenda.

Evangelii Nuntiandi (New Evangelization) and *Justitia in Mundo* (Justice in the World) make abundantly clear that actions for justice, peace and development in society are integral to spreading the Gospel. *Evangelii Nuntiandi* states "Evangelization would not be complete if it

---

[20] See Archbishop Renato R. Martino, "Foreword," André Dupuy, *Words that Matter: The Holy See in Multilateral Diplomacy Anthology (1970-2000)* (New York: Path to Peace Foundation, 2003), 7, 8.

did not take account of the constant interplay between the Gospel and [humanity's] concrete life, both personal and social" (*EN* 29). This basis for missionary activities expands the scope of evangelization beyond the limited goals of *conversio animarum* (conversion of souls) and *plantatio ecclesiae* (planting or establishing the Church).[21] This wider view is well expressed in a concluding statement of *Justitia in Mundo*:

> *If evil is structured into a society, its remedy must include social transformation, that is, changing the structures and institutions of society. Christian responsibility, then, must include both charity, personal acts of compassion in response to individual suffering, and justice, social and political action aimed at transforming the root causes of evil and suffering. Christians should be found in soup-kitchens, tutoring programs, and inner-city clinics, and on picket lines, in political campaigns and congressional lobbies.*[22]

Once again, we recall that this missiological underpinning supports the IMCS-Pax Romana understanding of their commitment through both advocacy at the UN and direct services to ensure the wellbeing of young students around the globe. They see themselves no less evangelizers than those undertaking primary evangelization missions. From these revised theological perspectives of anthropology, Christology, and soteriology, and from the way they have been understood and applied by these Catholic-inspired UN NGOs, we can draw the implication that every human situation, however secular, physical or "worldly," offers a possible encounter with God and a call to his kingdom. The deepest message of the incarnation is that "there

---

[21] Robert J. Schreiter, "Changes in Roman Catholic Attitudes Towards Proselytism and Mission," in Martin E. Marty & Frederick E. Greenspahn, eds., *Pushing the Faith: Proselytism and Civility in a Pluralistic World* (New York: Crossroad, 1988), 95, 96 of 93-108.
[22] *Justitia in Mundo*, in Milburn J. Thompson, *Justice and Peace: A Christian Primer*, (Maryknoll: Orbis Books, 2003), 198.

is nothing secular that cannot be sacred," as Madeleine L'Engle observes.[23]

Of all the theological categories and principles of Christian social engagement identified and enunciated by *Gaudium et Spes*, solidarity possesses an all-embracing dynamic. It includes a commitment to stand for the poor and with the whole human race seeking solutions to the grief and anguish of our time as well as sustenance for its joy and hope. It incorporates the other principles, offers us the opportunity to appreciate the contributions of these NGO UN activities, and provides us a tool to assess the fidelity of these NGOs to the articulated vision of their self-understandings.

Solidarity with & for the Poor

Solidarity is a central theological principle that validates these activities of Catholic-inspired NGOs as specifically Christian and participating in the economy of salvation. "The consciousness of the circumstances that make up our common life reveals the astonishing reality of our interrelatedness and interdependence." That we cannot be what we are and accomplish what we want to do without each other is both a political affirmation and a theological declaration. "We are members of each other," says Douglas Sturm.[24]

Solidarity draws its power from God, the source of unconditional rationality and relationality, in whose image we all are made. It is also a demonstration of God's presence in and concern for the fullness of humanity and all creation revealed by Jesus Christ—*Immanuel*—standing with the outcast and with those on the margins of society. It

---

[23] See Madeleine L'Engle, *Walking on Water,* in Eddie Gibbs and Ryan K. Bolger, *Emerging Churches: Creating Christian Community in Postmodern Cultures* (Grand Rapids, MI.: Baker Academic, 2005), 65.

[24] Douglas Sturm, *Solidarity and Suffering: Toward a Politics of Relationality* (New York: State University of New York Press, 1998), 7.

rests on the primary affirmation of all parts of creation as products of love that are both valuable and valued.

Further, solidarity provides a theological basis for challenging the interpretation of creation, humanity and nature as mere resources. It is an alternative way of being in the world in an unconditional commitment to stand with those who are oppressed. It is a God-given power to sustain, challenge and struggle against unjust and evil forces. It is a power that nurtures growth, creativity, mutuality and communion.[25] Through their activities toward solidarity amplified by their participation at the UN, these Catholic-inspired actors affirm that every creature has been created in love, by love and for love.

Gaudium et Spes presents solidarity as an urgent modern Christian moral and spiritual mandate. Though within the Catholic context the concept became popular only since Vatican II, its history dates back to the beginnings of modern Catholic social teaching, to Pope Leo XIII's *Rerum Novarum* (Of New Revolution) and other pre-Vatican II documents. [26] During this period of its evolution, the concept had assumed varied characterizations as "friendship, social charity, principle of socialization and interdependence, duty and element of civilization of love, value and virtue."[27] Without distortion, each of these

---

[25] Eleanor H. Haney, *The Great Commandment: A Theology of Resistance and Transformation* (Cleveland, Ohio: The Pilgrim Press, 1998), 58.

[26] 169.

[27] According to John Paul II in *Centesimus Annus*, celebrating the hundredth anniversary of *Rerum Novarum*, "what we nowadays call the principle of solidarity ...is frequently stated by Pope Leo XIII, who uses the term 'friendship,' a concept already found in Greek philosophy. Pope Pius XI refers to it within the context of 'social charity.'" Gradually, beginning with Pius XII, the term became more popular and assumed a broader meaning in the pre-Vatican II era. In Pius XII's *Summi Pontificatus,* the usage of the term had the connotation of "law" (*Summi Pontificatus* AAS 31). This shift in meaning continued with John XXIII, when it was categorized as a "principle" and was associated with his classical theme of "socialization" and his concept of interdependence (*Mater et Magistra* AAS 53). With Paul VI, solidarity became a "duty" (*Populorum Progressio* 17, 48). Referring to it as an essential element of a "civilization of love," he also expanded it to cover many modern aspects of the social question (*Octogesima Adveniens* 3). To John Paul II, solidarity is both a "value" and a "virtue" (*Sollicitudo Rei*

characterizations is situated within a broader background linking this concept with the common humanity that all persons share in God our Father, as well as the special bond of Christians in the Mystical Body of Christ.

These elements are summarized in Cortes' definition of solidarity as "the responsibility that all share in common because, as sons of Adam, they are children of God."[28] Today the term is often used in tandem with the principle of subsidiarity which asserts the right of individuals and smaller or local institutions to solve problems within their competence. In his encyclical *Caritas in Veritate* (Charity in Truth), Pope Benedict XVI sees the unity between solidarity and subsidiarity as necessary for solidarity to avoid giving way to a demeaning paternalistic social assistance and for subsidiarity to avoid social privatism.[29]

Some distinctive characteristics that *Gaudium et Spes* attaches to solidarity are quite useful in a theological assessment of Catholic-inspired NGOs at the UN. The conciliar document tends to see solidarity as a consequence of natural law theory with emphasis on its relation with the social nature of the human person, the common good and the universal destiny of goods.[30] It claims that "solidarity highlights in a particular way the intrinsic social nature of the human person, the equality of all in dignity and rights and the common path of individuals and peoples towards an ever more committed unity" (*Gaudium et Spes* 42).

Socialis 38, 40). See Pontifical Council for Justice and Peace, *Compendium of the Social Doctrine of the Church* (Ottawa: Canadian Conference of Catholic Bishops, 2005), 86, footnote, 421.

[28] See J. E. S. Hayward, "Solidarity: The History of an Idea in Nineteenth Century France," *International Review of Social History* 4:2 (1959), in Douglas A. Hicks, *Inequality and Christian Ethics* (Cambridge, UK: Cambridge University Press, 2000), 169.

[29] See Benedict XVI, *Caritas in Veritate* 57; also, the editorial commentary "In Defense of Politics," *Commonweal* Volume CXXXVI, Number 14 (August 14, 2009).

[30] Christine F. Hinze, "Straining Toward Solidarity in a Suffering World," 84.

This language resonates with that used by the UN in its universal declaration of human rights (UDHR). Not only does this correlation in language tend to support the claim of the influence on the UDHR exercised by the French Catholic philosopher Jacques Maritain, a member of the close group of editors consulted by those drafting the declaration. It also provides present Catholic-inspired actors a necessary tool for seeking the support of other Catholics in advancing the protection and promotion of these rights.

The Christian social ethicist and feminist theologian Christine Firer Hinze in her work "Straining toward Solidarity in a Suffering World: *Gaudium et Spes* 'After Forty Years,'" provides us a valuable window into the unique characterization of solidarity in *Gaudium et Spes* "as a fact, a norm and an embodied vocation."[31] According to Hinze, in *Gaudium et Spes* the *fact* of solidarity stems from our ontological relationality—"the 'is' of human interdependence that provides the grounding for the 'ought' of an affirmative response to it." This is illustrated in the *Gaudium et Spes:* 40-45 affirmation that "because we belong to each other, we are called to live with and for each other."[32] It is the prior reality of our existence that demands how we ought to act.

Solidarity is thus also a *norm* that "demands a responsive way of seeing, judging, and acting in relation to these realities." The essence of this normative character or virtue is "to recognize, to acknowledge, and to take appropriate responsibility for our *de facto* interdependence as human beings and as children of the same God." This is what Hinze, quoting Richard Rodriguez, terms "waking up to our 'we-ness' and living as if we are real."[33] It is rising above our individuality to embrace social responsibility as we read in *Gaudium et Spes* #30: "Let everyone consider it [their] sacred duty to count social obligations

---

[31] Ibid., 173.
[32] Ibid.
[33] Ibid.

among [their] chief duties today and observe [them] as such. For the more closely the world comes together, the more widely do people's obligations transcend their particular groups and extend to the whole world. This will be realized only if individuals and groups practice moral and social virtues and foster them in social living."

As we have seen earlier, most of the Catholic groups at the UN, especially those with international presence through their UN involvement, are awakening to this global connectedness that reflects the realization of our "we-ness" that Hinze refers to. This means living the social obligation advocated by *Gaudium et Spes* itself. Solidarity within their individual organization's international membership and apostolate is becoming more widely practiced. An example is the millennium development project for survivors of the HIV/AIDS pandemic in Nairobi, Kenya sponsored by the worldwide membership of the Augustinian Order. At the same time, a group's profession of solidarity is tested by how well it has concretized this connectedness. To that extent Hinze would conclude that for *Gaudium et Spes*, solidarity comes to Christians as an embodied *vocation*, a way of life which witnesses to the love of God in a new way that includes transformation of the world.[34]

The biblical and Christological perspectives visible in *Gaudium et Spes* highlight a bipolar character of solidarity: its universal and preferential dimensions. The universal dimension refers to our ontological relatedness on which is based our responsibility to participate with the rest of humanity in communal efforts for the common good. The preferential dimension, often used in the context of liberation theology and emphasized by *Gaudium et Spes* #1, refers to the special affinity we are called to have with those who are less privileged, the disadvantaged in society, particularly those impacted by systemic injustice within human societal structures. For liberation theologians, solidarity is "partisan," although if this aspect is overemphasized, solidarity

---

[34] Ibid.

becomes tainted with an exclusivist bias. The distinction between the two dimensions, universal and preferential, is then expressed as "coming together" and "going over to the other side."[35]

Properly interpreted, these poles of solidarity, though distinct, are not separated in practice, as illustrated by Christ himself. Thus, in the vulnerable, gracious act of Jesus, the compassion of God becomes for the Christian both a vocation and a model. We are called to bear witness in our world to his solidarity with and for the poor: first, because we are consubstantial with them, and second, because they especially need the genuine concern of the more advantaged members of society. We are thus called to be part of the universal human project for the common good of all with a preferential option for the poor, the disadvantage and the vulnerable.

In Jesus' own example we have the model for authentic witness. In Matthew's gospel, Jesus invites us to learn from him (Mt 11: 28-30). Thus, we may conclude that in Christ, as the bible presents him to us, we see not only the example of solidarity as "a fact, a norm and a vocation." We see as well a model. To respond to this call within the context of the modern world and its challenges, *Gaudium et Spes*: 3 "offers to co-operate unreservedly with mankind in fostering a sense of brotherhood to correspond to this destiny of theirs." It conceives this co-operation as the only way of bearing witness, under the guidance of the Holy Spirit, to Christ, who came into the world not to judge but to save, not to be served but to serve.

Incarnational Solidarity

In her conception of incarnational solidarity, Hinze further explores the scope and challenges of this Christological perspective and the conciliar teaching on solidarity. This work shows Hinze particularly useful and integral to the theological assessment we are here

---

[35] See Douglas A. Hicks, *Inequality and Christian Ethics* (Cambridge, UK: Cambridge University Press, 2000), 169.

undertaking, so that we can further interrogate the activities of these Catholic-inspired NGOs constructively and even suggest improvements for their performance.

The essence of incarnational solidarity confronting us in Christ's actions shows that this solidarity is not a merely sentimental expression of concern. Neither is it an abstraction, simply an ideal or just an interior attitude. It is rather "incarnated" reality. As the post-conciliar document, John Paul II's encyclical *Sollicitudo rei* Socialis (The Social Concern) proclaims "solidarity, then, is not a feeling of vague compassion or shallow distress at the misfortunes of so many people, both near and far. On the contrary, it is a firm and persevering determination to commit oneself to the common good; that is to say, to the good of all and of each individual, because we are really responsible for all."[36] This solidarity is that which, according to Jon Sobrino, "is another name for the kind of love that moves feet, hands, hearts, material goods, assistance, and sacrifice toward the pain, danger, misfortune, disaster, repression, or death of other persons or other people. The aim is to share with them and help them rise up, become free, claim justice, and rebuild."[37]

The baptism of Jesus is a particular concrete demonstrative act manifesting the incarnational dimension of solidarity with all its risks. William Reiser holds that the early Church universalized Jesus' solidarity with the people of Israel, ritually expressed when he received John's baptism in order to encompass the whole human story. Further, that solidarity revealed a divine purpose, namely the redemption and transformation of the human world in all its dimensions.[38]

---

[36] See John Paul II, *Sollicitudo rei Socialis,* # 38; also Robert A. Sirico and Maciej Zięba, O.P., *The Social Agenda: A Collection of Magisterial Texts* (Vaticano: Pontifical Council for Justice and Peace and Libreria Editrice, 2000), 66.

[37] Jon Sobrino and Juan Hernandez Pico, *Theology of Christian Solidarity* (Maryknoll: Orbis Books, 1985), vii.

[38] William Reiser, *Jesus in Solidarity with His People: A Theologian Looks at Mark* (Collegeville, Minnesota: The Liturgical Press, 2000), 54-5.

Jesus' baptism was more than a pre-figure of our own baptism through the sanctification of baptismal water by his immersion into the Jordan River as scholastic theology taught. It was partaking in the vulnerability of others, entering with them into the experience of weakness and powerlessness, becoming part of uncertainty and giving up control and self-determination.[39] He had no need of the baptism, Matthew writes, yet Christ filed out with his people for the baptism. It was more an act of identifying with his people in their brokenness because he felt the weight of their oppression by the structures of sin. Rather than standing aloof in the crowd, Jesus joined the people wailing, yearning, seeking their God and longing to cross over the threshold to the new life offered through the Baptist. This identification with the people came at the cost of risking his identity as the sinless one, as John the Baptist's hesitation to baptize him illustrates.

To be incarnate like Christ demands a sincere self-gift that involves "the immersion of bodies, the expenditure of time and energies in the midst of the blood, sweat, and tears of the real world, in practices of presence and service."[40] This reality becomes clearer in Hinze's contrast between "incarnational solidarity" and "virtual and sentimental forms of solidarity" practiced by a consumerist culture and economy. The virtual form substitutes sentimental gestures for political action or actual encounter. The incarnational, on the other hand, is "practical, embodied, and comes at a cost: the uncomfortable, challenging, disruptive aspects of face-to-face, shoulder-to-shoulder ways of acknowledging our 'we-ness.'"[41] True qualities of this incarnational way of being-with the other in solidarity include "to be humble, to be present and to be collaborative, in a non-paternalistic way." These qualities carry with them experiences sometimes inconveniencing and sometimes excruciating. The incarnate Savior, Jesus Christ, remains

---

[39] See Henri J.M. Nouwen, et. al., *Compassion: A Reflection on the Christian Life* (New York: Doubleday, 1983), 14.

[40] Christine F. Hinze, 174.

[41] Ibid.

our perfect example as we read in the Pauline Christological hymn (Phil. 2: 6-10).

From the way Christ lived out the implications of his incarnational solidarity, we observe that it involves not only mutual support but also a critique of the diametrically opposed attitudes toward the structures of sin found in the socio-economic and political arena as well as an examination of the care different generations give to each other. While Jesus identified with humanity in its pursuit of abundant life, he also chastised humanity for those activities and lifestyles that contributed to its own sufferings. Some examples of this are seen in the way he challenged the structures of his society. He put His life at risk by challenging the "business as usual" attitude in his time—he lived solidarity as a constitutive component of his salvific mission. It is this type of solidarity that the Roman Catholic Church-inspired NGOs advocate in partnership with the UN and exhibit in the various expressions of their self-understanding as articulated above.

NGOs of Institutes of Religious Life
Modeling Incarnational Solidarity

The UN presence of institutes of religious men and women presents opportunities for us to explore the dynamics of incarnational solidarity. One example is that taking up NGO work witnesses to emptying oneself. This aspect of incarnational solidarity means dying to oneself to increase life hopes for another. Incarnational solidarity is a meeting point between concept and contact, between theory and practice, belief and experience. It is filled with all the meaning that "the word taking flesh and pitching his tent among us" captures in God's act of incarnation so replete with realism and symbolism. By this act, God in our frail nature physically walked the street with his people, touched and was touched by them in ways that make our God real. Incarnational solidarity is thus a demonstration of our realism toward people we care for, people we are called to serve.

Jesus embracing our humanity in its manifold dynamics took on the risks and vulnerabilities that this inscrutable and priceless act of being-with embodies. God was immersed in our history with all its realities, withholding nothing of his person and capacities to be of service to our groaning creation. As in the case of Christ, incarnational solidarity does not deny but rather lives up to the risk of existing. This also describes the ongoing dynamism that generates constantly emerging agents of solidarity. In a similar way the act of religious institutes taking up their NGO identity and assuming the UN project may be called incarnational solidarity in all its realism and symbolism.

Taking up an NGO identity implies rethinking religious life along with institutions and services that institutes have lived with for all their years of existence, some for centuries, others for decades. Through the lens of Vatican II, many religious see the reality of this identity as a concrete significant "sign of our times" bringing close the "world church" realism, a post-Vatican II emergence, with responsibility to all people around the world. In other words, religious institutes are seen no longer as existing for the benefit of their members who are concerned about making heaven. This is a key aspect of incarnational solidarity: the realization of oneself in the act of living for the other in such a way that "I" is not the central focus but "We," that is "I" and the Other together.' Through this new identity as UN NGOs who speak not for themselves but for others, especially the most disadvantaged, members of religious congregations are becoming more aware that their lives are a commitment to serve others rather than a matter of simply perfecting themselves.

It is untrue that before now members of religious institutes neglected to incorporate service to the Other in their mission. The abundant educational, healthcare and material relief aid they provided to the communities they served bear witness to their long commitment to the Other. It suffices to recall that the United States House of Representatives honored United States Catholic Sisters on September 22, 2009 for their contributions to the development of the country through their long history of activities in education and caring for the needs of those living in poverty. The social work of the Ursuline Sisters dating back to 1727 and that of other sisters since 1880 were some of the examples cited in this award."

This observation is true not only regarding the United States but also of many other countries around the world. In her foreword to the book *It is Good for Us to be Here: Institutes of Religious Life as NGOs at the United Nations*, Prof. Joy Ogwu, the Nigerian Ambassador to the UN, acknowledged the immeasurable contributions of the congregations and orders of religious men and women to the development of many countries around the world. In her words: "in their long history of activities in education and care of the poor, members of Institutes of religious life have contributed immensely to the development of the world's human resource, including mine. More significantly, they have been a force for peace and justice. They were the pioneers in technologies, literacy and medical knowledge in many parts of the world. In our times, they continue to explore the frontiers of knowledge and understanding."[42]Nevertheless despite this testimony, in their service to the Other, members of religious institutes are more aware today of the distinction between charity alone and a charity that necessarily includes a commitment to justice. The demand for this kind of service is as borderless as the gospel imperative of throwing all away for the sake of a discipleship willing to go to the ends of the earth.

Concomitantly, the NGOs' authority at the UN to speak does not come from their identity as religious groups but rather from the voices they speak for, namely the people in the grassroots. Thus, sisterhood and brotherhood transcend the confines of individual religious groups to assume a universal sisterhood and brotherhood. It is such a selfless universalism that moves other UN actors to believe that these NGOs are genuine and sincere. Indeed, religious institutes do not

---

[42] See Joy Ogwu, "Foreword," in Emeka Xris Obiezu, et.al, *It is Good for us to be Here: Institutes of Religious Life as NGOs at the United Nations* (Indiana: Xlibris Press, 2015).

exist to serve themselves but rather to serve the people. Consequently, those outside these groups who address them as sisters or brothers can relate with them as they see these religious becoming agents of change for the common good. This reality too has begun to impact NGO understanding of the scope and meaning of their religious vows.

Thus, the spirituality and meaning of religious vows—poverty, obedience and chastity—are becoming clearer to most of these groups, at least among the members who take an active part in the UN apostolate. The UN apostolate helps many to see the evangelical nature of their vows, removing them from an overly individualistic attitude focused on the sanctification of individual members. *Lumen Gentium* prepared for this new understanding by shifting language regarding consecrated life from "state of perfection" to "living the gospel evangelical counsels."

Similarly inspired, the Vatican II document *Perfectae Caritatis* (Religious Life Renewal) proposed a threefold basis for that renewal: signs of the time, a return to the founding charism, and the gospel itself as basic rule. Such a renewal demanded that religious life and vows could no longer be seen primarily as ascetical practices but as witness to the gospel of Jesus and as needed prophecy for today. The three religious vows are indeed evangelical as a prophetic sign for today rather than a means of escaping historical reality in order to point at some heavenly future.[43]

Being evangelical, these vows are by nature public witnessing to the love of God for creation made manifest in the life and service of those who respond to the invitation to enter religious life. These religious are beginning to see solidarity with the poor and commitment to social justice as a necessary, concrete measure of the realization of Vatican II renewal. This reality will necessarily involve being converted

---

[43] See Patricia Walter, "Religious Life in Church Documents," *Review of Religious Life* 51(1992)555.

by the marginalized, critiquing societal and ecclesiastical values and structures and advocating systemic change at the roots of injustice.

Regarding the vow of poverty as an illustrative example, Joan F. Burke, SNDdeN narrates how her experience with social questions in the UN apostolate has enlightened many of her sisters' understanding of their vows as well as hers. Both direct interaction with impoverished people and advocacy with other UN NGOs gave impetus to her congregation's shifting from an earlier, limited grasp of the vow of poverty to a perspective appropriate for today. They now feel called both to model an alternative way of living and to restructure our world so that all may have enough. This has implications for all their ministries as well, for their renewed understanding influences every facet of their lives.

This is one particular way of responding to Vatican II's call to all consecrated life for renewal through the tripartite approach regarding signs of the times, original founding charism and the gospel as basic life rule. In its pre-Vatican II conception, the vow of poverty simply enjoined all bound by it to renounce free control of property and use of money or valuable goods without the lawful superior's permission. Such a limited view is devoid of an evangelical thrust, and it certainly is not an incarnational solidarity modeled by Christ.

The renewal initiated by Vatican II sheds bright light on social realities, exposing them as a powerfully instructive context for poverty for vowed religious. While many may strive to pursue by themselves this enlarged reinterpretation of vowed poverty's scope, those in a UN apostolate have a sharp awareness of the social conditions of our time quickly opened to them. As such, this apostolate readily allows many to make the connections that give the vow of poverty a global perspective, as at the same time the UN apostolate itself becomes an opportunity for solidarity and an evangelical witnessing.

Further, this apostolate helps its participants to connect the dots scattered among the multitude of church social documents, especially those with particular UN relevance: Pope John XXIII's *Mater et Magistra* and *Pacem in Terris*; Pope Paul VI's *Populorum Progressio*; Pope John Paul II's *Sollicitudo Rei Socialis*; and the Synod of Bishops' *Justice in the World*. Also, many religious congregations today include in their response to the call for evangelical poverty a desire to live as simply as possible, to listen to the voices of the world, to respond to the most pressing needs of our day by urging human behavior and institutions towards justice and charity and to collaborate generously with other persons and organizations serving the human family.

We do not claim here that these developments began with the UN apostolate. We rather observe that the UN apostolate created space for their realization and gave it support. Religious congregations did not absolutely need to be at the UN to respond to Vatican II's call for renewal, but the UN apostolate provided resources and urgency for a renewal already begun to be fruitful. Independent of a UN apostolate, several renewal workshops, seminars and events have been sponsored by a variety of religious institutes, sometimes in collaboration with others. Projects and institutions such as Justice, Peace and Integrity of Creation (JPIC) were established as a result.

The UN apostolate in its several forms and realizations should be counted among these concretizing projects. This apostolate increases and spreads enlightenment on social issues, especially in their magnitude and global connectedness. It thus enables and motivates international NGOs to form visible solidarity among themselves, to collaborate in commissions and committees of kindred NGOs and to form a wider supportive community with and among the several NGO communities at the UN. Many groups were thus aided in appreciating the connectedness of global social questions to their faith reality, to the value of the religious lifestyle in shaping a new paradigm and to the price of inaction.

Communion Ecclesiology in Action:
One though Many

The Church/world relationship is another area wherein Catholic-inspired UN NGOs mirror reception of Vatican II's significant theological shift in ecclesiology. As its title suggests, *Gaudium et Spes* (The Church in the Modern World) focused attention on the position of the Church in society, the locus of her ministry and her existence in time and space. Through a renewed outlook toward this relationship, the Church can realize its commitment to a solidarity informed by shifts in other theological categories as previously discussed. Such a renewed outlook leads to a genuine commitment to people and creation. Formed by this renewed outlook, the Church must be friendly, humble, docile and dialogical.

The pre-Vatican II Church-world relationship was triumphalist, an outlook in which the world posed question which it could not deal with without the help of a Church reaching into its deposit of faith to provide answers. This outlook is captured vividly by Pius XI: "All eyes often turn toward the Chair of Peter, sacred repository of the fullness of truth.... To the feet of Christ's vicar on earth were seen to flock, in unprecedented numbers, specialists in social affairs ... begging with one voice that at last a safe road might be pointed out to them."[44]

One can thus appreciate why the first Catholic-inspired UN NGOs felt their job was to ensure that the UN would follow Pius XI's papal "peace program." One can also see why the US Catholic Bishops were reluctant to welcome the UN San Francisco conference, as it neglected to model itself upon the papal program. Thus, Fr. Edward A Conway suggested that the Church send "someone who would...make sure that the Catholic viewpoint was advanced whenever critical issues

---

[44] See Pius XI, *Quadragesimo Anno*, 7.

were being deliberated and opinions requested at the appropriate United Nations agencies."[45]

This triumphalist understanding changed with Vatican II offering a new posture for the Church toward the world that is not triumphalist, isolationist or combative but rather humble, engaging and dialogical. With this outlook "the Church speaks to issues from a standpoint deeply within the society, winning support by persuasion and seeking common ground with others, including non-Christians."[46] This ecclesiology and its implications provide the impetus for, and the manner in which, later Catholic NGOs would participate in the UN.

The realization of this new world-Church relationship heavily depends for its support on the new ecclesiology of the council, one that repositions the Church as present in all its members so that the contribution of one part is the contribution of the whole. The bold claim of Catholic-inspired NGOs that they are drawn to the UN in the name of the Church and her mission justifiably expresses a visible way of being Church consistent with Vatican II ecclesiology. Among the people of God different groups are valued without confusion or contradiction as one Church.

This people of God ecclesiology is predicated on the notion of the Church as a communion within the Trinity as her ultimate source. This fundamental outlook at the center of the renewal spirit and the revolutionary shift of the council is most visible in her call for the co-responsibility and participation of all members in the life and work of the Church.[47] Thus, implications of the new ecclesiological self-understanding of communion extend to the Church's actual organization as a community of the faithful on mission. This ecclesiological insight

---

[45] See Joseph Rossi, *Uncharted Territory*, xii, 12, 1.

[46] *GS* in ibid.

[47] Dogmatic Constitution on the Church, *Lumen Gentium*, Austin Flannery, OP. ed., *Vatican Council II, Vol. 1: The Conciliar and Post-Conciliar Documents*, no. 37; Cf. Aloysius Wycislo, *Vatican II Revisited: Reflections By One Who Was There* (New York: Society of St. Paul, 1987) 50-54.

underscores the priority of the vocation of the whole community of the people of God over all diversities of functions and of charisms.

Ecclesial communion attempts a shift from the previous understanding of the Church as a hierarchical and institutional structure, synonymous with exercise of authority by a few people over others. Rather the Church is the entire community of the Christian faithful as members of the living Body of Christ. John Paul II uses the image of the functioning of a living body to illustrate the organic nature of the communal ecclesiology characterized by a diversity and complementarity of vocations and states in life, of ministries, of charisms and of responsibilities.[48] Just as the living body's functionality does not depend on the dominance of any of its parts but on the participation of each part in a collaborative dynamism, so it is with the Church, another living body of different components.

Walter Cardinal Kasper, applying the mystery underlying the reality of the Church, holds that attempting a unilateral system for the entire Church leads to dysfunction. As a mystery, the Church is composed of different aspects. No one has the whole truth; truth is found only together.[49] Even though the full shift intended by this new outlook still remains far from being realized, the participation of Catholic-inspired NGOs at the UN stands out as one of the examples witnessing to the reception of the council in various quarters of the Church.

These Catholic-inspired NGOs are not the authoritative voice of the Church like the Holy See is, and in fact they do not need to be. Yet they are there in the UN truly as Church realizing its mandate of salvific witnessing. It is the Holy See which carries out the official responsibility of advancing the mission of the Church within and among the member states, "the first UN" in realization of her privilege

---

[48] John Paul II, Post-Synodal Apostolic Exhortation, *Christifideles Laici* (On the Vocation and Mission of the Lay Faithful in the Church and in the World) (London: Catholic Truth Society, 1998) nos. 19-20.

[49] Cardinal Kasper interview with Robert Mickens, "The Whole Truth is only found Together," *The Tablet*, July 6, 2002.

of non-member state permanent observer status. Other Catholic actors continue the same *missio ecclesiae* in their capacity as members of the "third UN" equally as legitimate members of the Church. These actions, respecting all variations, are without confused or contradictory actions of one and the same Church. Therefore, when Catholic-inspired NGOs undertake their collaborations with partner NGOs from different faiths and no faith at all, they invariably make visible the Church in her commitment to ecumenical and interfaith dialogue and solidarity with their world in realization of her mission for a redeemed world.

As mentioned in chapter two, even with the perceivable distance between them, there are instance when the Holy See and these Catholic-inspired NGOs have partnered together on some UN activities demonstrating the collaborative dimension of Vatican II ecclesiology. A few mentioned include Jean Gartlan's 1950 representation of the Holy See in Geneva to monitor the UN Trusteeship Council deliberations on the status of Jerusalem, participation of the Augustinians NGO office in drafting the Holy See intervention at the UN conference on sustainable environment in 2002 and the 2011 representation of the Holy See at the European Union by Olivier Poquillon O.P. of the Dominican Order UN office. The Holy See has frequently co-sponsored events with Catholic-inspired NGOs such as with Franciscans International and Caritas International at the 2012 Rio+20 conference on sustainable development in Rio de Janeiro, Brazil.

Understanding this mission from the lay group point of view may not be as difficult as it may be from that of religious groups, especially those of a clerical nature. The Church of Vatican II in its document on the laity acknowledged their role within the larger mission of the Church as pertaining to the renewal of the temporal order. Living in the midst of the world, they are to address all its problems and concerns with the divine message of salvation. The Catechism of the Catholic Church #899 continued the same teaching, emphasizing the lay responsibility to permeate the social, political and economic realities of their times with the demands of Christian doctrine and life.

This lay role was articulated in pre-conciliar theologies of the laity, such as in Yves Congar's concept of the "distinction of planes," between "ecclesial-clerical and lay-secular action,"[50] which restricts the political arena as a field appropriate only to lay Catholics. Karl Rahner's ecclesiology of "Church in diaspora" is another theological support for lay Christian mission in the social realm. The Church of the diaspora is a production of Rahner's reflection on the situation of the Church in the modern world. In this reality, all the riches of culture – literary, artistic, scientific etc.--will no longer be specifically Christian or bear a Christian stamp, leaving the Church stripped of the absolute power to pontificate in all matters as it did in the past. Therefore the only way she can exist is in becoming and remaining "a Church of active members, a Church of the laity: a laity conscious of itself as bearing Church in itself, as constituting her, and not being simply an object of her – i.e. the clergy – to look after."[51] These teachings are well known to the lay Catholic-inspired NGOs working at the UN.

Yves Congar, Karl Rahner and various Vatican II documents relating to this issue may have provided the basic foundation for lay group participation in social establishments as in the case of lay Catholic-inspired UN NGOs. Yet this distinction remains problematic in many ways, and more so in the dynamics of a UN relationship of Catholic-inspired NGOs composed of both lay and religious groups. Concerning Congar's position in particular, as we read in Leonardo Boff, "the Church, in this sense, is synonymous with hierarchy," thus the legitimacy of laity-activities as belonging to the Church is in question. "It presupposes a functionalist sociology wherein each body is defined

---

[50] See Yves Congar, *Lay People in the Church*, trans. Donald Attwater (Westminster, MD: The Newman Press, 1965), 80, 81 in John Milbank, *Theology and Social Theory: Beyond Secular Reason*, 2nd Edition (Malden, MA: Blackwell Publishing, 2006), 229.
[51] Karl Rahner, *Christian Commitment: Essays in Pastoral Theology*, (New York: Sheed and Ward, 1963), 22-26.

by its practices and does not interfere with other segments of society. Therefore, the Church – [the clergy], is not to interfere in political arena"—which is the exclusive reserve of the laity.[52] Such a dualism continues an ecclesial dichotomizing tendency between the secular and the sacred that is narrow-minded, divisive, and elitist. By this division, greater importance is attached to the clerical duties administered *intraecclesiam,* while the secular duties which are to be performed by the laity may come to assume lesser significance.

More than that, going back to the alleged role of the relationship between lay and religious NGOs in the demise of the International Catholic Organization (ICO), the umbrella network for Catholic NGOs at the UN, we see how destructive an emphasis on this distinction can be to collaborative ministry. We recall the sentiment of the lay groups at the religious groups joining and rising to leadership positions in the ICO, which is linked with the cause of this organization's death.

This lay theology also has serious implications especially for many male religious groups of clerical status that want to include a UN apostolate in their mission. As within Congar's view, they experience great difficulty in discerning the extent to which such a dimension is appropriate to their priestly ministry. Also, on the other hand, the Catholic lay NGOs might, and sometimes do, see the presence of Roman Catholic clergy and religious congregations and orders in the UN as intruding into their exclusive (laity's) territory.

This is an issue not only for the UN apostolate. It surfaces also in other aspects of the life of the Church in the social plane where religious congregations, especially those of the sacerdotal group, may dare to enter. We see a similar rift also in other aspects of Church life where a part of the Church thinks the participation of other parts is an intrusion into their reserved privilege. In most of these situations effort is made to limit the level of participation of these others. This issue

---

[52] See Leonardo Boff, *Church, Charism and Power* (Maryknoll, New York: Orbis Books, 1986), 4, 5.

surfaces more in areas like liturgy and administration where some clergy still think that the laity should have a minimal participation. Quite importantly, most of these questions still remain open-ended and unanswered.

Finally, it is on this theological perspective that contemporary Christian social activists anchor their efforts towards a more just social, economic, ecological and political order as aspects of the liberating power of God's grace to free people and the entire creation here and now from the power of evil. Church-inspired NGOs do not view their work for social justice as mere social activism but as their contribution to the work of salvation, the mission of the Church. It is in this holistic dimension of salvation that we see a legitimate intersection between Christian faith and a secular mythos such as the United Nations project, whose language of peace we may say mirrors this overarching notion of salvation.

To live out this reality requires fulfilling what Hinze poses as four challenges and imperatives that incarnational solidarity presents to Christians: to "be attentive, be intelligent, be reasonable, and be responsible-loving."[53] Each situation demands its particular pattern of being present. As maintained in this work, this responsibility requires that members of Catholic Church-inspired NGOs in the UN not only consider the world outside the UN but also the UN itself as bearers of these signs calling for discernment and forcing these NGOs to reconsider their self-understanding and mission. They must be flexible enough to make necessary adjustments to meet with the demand of new responsibilities as they arise.

The last part of this chapter is to view the activities of the Catholic-inspired NGOs from these theological standpoints to determine how well they have fulfilled the articulated visions and implications of these theological self-understandings and principles.

---

[53] Ibid., 183.

Evaluating the Work of Catholic-Inspired NGOs
in Light of Theological-Pastoral Principles

Their mere presence in the UN system—a conglomeration of people of every variety—is itself a witness to their embracing solidarity, to being with the poor and with others for the sake of the poor. This is further witnessed by their receptivity and collaboration with non-Catholic partners who are sometimes admitted into Catholic groups such as Franciscan International and Maryknoll Brothers and Sisters. By their open receptivity, they have demonstrated the humble attitude of Vatican II ecclesiology that replaced a former self-understanding of the Church as dispenser of privileged truths possessed by no others. The Church now identifies itself as co-pilgrim with the rest of humanity in their search for the best solutions to the problems that beset our world today. The Church is now open both to teach and to be taught.

This is in accord with Jesus' own example of solidarity, by his act of queuing up for baptism with his people. His action offers richer meaning to solidarity as participating in programs with people seeking solutions to their common problems.[54] This provides justification for the claim of some later NGOs that it is legitimate for them to participate in UN programs because the UN is humanity's unified effort in search for solutions that commonly threaten our times. It identifies with the universal concern for, and pursuit of, lasting peace and human security.

Many of these groups, particularly those with a direct link to traditional Church entities such as Caritas Internationalis and NGOs of religious congregations, have added to their traditional practice of "face-to-face service to the poor and marginalized" an advocacy that challenges structures of oppression and marginalization. In this they

---

[54] For more reading on participation as a demonstrative of solidarity, see Emeka Christian Obiezu, *Towards a Politics of Compassion: Socio-political Dimensions of Christian Responses to Suffering* (Bloomington, Indiana: AuthorHouse Publishers, 2008), 88-90.

demonstrate the prevalent understanding of a new theology of sin and salvation, affirming that sin transcends personal morality to include evils rooted in the structures of society. The response of the NGOs not only identifies the root causes of suffering but is committed to eradicating them so that, to quote an Augustinian phrase, "we may not have to give charity forever." The way NGOs blend advocacy with personal attention to the victims of suffering frees their advocacy from the danger of impersonal generalizations. This failing is what Wendy McElroy calls shifting attention "from victims to victimhood," an attitude that stifles action for justice.[55] Significantly these NGOs have ensured the opportunity for victims of different kinds of suffering to attend UN-sponsored conferences, fulfilling a critical aspect of solidarity for the poor, namely allowing victims the chance to be heard. Rebecca S. Chopp maintains that solidarity does not imply that "the poor are simply to be helped, assisted along, or chronically 'underprivileged,' but [that they] must be granted their rights to speak, to eat, to work, to think."[56]

These activities are salvific partly because they are incarnational. Incarnation, an act of solidarity as described by *Evangelii Nuntiandi*, includes both announcing the love of God in Christ, who took flesh to save humanity, and immersing oneself in the conditions of the people and the place in which they announce that message. We described this as an acceptance of vulnerability. This rings true in the experience of the vulnerability that these NGOs accept in order for them to bear effectively the love of God to this community of people in the international arena where issues of human concerns are dealt with. Their participation demands an immersion in the culture, language and

---

[55] See Wendy McElroy, "Victims Versus Victimhood," Oct. 11 2005, 2 *http://lewrockwell.com/mcelroy94.html*, in Emeka Christian Obiezu, *Towards a Politics of Compassion: Socio-political Dimensions of Christian Responses to Suffering*, 87.

[56] Rebecca S. Chopp, *The Praxis of Suffering: An Interpretation of Liberation and Political Theologies*, (Maryknoll, New York: Orbis Books, 1992), 22-23.

conditions, not only of the people they represent, but also of the UN in its dynamics and dialectics.

The outlook of salvation understood in the age of Church-state dichotomy as a kind of doctor-patient relationship undermines salvation itself. In this earlier outlook, the patient is deemed contagious and is therefore isolated, receiving medication free from any direct contact with the dispenser. On the contrary their Vatican II inspired UN presence is a "being-with," understood as the incarnational and compassionate sharing in the vulnerability of the other, entering with the other into the experience of weakness and powerlessness, becoming part of their uncertainty and giving up control and self-determination.[57]

Urged on by this Vatican II outlook, they are sometimes exposed to and endure attacks, not only from secular society but also from people within their various groups and within the Church itself. Whatever is said of the UN by its critics is directly or indirectly predicated of those participating in it. Yet, I believe their success is heavily dependent on how faithful they remain in the face of these incarnational inconveniences. This was the lot of Christ, the sinless one who experienced sin for the sake of those he loves (II Cor. 5: 21). What is meant by this Pauline expression is made clear in the thought of Dietrich Bonhoeffer. According to him, the sinless one experiences sin by "placing himself in the very midst of the world of sin and death, taking on the needs of human flesh, humbly submitting to God's wrath and judgment over sinners, remaining obedient to God's will in suffering and death; born in poverty, befriending and eating with tax collectors and sinners."[58]

---

[57] Henri J. M. Nouwen, Donald P. McNeill, and Douglas A. Morrison, *Compassion: A Reflection on the Christian Life*, (New York: Doubleday, 1983), 12.

[58] Dietrich Bonhoeffer, *Discipleship*, trans., Barbara Green and Reinhard Krauss (Minneapolis: Fort Press, 2003 edition), 284.

Still, the witness of these NGOs does differ visibly from the manner in which Christ fulfilled this incarnational aspect of solidarity as illustrated above. The incarnational solidarity, the mystery of God entering into history and becoming one like us, is that he chastises us even while gently leading us to our full glory. He did not withdraw from choices that constituted an option for the poor, even at the risk of misrepresentation of his identity as the sinless one. Jesus' sinlessness, an act of solidarity, is his continuous choice of others and not of self. Reconsidered in the light of Christ's example, the NGOs' avoidance or oversight of the UN structural issues even when these might have an adverse effect on the poor is an inadequate witness to solidarity for the poor in a given circumstance. This attitude is incongruous with their articulated theological self-understanding as well as the solidarity principles of Vatican II that support their activities.

As we sum up this chapter, we agree that these activities contribute to theology, "making faith connections" by bringing UN issues into faith perspectives. Academic theology itself is thereby enriched as it struggles to interpret and evaluate human activities such as these in authentically Christian terms and as belonging to the economy of salvation—the Church's mission to continue the saving word and work of the risen Lord in space and time. The incarnational solidarity, the mystery of God entering into history and becoming one like us, is that he chastises us even while gently leading us to our full glory. This should become the pattern of NGO relations with the UN, an incarnational solidarity act. Being hopeful about the world is not the same as being "naively optimistic." Hope does not refrain from remarks, often quite critical, on imbalances and failures in the system within which we work. We again recall Augustine's understanding of the Christian's role in social institutions as working to increase opportunities for love and to diminish those of lust present in these institutions.

Finally, from all we have explored in this chapter, it is obvious that the real issue is no longer whether these Catholic actors should participate, or even be present, in the UN. The real question is how to improve their participation so that they may bear the desired fruit as witness to the basic theological and pastoral principle of solidarity that gives foundation to their activities. The enormous contributions of these Catholic NGOs toward alleviating the many kinds of suffering in our world can thus be strengthened by addressing UN shortcomings neglected up to now. Examples of these structural issues discussed here illustrate the magnitude of these systemic structural deficiencies and their effects which are conceptualized in Catholic social teaching as structural sin.

4

TOWARD A NEW MODEL OF
CATHOLIC-INSPIRED NGO/UN RELATIONSHIP

M any supporters of the United Nations, Catholics among them, make a much more positive evaluation of this world body than would be merited by dysfunctional Security Council power politics or the cumbersome bureaucracies so often criticized by media. These supporters steadfastly maintain that worldwide benefits of UN economic and social development programs and its response to contemporary global issues far outweigh even serious UN defects like the Security Council veto used by privileged "P5" for their narrow national interests against the common good. No matter how valid this political/moral tradeoff may be, it should not be tolerated as an excuse to overlook or trivialize the impact that structural defects have on the UN goal we hope for—the common good of all. Structural defects can even bring member states to abandon the spirit of global cooperation, provoking "international mistrust, aggression, greed and protectionism."[1]

---

[1] Douglas Roche, *United Nations: Divided World*, 27.

We will now look at issues of defective UN structures, recognizing and dealing with them as belonging to the theological category of structural sin and as an appropriate focus of Christian witnessing at the UN itself. In this chapter, we will explore the position we maintain in this work that, while continuing to collaborate in UN projects, Church-inspired NGOs should simultaneously engage in constructive criticism of the UN system so as to prevent it from exacerbating the already toxic problems of today's world. Such an engagement fulfills the second dimension of incarnational solidarity theology and further validates the suitability of Catholic UN participation. It thus assures us that, even in the face of dysfunctional structures, the UN is worth sincere, energetic and generous cooperation of all people. This in turn demands that Catholic NGOs employ an alternative paradigm for UN participation. The paradigm we recommend here is a "dialogical confrontation."

We will view through the theological lens of structural sin some UN deficiencies discussed in earlier chapters to show the need for this alternative way of Catholic participation. We will follow by exploring the meaning, implications and challenges of this new paradigm. Finally, we will evaluate advantages of this paradigm for the Catholic NGOs' own internal dynamics as international institutions.

UN Structural & Systemic Challenges
in Theological Perspectives

The alternative Christian presence of dialogical confrontation that we advocate in this work is based on the recognition that UN structural and systemic challenges are theological issues and as such merit a theological assessment. Accordingly, we will highlight a few examples of structural deficiencies in the UN system, viewing them through the theological lens of structural sin deserving confrontational responses from UN participants, especially Christians. Our challenge then is to interpret internal organizational issues so that they readily and obviously appear as structural social sin.

One approach is to observe how these UN structural, systemic or organizational deficiencies impact either directly or indirectly disadvantaged people throughout the world. Because of this impact on the totality of peoples, the various documents of Catholic social teaching could condemn such structural deficiencies as constituting systemic injustice and so label them social or structural sin. Reflecting upon such principal UN goals as world peace, security and development, we can assess how UN structures either promote or frustrate their achievement.

Similarly, we can apply this critique to foundational UN documents like the Charter and the Universal Declaration of Human Rights (UDHR). For instance, looking at the disparity between the rights to immigrate and to emigrate, we can easily see how the UDHR maintains structural imbalances between countries by offering a thematic framework for perpetuating harsh border and immigration policies. Theologically speaking, Christian UN participants indifferent to such harmful systemic deficiencies are indifferent to Christ being crucified again in the poor.

Understanding Structural Sin

The category of structural or social sin comes from the contemporary theological reflection that recognizes moral evil as not limited by earlier narrow understandings. This evil cannot be constrained by a specifically religious vocabulary or reduced to purely private or personal categories.[2] Concomitantly, the notion of original sin must be broadened from simply a universally inherited consequence of Adam's fall to the inclusion of other wider views. One of these complementary views is described by Alister McFadyen as "a

---

[2] Alistair McFadyen, *Bound to Sin: Abuse, Holocaust and the Christian Doctrine of Sin* (New York: Cambridge University Press, 2000), 5.

distortion of our fundamental way of being in the world."[3] Such broadening admits integration into the entire original sin tradition of a societal aspect: "the systemic and structural distortion of the conditions of human sociality, of the most basic patterns of disposition which constitute our personal identities, and which underlie our actions."[4] Loosened from former individualistic morality limits, sin, whether personal or original, can now be more comprehensively viewed. As the renowned Peruvian theologian and father of liberation theology, Gustavo Gutierrez puts it, sin is "the radical alienation present at the heart of every situation of injustice. It is also an interior personal fracture."[5]

Structural evil cannot be blamed on one solely responsible individual. It nevertheless is a species of moral evil because it results from human choices or sins though it continues onward with a life of its own. Thus, the American Presbyterian minister, theologian, and activist, Richard McAfee Brown warns "we misunderstand injustice if we see it only in individual terms and assume that if we can just change (or get rid of) a few unjust individuals, we will have cleared the path for justice."[6]

American theologian John Bennett makes a significant contribution to appreciating the distinction between personal sin and structural sin when he recognizes their differences both in ontology and in the ways that they may be overcome. "Deliberately chosen evil [personal sin] can be overcome by an inner change of persons, by real repentance and moral conversion," but, "evil which is not deliberately chosen...can only be overcome by a variety of means which include

---

[3] Ibid., 17.

[4] Ibid.

[5] See Gustavo Gutierrez, *A Theology of Liberation: History, Politics, and Salvation*, Trans. Sister Caridad Inda and John Eagleson, revised edition. (Maryknoll: Orbis Books, 1989), 103.

[6] Richard McAfee Brown, "Toward a Just and Compassionate Society: A Christian View," in *Cross Current*, summer (1995), 166.

knowledge of cause and effect and large-scale changes in institutions and external circumstances by social action."[7]

Though recently articulated by contemporary theology, structural sin is not original to it. Gregory Baum reminded us that the Bible consistently refers to sin in the twofold language of personal and social, or, as the latter is frequently expressed, the "sin of the world." In biblical understanding, social sin is not simply the sum total of the personal sins of individual citizens of nations or of members of institutions. While personal sin refers to an evil act knowingly and freely chosen by an individual, social sin refers to communal actions resulting from false or distorted structures or systems. It is "the structure of evil, built into society, which wounds people, distorts their inclinations and prompts them to do evil things."[8]

We seem to be held helpless in the firm grip of structural sin, often not even aware of it, and that is why it is most difficult to deal with. Structural sin has the characteristic of a profound collective blindness. Examples of this collective blindness to UN structural sin are the tyrannical monopoly of the big powers, the P5, the lack of equitable and universal participation in Security Council decision making, inequitable gender distribution of Secretariat staff and inconsistencies of UN foundational documents like the Charter and the Universal Declaration of Human Rights.

These problems militate against UN organizational goals such as the protection of the common good, of human life and dignity, and of peace and security Many UN actors, including dedicated advocates, appear unaware of these structural flaws or at least are blind to their impact. They would claim even not to see how the composition and

---

[7] John Bennett, *Social Salvation: A Religious Approach to the Problems of Social Change,* (New York: Scribners's, 1935), 9, cited in Michael Bourgeois, "Historical anticipations of Critical Theology: Why Social Theory Matters for Theology," in Don Schweitzer and Derek Simon, *Intersecting Voices: Critical Theologies in a Land of Diversity,* (Ottawa: Novalis, 2004), 43.

[8] Gregory Baum, *Religion and Alienation,* 172-174.

modus operandi of the Security Council puts world security in jeopardy.

Sinful structures become even worse when personal evil is simultaneously strengthened and disguised by social relationships. According to Valpy Fitzgerald, "a particular system, (a historical system of relations between people) can easily create a series of situations which make necessary – and thus apparently reasonable – that conduct which favors one's own greed…at the expense of the life and dignity of many others."[9] This can be observed both in systematic violations of human rights and in the endangerment of other sentient beings and creatures held in social, economic, political, religious and family relationships.

Such a mutually enabling relationship between structural sin and personal sin is evident in the Universal Declaration's affirmation of the right to leave one's country without a reciprocal right of entry elsewhere. This disparity lets governments enact strict and inhuman border policies that encourage migrant human rights violations both at and within international borders. Thus, for migrants, structural evil imposes a deprivation of the common good which has always included "subcategories like mutual accountability, subsidiarity, and participation."[10] Powered by rampant accumulation, domination and self-interest, sinful structures generate injustice that endangers creation, divides humanity, increases misery and inflicts unnecessary deaths. UN actors themselves may never discover the consequences of their actions because effects of their participation in structural sin are felt far away in remote and rural areas.

Subjecting the UN system to a critique of structural evil is warranted precisely by the UN's position in the universal search for global

---

[9] Valpy Fitzgerald, "The Economics of Liberation Theology," in Christopher Rowland, ed., *The Cambridge Companion to Liberation Theology*, (Cambridge, UK: Cambridge University Press, 1999, reprinted copy, 2002), 224.

[10] Cahill, in *Globalization and Catholic Social Thoughts*, 44.

governance with the wellbeing of the totality of the world's people as its foundational goal. As an agent of global governance -- an arrangement for better management of the world's issues for the common good of the world's people -- its structures and systems have no other purpose than to ensure goal achievement. Thus, this same goal forms both the framework and the criteria for assessing these structures and systems.

The structures have no reason for being other than the achievement of the goal. Therefore, to refuse to expose them to criticism using the critique of structural sin is to let them continue to hamper the realization of full life for the people. This was the case with past structures and systems in society and institutions that perpetuated throughout history varied forms of injustice be they racism, slavery, patriarchy, xenophobia or sexism. All these kept people from realizing the full life God has promised his people. They were inherent in governance structures or societal organizations, so in most cases they were overlooked as being merely organizational elements or internal dynamics of those institutions where they thrived--until they were challenged and overcome.

Revisiting the UN Structural & Systemic Challenges

From our earlier discussion of Security Council dynamics, it is entirely beyond any doubt that politics of self-interest and moral relativism — imperial proclivities—underlie the P5 frequent resort to the veto. These proclivities are responsible for the Security Council's pathetic response to global crises, especially to war and other serious human rights violations. These proclivities to systemic injustice are also common to other structures of evil. Lives are lost all around the world every day because of the superpowers' struggle for economic interest, lust for power and maintenance of regional spheres of influence. This was as clear in conflicts throughout history as it is today.

It is clear that persisting Middle East crises, aside from their particularly unique specifics, are deeply rooted in the silent struggle for control in the Arab world among Security Council permanent members, among China, Russia and western superpowers, particularly the United States. While the entire range of Middle East crises cannot be attributed simply to struggles among Security Council P5 members, it is nevertheless obvious how these P5 struggles do contribute to the frustrations caused by Middle East crises as they persist.

On December 5, 2016, Russia and China vetoed a Security Council resolution for a truce and ceasefire in Syria despite the dreadful and worrisome humanitarian conditions there. Two hundred thousand (200,000) people were still trapped in rebel-held area of Aleppo, which was affected by severe food and aid shortages. The vetoed resolution was crafted to demand humanitarian aid access and an end to the violence throughout Syria. This was the sixth time Russia had vetoed a resolution on Syria since 2011 and also the fifth time China had blocked action.[11]

The Russian UN ambassador Vitaly Churkin cited as an excuse for their veto the rebel tactic to use a ceasefire as an opportunity to regroup and to reinforce. In his words, "These kinds of pauses have been used by fighters to reinforce their ammunition and to strengthen their positions and this will only worsen the suffering of civilians." However, his U.S. counterpart, Michele J. Sison, U.S. Deputy UN Ambassador, rejected this excuse claiming that "Russia has been more focused on preserving its military gains than helping Aleppo's citizens."[12]

Joining the tirade against Russia and China, British Ambassador Matthew Rycroft disputed Russia's further explanation that a purpose of

---

[11] Michelle Nichols, "Russia, China block U.N. demand for seven-day Aleppo truce," *Reuters* online edition (Monday, December 05, 2015), *http://www.reuters.com/article/us-mideast-crisis-syria-un-idUSKBN13U2LX?il=0*, retrieved December 06, 2016.
[12] Ibid.

the veto was to allow for more time for consultations between Washington and Moscow or among members of the Council. It was rather "because of their (Russia's and China's) long-standing, misplaced faith in a despot who has killed nearly half a mission of his own people." Chinese UN Ambassador Liu Jieyi maintained the position that their veto was solely for the sake of more negotiations on the draft resolution text that would ensure reaching Council consensus. Liu Jieyi accused Rycroft of "poisoning" the atmosphere and "abusing" the forum with his remarks.

As co-drafter of the resolution together with Egypt and Spain, New Zealand UN Ambassador Gerard van Boheme's frustration over this veto action graphically captured the point we have made in this work repeatedly about the use and impact of the veto along with the political bickering among the P5. He said the failure to act was "deeply damaging to the [Council's] reputation and catastrophic for the people of Syria."[13]

Further, a better Security Council structure could more effectively handle such issues as the invasion of small countries by some P5 members. To many people, P5 hegemony and the battle behind Security Council bickering were why the UN could not stop the U.S. invasion of Iraq, the Russian invasion of Georgia and the more recent tactical annexation of Crimea. Human lives, property, culture and history wantonly wiped out in these crises seem to count for nothing.

We must again recall that each of the five Security Council permanent members are among the top nine possessors of the more than 25,000 of the world's nuclear weapons. These five countries consistently frustrated negotiations for an international small arms treaty, even ensuring that the treaty adopted in 2013 did not endanger any commercial interests.

---

[13] ibid.

United States opposition was behind the inability of the first conference on small arms in 2001 to construct a more substantial Programme of Action (PoA) that later could lead to the treaty. The reasons, otherwise known as "redlines," for US hesitance as contained in the speech of its representative Ambassador John Bolton include US government unpreparedness to "accept controls on legal manufacturing or trade in small arms and light weapons, prohibitions on civilian possession of small arms, restrictions of small arms and light weapons transfers to governments, any legally binding instruments, and any mandatory review structure and any language supporting the role of non-governmental organizations." This hesitance provided a ground for other governments to undermine both the comprehensiveness and the content of the final document of the Programme of Action.[14]

This negative impact of the US was explicitly criticized by the Conference President Ambassador Camilo Reyes Rodriguez of Colombia in his closing statement: "...I must, as President, also express my disappointment over the Conference's inability to agree, due to the concerns of one State, on language recognizing the need to establish and maintain controls over private ownership of these deadly weapons and the need for preventing sales of such arms to non-State groups."[15] The US persisted in its efforts to frustrate or at least weaken the treaty Note how in a later development the U.S. objected even to small ammunition being included in the treaty. A major reason or this obstructionist U.S. position came from strong domestic resistance fomented by the National Rifle Association (NRA).[16] In the last days of the treaty negotiations, many critics feared that some U.S. positions taken to weaken

---

[14] Natalie Goldring, "The 2006 Review Conference on Small Arms and Light Weapons: A Study in Frustration," *Disarmament Diplomacy* no. 84 (Spring, 2007). *http://www.acronym.org.uk/old/archive/dd/dd84/84ng.htm.*

[15] ibid.

[16] Scott Stedjan, "US Opposes Small Arms 'Ammunitions' within a Global Arms Trade Deal," *The World Post,* (2011), *http://www.huffingtonpost.com/louis-belanger/us-opposes-small-arms-amm_b_829908.html.*

the outcome document would even align the U.S. itself with countries like Russia and China.[17]

The global governance system continues to entrust the security of the world into the hands of the five nations that have the most weapons of terror, yet people seem unable to connect the dots that would reveal this anomaly as structural sin rampant in the UN system.

Another flaw of the Security Council supported by the UN Charter consistent with structural sin concerns the admission of new UN members. Though the Charter at first proclaims that membership is open to all "peace-loving" nations, it then reserves actual admittance to nations recommended by the Security Council. Charter, Art. 4 (1) "Membership in the United Nations is open to all other peace-loving states which accept the obligations contained in the present Charter and, in the judgment of the organization, are able and willing to carry out these obligations." Charter 4 (2) "The admission of any such state to membership in the United Nations will be effected by a decision of the General Assembly upon the recommendation of the Security Council."

Any honest side-by-side comparison of these two Charter provisions would make obvious what was long recognized by those convinced that the P5 intentionally structured the UN Charter to continue the

---

[17] According to Suzanne Nossel of Amnesty International, On July 12, 2012"the U.S. government now preferred[d] a treaty that only requires countries to take 'into account' a range of considerations – including human rights concerns, national security, and regional stability – before deciding to ship weapons to countries where the risk they will be used to commit serious violations of human rights is high. Especially troubling is the United States' assertion that 'we want to ensure that states are asking the right questions and striving to strike the right balance when making decisions about the export of conventional arms.' This fence-straddling approach won't stop the flow of guns and bullets, tanks and gunships into the hands of dictators, armed militias and others." Suzanne Nossel, "US Joins Russia and China in Trying to Weaken Arms Trade Treaty" (July, 13, 2012) *http://blog.amnestyusa.org/us/us-joins-russia-and-china-in-trying-to-weaken-arms-trade-treaty/*.

subjugation of weaker and smaller nations. This inherent contradiction in the foundational document of the UN allows ready manipulation by the P5. The imperialistic prerogative of the veto would make UN admission difficult for states perceived as threats to any of the P5 or their clients.

For example, Palestine's admission to the UN is unacceptable to the United States because of its relationship with Israel. The US has stymied any Security Council vote that would admit Palestine to UN membership. The US has even tried to keep the General Assembly from upgrading Palestine's UN status to Permanent Observer State—a futile attempt without a veto.

In the preceding chapter we asserted that one characteristic of suffering in our time is deprivation, and the worst of deprivations is, according to Douglas Sturm, alienation. Alienation is perhaps the best descriptive name for the burden carried by those weighed down by the superpower veto. The five most powerful nations keep the less powerful from full and equal participation in the UN where they could hope for recognition of their dignity or realization of their identity. Such is the burden of Palestine.

A further example of UN foundational document inconsistency deserving critique in terms of structural evil is the Universal Declaration of Human Rights, Article 13 (2). This somewhat deceptive provision states that "Everyone has the right to leave any country, including his own, and to return to his country." On its face and without critical analysis, this provision seems to protect all people and sovereign states fairly when applied equally. But considered within the dynamics and realities of migration, it condones and continues institutionalized imbalances by not completing the "right to leave" one's country with the reciprocal "right to enter" another country of choice. This ensures that only emigration is guaranteed as a human right and raises the enigmatic question of how the right to emigrate can be realized without the right to immigrate.

In actual practice, the UDHR denies people the very right it claims to ensure. People are deprived of their right to emigrate by the mere denial of their right to immigrate.[18] In the reality of today's world, the right to emigrate remains problematic in the face of strict immigration and border policies. Government exploitation of this flaw produces immigration policies that increase human suffering and leave the world more volatile than secure. Despite all the human rights conventions designed to protect the right of every person irrespective of status—citizen or migrant, regular or irregular, resident or refugee—this disparity remains a grave obstacle to international relations.

The adverse effects of this foundational inconsistency, whether moral, ethical, economic or social, are many and widespread. But let us ask who suffers most under the present arrangement. Countless people, often refugees fleeing violence, oppression or natural disaster, die on their way to receiving countries. Governments spend huge amounts, approximately twenty-five to thirty billion dollars each year, on enforcement of immigration laws. The disadvantaged are burdened by inequalities, for while citizens of wealthy countries travel or stay almost anywhere in the world without much trouble, the poor meet constant obstacles and setbacks. Skilled workers enjoy easier mobility than unskilled ones, or vice versa depending on the particular needs and wants of the receiving country's elite.[19]

A few examples may bring home this reality. A two-year multiple entry visa for the United Kingdom costs five hundred thirty-six US dollars ($536) for citizens of developing countries while citizens of developed countries usually do not even need a visa for travel there. Further, many countries demanding visas from citizens of poor countries frequently allow them only a short period of stay, requiring the poor

---

[18] Pierre Sane, "Foreword," *Migration Without Borders: Essays on the Free Movement of People,* Antoine Pécoud and Paul De Guchteneire, eds. (Paris: UNESCO Publishing, 2007), ix of ix-x.

[19] Antoine Pécoud and Paul De Guchteneire, "Introduction: The Migration Without Borders Scenario," in *Migration Without Borders,* 4, 5.

to pay repeatedly for visas for repeated travels. Moreover, the period it takes to obtain these visas raises flight costs for the poor up to double the flight costs for the rich. And often remaining unnoticed is the inhuman treatment people from poor or developing countries suffer at the international borders just because of their nationality.

These situations are as demoralizing as they are finically draining. Yet up to now no migrant rights discussion at the UN or in its related organizations has bothered to address this problematic fundamental issue of the right to leave a country without the corresponding right to enter another. Indeed, concerning the right to leave one's country not coupled with the right to enter another, even ordinary experience would suggest such an outlook not to be unreasonable. "The right to leave one's own house does not imply the right to enter your neighbor's house." The right to enter another territory should be understood as moderated by sovereignty rights and must be respected as such. We acknowledged the 1951 Refugee Convention and other related treaties responding to the needs of migrants and refugees. However, the case made in our work by referring to this non-complimentary provision in the UDHR is that it exacerbates the situation of vulnerable migrant and refugee groups hurt by structural sin manifested by unjust exploitation by some governments in the guise of protecting national sovereignty.

The widening gap between unbridled sovereignty protection and universal solidarity towards refugees and migrants has deepened the crisis brought about by unprecedentedly large movements of refugees and migrants with their associated vulnerabilities. This situation cannot be ignored or glossed over simply by referring to existing but rarely implemented international instruments while witnessing the loss of life of fellow world citizens in a number that we have never seen before. Also considering that the UDHR and the 1951 Refugee Convention were born out of a particular time and context, we must admit that changing times and situations weaken the applicability of these foundational documents and instruments. A major task of the late 1940s and early 1950s was to promote global solidarity to support endangered populations whose autocratic and oppressive regimes would not permit flight from home or return. The UDHR and the 1951 Refugees Convention were great achievements in their time, but it remains true that with few exceptions so many countries were opening their borders to these people that the right to enter another territory was not as problematic as it is today.

Our treatment of this topic aims to awaken global consciousness to the reality we live in so as to inspire a collective search for a genuine and comprehensive action plan response guided by courage and political will. A step in this direction is the earlier mentioned September 19, 2016 UN Summit in New York on the Large Movement of Refugees and Migrants and its inspired process on global compact for safe, orderly and regular migration (GCM). The plight of migrants and lack of efficient policies responding to their needs are the key reasons behind the UN-led GCM process demonstrating also the desire of world leaders' commitment in solidarity to seek better ways to save lives, protect rights and share responsibility on a global scale.

We hope this will lead to re-evaluating and adjusting the existing instruments so as to overcome their inherent vulnerabilities to being manipulated into inhibiting the realization of their intended goal. This matter was repeatedly raised during the 2016 Global Forum on Migration and Development (GFMD) held in Dhaka, Bangladesh December 8-12. The chair of the Forum, the Bangladesh Foreign Secretary, H.E. Md. Shahidul Haque made the case for the urgency and necessity of this radical and critical review in his welcome remarks of the conference/forum.[20] High ranking UN experts, diplomats, staff and non-government actors at the Forum demanded that the expected global compact on safe, orderly and regular migration should not fail to undertake a critical review of existing instruments which many acknowledge are obsolete and ineffective.

---

[20] *https://www.gfmd.org/.*

Even if these structures were justified in the past, changes in world realities and international relations have rendered most of them obsolete or even counter-productive. In any case, these structures actually inhibit necessary reform. The UN collaborates with international institutions such as the *Institute for Democracy and Electoral Assistance* (IDEA) in initiating, conducting and supervising constitution reviews around the world, yet review of even parts of UN foundational documents do not get similar attention. In fact required review processes and procedures make it difficult to conduct a review that would be proper—let alone effective.

It is true that modifications of some articles of the Charter had been achieved over the years such as the review of the membership of the Security Council in 1966 that increased the number of non-permanent members to ten. Also, we had mentioned earlier the reviews of the ECOSOC NGO consultative status in 1950, 1968 and 1996. Equally some NGOs and academics have undertaken reviews of the UN foundational documents and produced proposals for UN reform as exemplified by Thomas Weiss and his colleagues mentioned in chapter one of this book. There also has been a variety of reviews of the UN carried out by committees at the prompting of the UNGA or the UN Secretary-General. However, these were not taken up because of scant widespread support as well as the bottleneck suffered by the review processes and procedures prescribed by the Charter.

This is the case we are making. In any game where the field and rule of play are not equally accessible, open, and applicable to all players, there injustice thrives. And structures that sustain such situations are unjust and sinful structures in Christian theological language. How else would the Palestinian people seeking their human right for self-determination interpret their situation considering how the United States exercises its veto in alliance with Israel? Why would the many migrants suffering under various hardships sanctioned by the Universal Declaration not resent the entire UN and the Declaration itself as attempts to prolong western hegemony, domination and suppression of others? Why do small countries have to play stooge to the military and the economy of rich and powerful countries for their voices to be heard and for their issues to make it to the discussion agenda of an organization that claims to maintain the equal right of all members?

How is it justified that United States President George W. Bush never appeared before the International Criminal Court (ICC) for invading Iraq in defiance of the UN and with a war based upon lies besides, while leaders of small countries who do the same but on smaller scales are forced to face the wrath of international law? As clear truth of unlawful acts of torture committed by Security Council permanent members continues to emerge, what becomes ever clearer is their impunity before international law. It is a further abomination that these atrocities and the double standard that shields Security Council perpetrators, as in the case of George W. Bush, can be arguably defended. The immorality of the Iraq War cannot be adjudicated by the ICC since it is a crime of aggression over which the ICC does not yet have jurisdiction. Worse still, if and when the ICC does get jurisdiction, no such charge will be retroactive.

It may be next to impossible to counter or even confront these structural sins. They have been with us for generations, as witnessed in the fifth century by Saint Augustine's parable in his *City of God* of the sea pirate and the emperor. Augustine writes, "Thus it was an apt and honest response that a captured pirate gave to Alexander the Great when he was asked why he was involved in such an evil profession. He said 'because I do what I do with a tiny ship, I am called a pirate. But because you do the same thing with an enormous navy, you are called emperor."[21] It is important to mention that the issues discussed here do not exhaust all that could be termed structural sin within the structures of the UN system. As further examples we can point to injustices built into the system of UN finance such as the imposition of

---

[21] Augustine, *De Civitate Dei*, IV: 3, 4.

a ceiling on the contributions of wealthy nations to the UN budget allowing them to pay less than others—especially the poor countries.

A practical exercise to determine whether organizational flaws are structural sins may be simply to ask a set of revealing, upsetting questions. Who benefits from the present structurally arranged status quo? Who loses? Who reaps profit? Whose interests are served? Are the many disadvantaged people further hurt? Are lives of the privileged few enhanced all the more? What are the differential outcomes for the one percent (the elite) versus the ninety-nine percent (the masses)? And if the reverse were to be the case would the rich, the powerful tolerate it? Why does the rest of the world have to kneel in supplication, begging and waiting on five countries or sometimes one person before the UN could act? When has one head become better than two—or, in the case of the UN, when have five heads become better than one hundred eighty-eight?

In summary, do the structures serve the hopes enunciated by the UN goal "to develop friendly relations among nations based on respect for the principle of equal rights and self-determination of peoples; to achieve international cooperation in solving international problems of economic, social, cultural or humanitarian character; promoting and encouraging respect for human rights and fundamental freedoms for all without distinction as to race, sex, language, or religion; and to be a center for harmonizing the actions of nations in attainment of these common ends?"[22]

In turn, these same questions make it incumbent upon gospel motivated participants in UN structures to ensure that they are constantly raised and never forgotten. In that way occasions of sin are minimized or completely eliminated, and occasions of love abound. Why should the UN, which during its seventy years has neglected to choose a

---

[22] See UN Charter, Chapter I, Article 1, in Leland M. Goodrich and Edvard Hambro, *Charter of the United Nations: Commentary and Documents* (Boston: World Peace Foundation, 1946), 339.

woman as Secretary-General, go unchallenged by those who work in the UN system from gospel imperatives? We celebrated the inclusion of three women on the shortlist of candidates to succeed Ban Ki-moon: Irina Bokova the Bulgarian Director General of UNESCO, Vesna Pusić the Deputy Speaker of the Croatian Parliament, and Natalia Gherman former Moldavian Minister of Foreign Affairs. But the election of António Guterres in October 2016 proved again the wise warning not to count our chicks till the eggs are hatched—especially so as we remember that this is not the first time a woman's name appeared on the list.

Do these imperatives not insist on the equal and fair play rules applicable to all? Such neglect cannot hide under the cover of the structures being merely a matter of internal organizational issues. That is a charade that has covered continued injustice and discrimination infecting many institutions. For instance, the unchallenged privilege and use of power by clerics over the other members of the Church or the racially inflamed police brutality in societies like the United States are passed over as simply internal and organizational affairs.

Catholic UN participants betray their prophetic calling by blindness to sinful UN structures, seeing them only as internal organizational issues not meriting theological critique while distracting themselves with positive UN projects. By being devoid of the charity that is honesty, they would betray the UN itself as well. Such a betrayal would ensure that the UN would continue to lose credibility with the world's disadvantaged who remain unconvinced that this world body exists for their good. It is a betrayal of their prophetic calling, for the reaction of Jesus to similar situations in his time was a condemnation of structural sins. He never overlooked them as mere internal organizational issues not meriting his attention and the intervention.

These systemic weaknesses underlying selfishness, individualism and indifference towards the fate of the world's people ultimately lead to a critical question: What are we to do with the United Nations? This question cannot be reduced to a matter of academic interest to scholars of international relations and politics. On the contrary, it is both a practical and a theological concern crucial to the assessment of Catholic Church-inspired NGO participation in the UN. An NGO that turns a blind eye to the structural sin in the system in which it participates is de facto guilty of conspiring with the evil structure it claims not to see. We have maintained from the beginning of this work that we need an alternative way to witness, one that arises from a theology of incarnational solidarity enshrined in Catholic social teachings that will respond effectively to these issues. That alternative is what is proposed here and is appropriately called dialogical confrontation.

Dialogical Confrontation as an Alternative Christian Witness

The social or structural category of sin is dismissed by some theologians as an uncritical rhetorical flourish that "baptizes as sin what secular thought identifies as pathological."[23] Such is the claim of those insisting that UN structural deficiencies are organizational and internal to the system and thus do not merit either Christian theological critique or Christian advocacy. We concur with Alistair McFadyen's response to this claim: "To speak of what damages human beings as sin is to claim that the essential character and defining characteristic of such pathology, however else it may be described and identified in non-theological languages, is theological: the disruption of our proper relation to God."[24] Drawing on the expanded theology of salvation which includes a socio-political dimension discussed above, we hold that it is imperative for UN Catholic actors to respond to all forms of structural injustices. All these sinful structures increase human suffering and decrease the opportunity to gain the full life and personal fulfillment promised to all by God.

---

[23]Alistair McFadyen, *Bound to Sin*, 11.
[24] Ibid.

Moreover, we maintain that the critical question of what we are to do with the United Nations in the light of its structural weaknesses compels theologians to ask this further question: What level of participation should Church people have in institutions which are to a large extent responsible for reinjuring even more gravely the very wounds they are called upon to heal? We reject a fundamentalist attitude that, given the UN's complicity in these structures of sin, the only options available to Church-inspired NGOs are either complete dissociation or a severely restricted involvement. Such a view seems disturbingly close to the pharisaic criticism against Jesus for associating with tax collectors and sinners, dining and mingling with them (Luke 5: 30-32). We contend that Christian groups, especially Catholic-inspired NGOs, should not hesitate to participate actively in the UN as their resources permit and empowered by solid theological principles enunciated in preceding chapters. Doing so will experientially demonstrate that, in spite of all its structural limitations, the UN is a legitimate sphere of Christian service.

Reluctant or conditional participation could prove just as injurious to the Church's mission in the modern world as complete withdrawal would be. To work for reform from within the present structure would show that the Church has both the ability and the motivation to attack unjust structures and to contribute to radical structural transformation. To achieve this from the perspective of the Catholic-inspired NGOs, we propose an approach that responds to the obvious deficiencies of the UN while still supporting those policies and programs that foster the general welfare of the world's people. The dynamics of this relationship is what is captured in the paradigm of *dialogical confrontation*.

Meaning of Dialogical Confrontation

Dialogical confrontation is a way of relating which encourages and sustains participation in complex, multiple-sector institutions like the

UN. Such institutions are worldly in the full sense of the word. They are places where both grace and sin operate, places of the City of God and the human city harboring both a yearning for cooperative existence and the lust for domination. In the realism of Augustinian thought, this is the truth of the dynamism of every human institution, each of them being maintained by constant struggles between grace and sin.[25]

Often the evils one sees and addresses in other institutions are present in one's own institution, and unhappily at times even worse. We have cited as an example of such a situation the various ways that veto privileges of the five permanent Security Council members give them an undue edge over all other nations. The vulnerability of this privilege before tyrannical tendencies limits full participation of all other UN Member States in the major decision-making of the organization, for there is constant threat that the superpowers will put their self-interest above the common interests of all. Opportunities emerge for larger, stronger nations to dominate the smaller and weaker. These are among the very same contemporary evils that the UN seeks to redress as it confronts tyrannical and despotic governments.

According to Augustine, the Christian participant in any institution ought to labor to decrease not just sin but also the opportunities for sin so as to create more space for love. Dialogical confrontation presents the opportunity for Catholic-inspired NGOs at the UN to respond to its institutional sinful elements, its structures that hide inherent injustices. This aspect of UN ministry is too often neglected by traditional NGO approaches that simply collaborate with the UN system in its programs for peace, security and development. What we expect from dialogical confrontation is envisioned in the thought of Walter Brueggemann on the challenge of prophetic ministry: this ministry is tasked with nurturing, nourishing, and evoking a

---

[25] Monika K. Hellwig, *Public Dimensions of a Believer's Life: Rediscovering the Cardinal Virtues* (New York: Rowman and Littlefield Publishers, 2005), 113.

consciousness and perception alternative to the consciousness and perception of the dominant culture around us.

Prophetic ministry has already been initiated by NGOs introducing a new language capable of unmasking hidden discriminatory tendencies. One example cited here is the fashioning by the NGO Committee on Social Development of new language defining poverty and people living in its grip. While this contribution is not to be denied or trivialized, the task of prophetic ministry is not yet completed without unmasking the systemic sin in the UN system that allowed discriminatory tendencies to go unnoticed in the first place. Leaving its task unfinished is like treating symptoms of a cancerous disease without ever getting to root causes.

In this way dialogical confrontation complements and fulfills traditional approaches currently pursued by NGOs. What is demanded is courageous and continuous NGO collaboration with UN projects while just as courageously constantly seeking ways to respond to the sinful elements and structural injustices in the UN itself. This is consistent with the Jesus paradigm illustrated in the theology of incarnational solidarity—the mystery of God entering into history, becoming one like us and chastising us even while gently leading us to full glory.

In his compassionate response to the conditions of his time, Jesus perceived the connection between unjust structures and the various sufferings his people experienced. Including a social dimension in his compassionate agenda, he undertook a repeated and direct challenge to the socio-political institutions of his time. Jesus would hardly approve limiting compassion to individual instances and private charity. While alleviating the immediate material needs of the suffering, Jesus worked to eliminate, or at least diminish, the structural causes of those sufferings. In his journey to Jerusalem and his ministry once he arrived there, including a confrontation with temple abuses, we have examples of Jesus' compassionate attack on the socio-political and religious structures of oppression in his time (Mk. 11: 15-18).[26] In the face of unjust systems and corrupt institutions, especially those in which they participate, Christians cannot fulfill their responsibility adequately by simply working with good and convenient programs on the side. Catholic-inspired NGOs ought to appreciate the seriousness of the relationship between the structures of sin and the suffering of people so as to act with dialogical confrontation for the sake of the people whose interest they are called to serve.

This paradigm's confrontation is structured in, and inspired by, Christian compassion, genuine love for the institution and that for which it professedly stands. Motivated by love, this paradigm is able to view criticism of sinfulness as a form of compassionate charity owed the institution by all its loving participants, especially those who are Christian, so that the opportunities for grace may be increased. It never seeks to demonize people responsible for these structures nor destroy the system altogether. That simply is not the major aim of compassion.[27]

Aware of widespread UN structural inadequacies, these actors like Jesus are expected to speak out. Undertaking such compassionate criticism of UN structural weaknesses diminishes opportunities for human sinfulness which can occur through distorted concentrations of power, as is the case with the Security Council and its permanent members privileged with the veto. In this case we may hope that a system will emerge wherein people at their worst can do the least amount of harm and people at their best can have the greatest freedom to do good works. Only in this way can a religious congregation like the Augustinians—that conceive their UN relationship in terms of *empire-community* encounter—hope to counter the imperial tendencies of

---

[26] See Ched Myers, *Binding the Strong Man: A Political Reading of Mark's Story of Jesus* (Maryknoll, New York: Orbis Books, 2005, 15th printing), 277-291.

[27] Gregory Baum, "Critical Theologies in Canada: From Solidarity to Resistance," in Don Schweitzer and Derek Simon, eds., *Intersecting Voices: Critical Theologies in a Land of Diversity,* (Ottawa: Novalis, 2004), 59.

accumulation, domination and self-interest in the UN with their communitarian alternatives of witness, service and fellowship.

Given our knowledge of the situation, inertia on this issue is tantamount to sin. The four popes addressing the UN asked for its reform. They were Paul VI in 1965, John Paul II in 1995, Benedict XVI in 2008 and Francis in 2015. As we recall from our discussion in chapter one, Benedict XVI so recognized the enormous pressing need for UN reform that he warned not even the recent global recession should minimize its urgency. In fact, in his perspective, healing the UN organizational power imbalance would itself facilitate a faster and more lasting recovery from the economic recession. According to the pontiff, "One also senses the urgent need to find innovative ways of...giving poorer nations an effective voice in shared decision-making. This seems necessary in order to arrive at a political, juridical and economic order which can increase and give direction to international cooperation for the development of all peoples in solidarity."[28] His *Caritas in Veritate* teaches that without working for truth, "...social action ends up serving private interests and the logic of power, resulting in social fragmentation, especially in a globalized society at difficult times like the present."[29] "Truth" here should include seeing to it that the UN lives up to its purpose by maintaining structures enabling its ideals to be realized.

Pope Francis continued on this call for a radical transformation of the UN system with specific reference to the Security Council. "...the experience of the past seventy years has made it clear that reform and adaptation to the times is always necessary in the pursuit of the ultimate goal of granting all countries, without exception, a share in, and a genuine and equitable influence on, decision-making processes. The

---

[28] Benedict XVI, *Caritas in Veritate*, #67.
[29] Ibid., #5.

need for greater equity is especially true in the case of those bodies with effective executive capability, such as the Security Council..."[30]

The fundamental aim and final goal of this confrontational enterprise is mutual collaboration for the common good, which also would keep us from adopting self-righteous, judgmental attitudes of philosophical or theological individualism. Neither does it promote the utilitarianism of individualistic models of relationship with their impersonal traits that treat the "other" as mere instruments for promoting one's own agenda to use and abandon others to their own iniquities.

"Use" is at the core of this kind of functionalist relationship. Thus, Catholic NGOs do not "use" the UN and its system to achieve their purpose. On the contrary, our theological position of a "personal relationship" enables us to see the common limitedness of all humanity and the resulting common solidarity that enjoin all to identify with each other in good times and bad but without acquiescing in common sins. The NGOs participate with the UN as a universal human endeavor for common good. This is why the confrontation is framed as a necessary consequence of compassion, for if these issues are not challenged, they remain obstacles to the UN organizational goal.

The dialogical dimension of this approach relies heavily on the values and strength of partnership. It implies a mutual collaboration with others to achieve goals. It requires entering into or intensifying the dialogue Catholic NGOs have with other NGOs and with other disciplines and worldviews. This implies increasing participation in various NGO networks as well as in committees and caucuses beside those of their own groups. The solid record of collaboration by Catholic-inspired NGOs with other UN NGOs confirms with David Hollenbach that dialogue across boundaries of diverse traditions is not

---

[30] Pope Francis, "Address of His Holiness Pope Francis to the Seventieth Session of the UN General Assembly."

only possible but necessary for fruitful Christian engagement with public life.

Christianity's presence in this arena is complementary and not antithetical. It need not be divisive but rather can promote solidarity.[31] We already met the same sense of engagement in Pope John XXIII's *Pacem in Terris*. He saw this participation and partnership as a moment of discovering and adhering to the truth and so cautioned that such engagement should not be abandoned because of a history of past failure. "What was formerly deemed inopportune or unproductive," he remarked, "might now or in the future be considered opportune and useful."[32]As Augustine saw clearly, the heavenly city so long as it is on earth not only makes use of earthly peace but also fosters and actively pursues it together with the whole human family under a common platform regarding all that concerns our purely human life as long as it does not interfere with faith or worship. Though apparently merely earthly, such achievements embody Augustinian community values that Christians are to realize in any institution.

This paradigm does not assume that Catholic actors have at hand specific model alternatives to replace the present UN system. Yet, there are real world examples within the UN and their constituencies of how Catholic NGOs can realize the responsibilities of dialogical confrontation to bring about incremental change at the UN. Catholic NGOs must evaluate various UN reform proposals so as to be ready and able to collaborate with them and their advocates. A few examples of proposals worth considering include the 2005 approach led by then Secretary General Kofi Annan and documented in his work *In larger Freedom*. It argued, among other suggestions, for an expansion of the Security Council to 24 members. This ambitious goal was to be achieved by either of two plans. Plan A would create six new

---

[31] David Hollenbach, *The Global Face of Public Faith: Politics, Human Rights, and Christian Ethics* (Washington D.C.: Georgetown University Press, 2003), xii.
[32]*Pacem in Terris*, 159, 160.

permanent members and three new non-permanent members; plan B would create eight new seats in a new class of members who would serve for four years subject to renewal and one non-permanent member divided among the major regions of the world.[33]

More structurally based proposals for UN reform have been put forward by groups of civil societies and non-governmental organizations. Review of the UN Charter is proposed by the World Alliance to Transform the United Nations (WATUN) with its slogan "Global problems, require global solutions: Let's transform the UN to make it democratic and effective."[34] Parliamentarians for Global Action (PGA), an issue-oriented association of parliamentarians, advocates the creation of a United Nations Parliamentary Assembly (UNPA) which would reflect the aspirations of 'we the peoples of the United Nations' better than governments reflect them now. At present no Catholic NGOs have joined with any of these groups. This is a shortcoming among the later Catholic NGOs as we observed in our chapter two.

We mentioned in chapters one and two the tremendous work of Catherine Schaefer and other representatives of the Catholic Association for International Peace (CAIP) in ensuring the inclusion of article 71 into the UN charter so as to provide for NGO consultation by the Economic and Social Council, ECOSOC. These pioneers of Catholic NGOs at the UN were quick to criticize a totally government-constituted UN as a contradiction to the organization's ideals. Such a UN would have gone against the opening words of the Charter Preamble – "We the people of the United Nations." These pioneers were also part of the movement that first addressed the gender inequality ingrained in the

---

[33] See Kofi Annan, *In Larger Freedom: Towards Development, Security and Human Rights for All* (New York: United Nations, 2005), 61.

[34] *http://transformun.org/*.

UN administrative structure. Their initiatives began the inclusion of women in UN Secretariat administrative roles.[35]

However, our paradigm is somewhat cautious regarding the explicit Church identity promotion, as this early group took 'Catholicizing' the UN as part of their mission. Dialogical confrontation attempts to retain the good in the traditions of early Catholic NGOs while enhancing their potential for fulfilling the Christian duty of diminishing the occasions of sin and increasing the space for grace, love and mutuality in explicitly secular institutions. At the same time dialogical confrontation avoids a retreat into a sectarian ghetto mentality that would arrogantly condemn a "sinful world" in contrast to a "holy Church."

We hope we can retain the zest and bravery of the earlier Catholic NGOs in taking on the UN system while not losing the fresh spirit and genuine solidarity of the newcomers. This would mean that the later NGOs, like their earlier colleagues, would realize that their prophetic responsibilities demand not merely UN participation but also criticisms of the inconsistencies and structural deficiencies in the UN system. In a theological perspective, they should see the UN as St. Augustine saw every human institution—a mix of grace and sin, of the city of God and the earthly city, of compassion and lust for domination. In the midst of these complexities, Christian participants have the role of collaborating with the system's program, unless to do so would embrace such a total enmity against the reign of God that they would be blocked from working to limit the opportunities for sin or to increase the space for grace.

We can already point to some progress achieved in this direction. Most recently in the 2016 election process of the ninth Secretary General of the UN, some members of the NGOs of religious congregations of men and women were part of the movement advocating inclusion of women on the shortlist of candidates for the UN Secretary General.

---

[35] See Joseph S. Rossi, "The Status of Women:' Two American Catholic Women at the UN, 1947-1972)," 310-15.

They sought and obtained the support of the US mission to the UN in moving forward.

Also, there is an informal group of member states advancing the same cause of UN reform, so liaising with such a group would be an opportunity for Catholic NGOs to realize this aspect of their role. It is with such relationships that NGOs have always succeeded in pushing their agenda in the UN policy making process. This was the case during the days of the formulation and negotiation of the Universal Declaration of Human Rights. We may also cite as examples several NGO committees liaising with friendly Member States during the open working group process leading to the SDGs, the 2015 financing for development (FfD) meeting in Addis Ababa, the 2016 Paris Conference on Climate Change COP21 and the New York Declaration on Large Movement of Refuges and Migrants, September 19, 2016. We can surely look forward to additional incremental successes these real-world NGO activities can further achieve.

We want to see Catholic NGOs embark on systematic study involving experts on the present structure of the UN in light of its mission and goals and make recommendations for possible reforms where necessary. The report of such a study would equip them with talking points for advocacy in this regard. In fact, this is what other agencies and organizations are already doing. For instance, the International Peace Institute, an ECOSOC NGO as are so many Catholic groups, recently launched the report of its committee on UN reform.[36] Catholic NGOs have the capacity to achieve such an informed study, as many of them have universities, colleges and other specialized institutions staffed with recognized experts.

For example, the Augustinian NGO can enlist among its constituencies the analysis and advocacy of the many schools, shrines, parishes

---

[36] "Pulling Together: The Multilateral System and Its Future," *Report of the Independent Commission on Multilateralism of International Peace Institute, 2016, https://www.ipinst.org/2016/09/icm-final-report.*

and other institutions which it represents at the UN. These are active at the grassroots of the many nations where they are present. The Augustinian NGO can also call on these several institutions and members to petition their government UN missions, realizing as we mentioned in chapter one that the real political powers that play out in the UN are in the capitals of each member state. Augustinians have institutions able to advocate in more than eighty UN member nations including three of the Security Council P5. Other Catholic NGOs who share similar goals and purposes can multiply these efforts many times over through collaboration.

Although the time, energy and resources of any NGO are limited, we may conversely observe that their agendas and activities are also limited. So Catholic NGOs should not be discouraged from advancing their goals at the UN or from promoting national advocacy efforts. Even with their diversity and differences as we mentioned in chapter two, they can still effectively draw from the strength of their common backgrounds what they need for collaboration that will counter the challenges of less than abundant time, energy and resources. Their UN NGO work centers on the common good of humanity, preferential option for the poor and the care of creation – all of which are also mandated by Catholic social teaching.

Regarding their collaboration with existing coalitions of either civil society or Member States, Catholic actors are rather called to develop an openness allowing them to engage while always keeping in mind the principal focus of any engagement: a better UN for the betterment of the greater number of the world's population. Achieving this demands valuing compromise as a positive relational and diplomatic attribute that must be diligently employed by all participants in the UN, including those with a prophetic responsibility. However, in their sacred role as voice of the voiceless and marginalized, Catholic NGOs must endeavor at all times to avoid sacrificing these people to unbridled compromise.

The mutual openness demanded by this paradigm must at the same time preserve the integrity and catholicity of Catholic NGOs lest there be unwittingly encouraged a "translation of theological realities into secular and pragmatically atheistic categories."[37] In other words it demands of these NGO members a constant awareness of their Catholic identity. One way that Church participants have maintained this integrity is by ensuring that hope and not optimism sustains the struggle. Distinction between hope and optimism in many cases draws the dividing line between a religious as opposed to a secular spirit in a struggle for systemic change. "Optimism," Gregory Baum writes, "prompts people to overlook the destructive possibilities of the present and paint for themselves a rosy picture of the future [while] hope dares to confront the evidence of possible future."[38] Naïve optimism, not well-founded hope, would support cooperating with the UN and its programs while overlooking its inadequacies.

Retaining their Catholicity at all times demands operational awareness of the basics of the NGOs' theological self-understanding as well as of the theological and pastoral principles of Christian social action. Consistent reliance on their support groups, such as the Religious at the UN (RUN) and other opportunities for collective faith-sharing among Catholic-inspired NGOs, remains fundamental as well. That is one reason the demise of the International Catholic Organization (ICO) remains a great loss to this apostolate.

Finally, we may rightly conclude that, by adopting this alternative form of participation, these NGOs may actually retrieve ulterior motives, if any, lurking behind the founding of the UN. Thus, they may come to discover whether the UN was really created with genuine concern for the development of the world's population, or in fact was intended from the beginning to serve the economic and military

---

[37] Alistair McFadyen, *Bound to Sin: Abuse, Holocaust and the Christian Doctrine of Sin* (New York: Cambridge University Press, 2000), 13.
[38] Gregory Baum, "The Meaning of Hope in Evil Times," 79.

security of the nations that were victorious over the Axis powers in World War II, as many have suspected.

This discovery might serve two purposes. First, it could help to strategize future UN participation of Church NGOs, raising their consciousness on whether they were intended from the very beginning to be slaves of the empire or servants of the people. This could be especially vital to members of institutions of consecrated life who continue seeking validation for their new UN NGO identity. Second, by discovering and confronting for the future varied historical motivations, the UN can achieve an "assured cooperation, with sincerity of will and energy, with the purpose of a generous participation, not only of this or that party, not only of this or that people, but of all people, yes, rather of all humanity."[39]

Prospects & Challenges
of Dialogical Confrontation

This new paradigm also calls upon all Church-inspired NGOs to understand that a compassionate response toward UN structural sins is not the responsibility of just a few. It rather is a task demanded of all NGOs of and by Church-inspired identity. There should no longer be a chasm between advocacy groups and relief groups, or between earlier and more recent NGOs. Neither can this reformation be pursued from the narrow perspective of self-interest. In fact, this new way of relating with the UN could improve the relationship between the advocate-centered and relief-centered NGOs and between the pioneers and the newcomers. It provides opportunity for a collaborative coming together of all the varied Catholic-inspired NGO types – the conservatives, the liberals and the in-betweens – who until now would never meet each other. Whatever their point of advocacy, they won't be effective if these UN structures remain as they are. For instance, some members of the P5 have been accused of being promoters and

---

[39] Joseph Rossi, *Uncharted Territory*, 39.

sponsors of many activities contrary to pro-life positions. Privileges such as we have recounted give the P5 some monopoly of definition and decision affecting issues at the heart of these diverse Catholic-inspired NGOs. Indeed, nothing gets done if these UN bigwigs stand in the way. So, collaborating on challenging these structures is to the benefit of all Catholic-inspired NGOs, irrespective of ideology.

There are numerous possible obstacles to forming an alliance for UN transformation proposed by our model of participation. Significant among them is the fatalism syndrome – "there is nothing I can do." NGO representatives may spontaneously feel that way when they first compare the enormity of UN structural inadequacies against their limitations to challenge them. This helplessness may be the primary obstacle to achieving the dialogical confrontation model, as one feels overwhelmed, outgunned and discouraged in the face of such an enormity. In truth, the gravity and dynamics of these problems—the structural inadequacies of the UN systems – are indeed no less than enormous.

Additionally, when the topic of UN structural reform is raised at any UN event, also raised is powerful resistance from those who benefitted from the status quo, especially members of the UN bureaucracy. This deeply frustrates individuals and groups favoring UN structural reform. Frustration was the gut feeling of many NGO representatives when we spoke about joining the movement for UN transformation and for Charter review. This frustration is rooted in the provision that Security Council approval is a condition for any significant UN renewal or transformation. The UN Charter, Article 109(2) demands: "Any alteration of the present Charter recommended by a two-thirds vote of the conference shall take effect when ratified in accordance with their respective constitutional processes by two thirds of the Members of the United Nations, including all the permanent members of the Security Council."[40] How can anyone change an empire if systemic change comes only when all imperial actors concur?

Added to this fatalism is another challenge of powerful impact: the subsuming attitude of the UN systems that limit the option of dialogical confrontation. The very dependent nature of NGOs' UN participation allowed by the Charter and other UN instruments constitutes an obstacle to living out the prophetic imagining of dialogical confrontation. If they do not conform to any of the various categories of UN relationship approved by the Charter, NGOs have no other way of participating in the UN system. They become vulnerable to losing their accreditation or affiliation if they violate any conditions of their admittance or if they are perceived as a threat by a Member State or the wider organization. Even though the predominant reason for an NGO to lose its accreditation is the failure to submit a quadrennial report of its activities yet a member state can still eliminate an NGO's presence by raising an objection to it.

The ECOSOC procedure in dealing with NGO matters is on the condition that there is no objection from any Member State. So the system enjoys from its very beginning a self-protection from any challenge raised by alternative voices because it enjoys structures for moderating or eliminating NGO activities. This situation leads to the NGOs being co-opted and domesticated by the system. Revolutionaries turn into conformists.

It is uncomfortably noticeable how NGOs reverence their accreditation and the ability to adapt to the UN system's way of speaking and acting, of mastering the art of being diplomatically correct in language and demeanor. They become as Stanley Hauerwas describes "chartered by the Emperor."[41] How the UN system often legitimizes its

---

[40] See UN Charter Chapter XVIII, Article 109 (2), in See Leland M. Goodrich and Edvard Hambro, *Charter of the United Nations: Commentary and Documents*, 204.
[41] Stanley Hauerwas, and William H. Willimon, *Resident Aliens* (Nashville, TN: Abingdon Press, 1989), 39, 41.

outcome documents by reference to civil society consultation seems to support Hauerwas' description. Succumbing to this situation is inimical to the missionary implications of the incarnational solidarity that justify this relationship in the first place.

One example of the effects of the UN's subsuming of NGOs is the loss of the voice of the people through the subtle attitude insisting that NGO speech adapts to UN jargon for their voice to make sense. In this way, the true message of the voiceless that these NGOs represent is not clearly heard. It can be completely silenced. Bringing the voices of ordinary people to the UN arena is a prime reason for the NGO vocation and its authority as well. If NGOs cannot make an alternative narrative heard, it will be difficult to turn the conversation away from overly political and economic tones.

In other words, what is compromised is the NGO responsibility of ensuring that UN policy discussions are carried out within an ethical and moral framework that help movement from the prevalent deliberative pattern of cognitive empathy without real practical import. Such tendencies are also discernable in the reluctance of many NGOs at the UN to speak up on issues that are considered not palatable to the governments. One would think that this would not be the case as NGOs are generally known to be comfortable challenging government comfortability. Unfortunately, this is becoming the new normal within the advocacy-oriented NGOs working in a diplomatic terrain like the UN.

For instance, the NGO Committee on Migration is experiencing untold difficulty soliciting the support of other NGOs in its advocacy to introduce a proposal for the migrants in crisis in transit. The proposal includes a comprehensive action plan that would more effectively respond to recent deadly ordeals of many migrants at the sea. The reluctance is simply because Member States are not in favor of it but rather prefer the focus on migrants in countries in crisis promoted by the U.S. and the Philippines. On the other hand, experience shows that almost none of the issues the UN works on today were introduced by the NGOs through sometimes a long time of difficult advocacy.

Migrants in crisis in transit proposed by the NGO Committee on Migration calls for action to help and rescue, as well as protect and defend the human rights of all migrants in transit, especially those encountering crises of any kind: physical, legal, psychological etc. This would include seeking comprehensive action to respond to large movements of people at any stage of their movement. The initiative, Migrants in countries in crisis, advanced by the U.S. and the Philippines proposes a narrower approach of limited action focused upon rescue of migrants trapped in countries in crisis. It drew on the experience during the Libya crisis when the government of Philippines opened access to its rescue to migrants escaping violence irrespective of their nationality. The U.S. government collaborated in this initiative by providing funding.

Those Member States which exploit this situation know exactly what they are doing by their gambit. They are well aware of the power that peoples' life experience narratives hold over policy discussions. In turn, by abdicating their role, the NGOs lose their constituencies. The source of their authority and thus their credibility at the UN become questionable. Put in the language of the oracle of Isaiah the prophet, this situation has double disastrous outcomes — the people perish for the lack of prophets and NGOs risk their own demise for their authority is wiped out at its source.

This is why dialogical confrontation can sting the conscience of Catholic actors who trade their prophetic role for "gaining an entrée to the existing public debates and being heard there, rather than with challenging the system or espousing any utopian cause."[42] They would seem fulfilled by identifying with various UN programs, writing periodic letters to commissions, crafting statements at conferences and

---

[42] Duncan Forrester, *Christian Justice and Public Policy* (New York: Cambridge University Press, 1997), 32.

hosting human rights events often self- attended. But they also cannot deny that these statements are as helpful as reams of others occupying space in the impenetrable UN archives.

Of course, it is necessary for NGOs to be knowledgeable in UN language and procedure. Otherwise they could never represent their constituencies effectively. They must be able to carry the needs of the people into the heart of UN policy debate. In other words, it is essential that they acquire the skill to translate and adapt the voices and needs of their constituency into the UN jargons when needed. But to take comfort and satisfaction in this alone without raising a voice against structural issues, without unmasking UN structural sins and without initiating responsive systemic actions betrays both their self-understanding and their presence as an alternative community of a prophetic people.

NGO representatives are neither diplomats nor international civil servants. Their identity enjoys no other option than embracing the holistic demand of the prophetic presence as prescribed by incarnational solidarity. If Catholic NGOs abdicate this responsibility, Catholic presence at the UN would look like another of Stanley Hauerwas' descriptions: a "Church that had ceased to ask the right questions as it went about congratulating itself for transforming the world, not noticing that the world had tamed the Church."[43] Or it may lend credence to the perception that the church seeks and maintains a UN relationship only because of its desire for power.

It could be argued that these Catholic actors find in the Church the same limiting situation that seeks to clip the wings and seal the voices of prophets, turning them into conformists instead of the revolutionaries intended by their divine call. In the Church, on the one hand the place and tasks of all the parts are distributed to each from the divine source, but on the other hand the clerical sector arrogates to itself the role of sole arbiter of all Church roles. This sector controls all the other

---

[43] Stanley Hauerwas, and William H. Willimon, *Resident Aliens*, 39, 41.

parts of the Church, the religious and laity. The clerical sector sees itself as the validation of the prophetic action of all others, whose prophecy must always either conform to clerical expectations or else be officially judged inauthentic.

This is manifest in various cases and processes perpetrated by the Congregation for Institutes of Consecrated Life and Societies of Apostolic Life (CICLSAL) that still deny some religious congregations an autonomy that would enhance their prophetic nature. Examples include the prohibition of religious brothers having leadership over priests in male priest/brother institutes and the recent case between the Congregation and the Leadership Conference of Women Religious (LCWR). Some religious groups because of fear have failed to protest the Congregation's policies as their prophetic responsibility would demand of them. By this choice of self over others, some priests keep quiet and play by the Congregation's rules, depriving their brothers of the opportunity to exercise their God given rights. The same is to be said of the Conference of Major Superiors of Men (CMSM) in the United States, which has maintained silence over the Congregation's case against the Leadership Conference.

The basis of being a Catholic religious man or woman, "brother or sister" as they are commonly known, is by consecrating oneself to Christ through the profession of the three vows of poverty, chastity and obedience. Among the male institutes of religious life some groups go further, that is in becoming priests. There are also some mixed communities composed of brothers and priests. Sometimes, unfortunately though, this clerical or priestly status has become a cause of discrimination within mixed religious communities with the priests exercising or enjoying undue privilege over the brothers. CICLSAL's refusal to allow brothers in mixed communities to take on some levels of leadership positions that would place them over the priests, such as superiors of the house or general superiors of their institutes, is an example of the institutionalization of this privilege. Many see this as an expression of blatant clericalism. The CICLSAL is the administrative department of the Roman Catholic leadership "responsible for everything which concerns institutes of consecrated life (both of men and of women) regarding their government, discipline, studies, goods, rights, and privileges."[44]

The UN situation is analogous. Member States ("First UN") hold control over the NGOs ("Third UN") by prescribing the rules for their operation. Yet the "Third UN" is to function as a check and balance over the "First UN" and even over the "Second." Perhaps the experience of Catholic groups within the Church, where their charismatic function should check and balance other Church sectors, may have contributed to their domestication at the UN.

This reality warrants a reconsideration of the nature and manner of NGO UN participation, a necessity and a possibility to the extent that the NGOs understand their presence in terms of, or as incorporating, prophetic imagination. But some NGO representatives do in fact see their work as explicitly excluding the responsibility of challenging UN structures. Accordingly, they claim that they are not at the UN to change it. Thus, it becomes increasingly necessary for discussions, such as we are undertaking here, to take place among these Catholic groups especially as their memberships continually question the value of their presence asking what their mission is really about.

Theological reflection is a helpful way to proceed, as our findings in this work make evident. The suggestion of dialogical confrontation made here is seminal to this discussion as it showcases the demands of such alternative participation based upon prophetic witnessing supported by incarnational solidarity. From the nature of the UN any challenge for change in its structure could come only from within, so it is appropriate that the discussion of alternative models of witnessing ask the question: if we lose the opportunity of participating this

---

[44] "Congregation for Institutes of Consecrated Life and Societies of Apostolic Life," http://www.vatican.va/roman_curia/congregations/ccscrlife/documents/rc_con_ccscrlife_profile_en.html, accessed March 31, 2016.

way at the UN as provided by the Charter, would there be other ways of taking up a UN apostolate that would fulfill this purpose – of critiquing and helping to dismantle the prevalent and dominant UN culture so as to liberate the organization for the common good of all – the peace, security and development of all the people of the world?

The awareness that they face a similar reality within the Church could help Catholic groups re-evaluate their task of Church renewal that Vatican II calls for. When the Church, hijacked by clerics, protects herself from all forms of critique by co-opting and domesticating religious life, what opportunities are there for religious themselves to return in fidelity to the revolutionary spirits of their respective founders. How do they embark on dismantling the routinization and institutionalization of alternative communities formed and envisioned by their founders so that they may once again fulfill the dual tasks of questioning structural injustices of Church and of society?

We suggest that the first step in dealing with these obstacles is to identify the real fatalism in the NGO-UN experience. Canadian theologian and social justice advocate Mary Jo Leddy identifies this real fatalism with two errors frequently made by social activists. The first is to assume that structural change must necessarily be immediate and total. The second is to misconceive power as absolute control implying an "all-or-nothing wager."[45] Leddy maintains that both errors give rise to a sense of powerlessness which corrupts as obviously and disastrously as absolute power.[46]

In the face of defective UN structures that cry out for change, many NGOs committed to change sadly realize they lack the "all-or-nothing" kind of power. They accept their inability to confront all UN structural issues at once, and so they may doubt that they can bring about any change at all. This sense of powerlessness, of dreams destroyed, can lead not only to resentment and sometimes violence but,

---

[45] Mary Jo Leddy, *Radical Gratitude* (Maryknoll, New York: Orbis Books, 2002), 78.
[46] Ibid., 80.

in an even more disastrous manner, also to a group sabotage of its own professed ideals.[47] The result may be either the complete abandonment of the project or the employment of self-contradictory means.[48]

But contrary to typical NGO assumptions, real power may not ultimately be located in institutional positions, money or numbers but instead in the quality of personal relationships. Real power is relational and interactive, promising and transformative, causing people to relate to one another in a non-manipulative and selfless way manifesting mutual commitment to the common good. This deeper and more accurate understanding of real power dovetails with actual experiences of solidarity binding NGOs with each other and with those who are truly poor united in the pursuit of the common good. Further, NGOs must see that this power already resides with them for that is how NGOs have already made advances at the UN. These already achieved successes should encourage more engagement in structural change activity. It may also be helpful for NGOs to realize that this power extends to, and makes them indispensable in, the UN structure. Instead of holding back from engaging in this important aspect of it for fear of being expelled from the UN, they should realize that if they are united in this action, they would wield immense power: the UN cannot afford to expel all the NGOs or to do without the NGOs at all.

The second step out of this frustrating situation is for NGOs humbly and truthfully to acknowledge what they can do[49] and to accept the truth that they cannot accomplish everything. They should not even attempt to do so, for then they might achieve nothing at all instead of something. To discern what they can do, they need to reflect on how change occurs within institutions, particularly those posing enormous, even overwhelming, challenges like the UN.

---

[47] Ibid., 80-84.

[48] According to Mary Jo Leddy, "the desire to be totally in control and the feeling of being totally out of control can lead, in different ways, to violence." Ibid., 83-4.

[49] Ibid., 96.

Malcolm Gladwell in *Tipping Point* offers the wisdom of "how little things can make a big difference"[50] such as finding some one thing in the system that can be changed that then would bring change exponentially to the entire system. Although the whole system cannot instantaneously change, the simple identification of one thing within the system that is susceptible to immediate change can begin an inexorable process of eventually complete transformation.

For example, Joan F. Burke of the Sisters of Notre Dame de Namur advised NGO representatives to be advocates of systemic structural change by becoming ardent believers in change that is incremental.[51] That was how those Catholic NGOs in the early UN days attained inclusion of women and their issues in both the main UN agenda and UN administration as well as attaining NGO inclusion into the UN system itself. The same is true of NGO success in establishing the office of UN Women as a major UN agency. These NGOs can remain the UN's conscience awakening the system to its own potential.

Following these examples of effective incremental change, NGOs can take every opportunity to point out inconsistencies in UN systems and speeches, showing how they are incompatible with UN principles and are obstacles to its goal. Each of these many opportunities could itself address several facets of the imperialistic dominant culture within the UN system that stifles alternative consciousness by presenting itself as the only possible way.

Another opportunity for incremental change follows consideration of how system failures are sometimes glossed over as individual personal failures, a strategy to protect systemic structural evil by shifting blame onto individual sins. But structural evil is not a sum total of individual evils, and in many cases the very opposite is the operative dynamic. Individual sins are often aided and abetted by structural sin.

---

[50] Malcolm Gladwell, *The Tipping Point: How Little Things can make a Big Difference* (Boston: Back Bay Books, 2002), 10-11.

[51] Joan F. Burke, SNDdeN in conversation with the author, New York: 2008.

If NGOs expose strategies justifying UN systemic imbalances and protecting them from critique, they begin to set the UN on the path of mentality change by which systemic change is ensured. The mantra becomes real: "You cannot expect different results by using the same, usual means."

Appreciating the power that Member State governments enjoy over the UN system, NGOs can coordinate with local, national and international resources to mount on these levels significant campaigns for UN structural reform. Such coordinated and simultaneous NGO advocacy may promote significant change or at least the awareness that it is needed. This echoes once more the Augustinian triad dimension of community.

Above all, NGO representatives and support staff must never neglect the basic need to bring contemplation to their activism as they face obstacles to dialogical confrontation. This integration is at the core of Christian social responsibility. Without contemplation, activism suffers suffocation and becomes sterile or even counterproductive. From my own experience of the UN apostolate and of other social justice activities to promote change, I realize that even with the best planned and executed projects, a high energy level is still required to sustain perseverance. This is especially true when enormous effort seems to achieve tiny results.

High energy levels can come by way of hope, a precious virtue that Christians bring to ministry. Hope is a gift given in and sustained by contemplation, being with the Lord of the work. Hope keeps us from throwing our hands up in despair.[52] This hope—a high-energy attitude—readies us to size up opportunities and to seize them. Gregory Baum observes that our hope generates in us the confidence that, even though our expectations and efforts may be continually frustrated, the

[52] Joseph Stoutzenberger, *The Christian Call to Justice and Peace* (Winona, Minnesota: St Mary's Press, 1987), 23, 29.

future will be blessed.[53] This conviction, says Vaclav Havel, keeps us striving, not just because we stand a chance to succeed, but because our goal is good. Hope builds not on the certitude that things will turn out well, but on the fact that they make sense.[54]

Experience teaches how quickly one can get so overcome by UN ministry demands that prayer can be shoved into the background or completely forgotten. It is so true. We notice how we begin to drift aimlessly when our actions become empty of prayer and devoid of constant communication with the Lord. The first UN Secretary General Dag Hammarskjöld so grasped the need for constant quiet return to the source of our work that he dedicated a room at the General Assembly building lobby for meditation. In the words of the Nigerian Ambassador to the UN, Her Excellency Joy U Ogwu, there is no place like the UN for us to take to heart St. Paul's warning that we are battling not with flesh and blood but with principalities and power.[55] Thus it is only with a superior power that such powers and principalities can be surmounted. As Karl Barth spoke to fellow Christian of his time, we say to Catholic actors today, lay and religious "To clasp hands in prayer is the beginning of an uprising against the disorder of the world."[56]

NGOs should heed Gregory Baum's caution not to regard the work of challenging UN structures as "a promethean project, thus failing to stress God's unmerited grace that empowers people to act on behalf of justice."[57] The only way to achieve what is proposed in this alternative model of UN participation is by linking together in an

---

[53] Gregory Baum, "The Meaning of Hope in Evil Times," *ARC XX* (Spring 1992), 79.

[54] Vaclav Havel, "Reflecting on Hope…." From *Disturbing the Peace,* written or spoken while he was in prison.

[55] See Joy Ogwu, "Foreword," in Emeka Xris Obiezu, et. al., *It is Good for Us to be Here: Institutes of Religious Men and women as NGOs at the UN* (Indiana: Xlribris, 2015).

[56] See Karl Barth, in Robert McAfee Brown, *Spirituality and Liberation: Overcoming the Great Fallacy,* (Philadelphia: Westminster Press, 1988), 13.

[57] See Gregory Baum, "From Solidarity to Resistance," 56.

unbreakable chain our prayer and our action, contemplation and prophetism. Cut off from the Lord of the work we can do nothing.

Religious groups at the UN have the luxury of spaces and programs helping them pay due attention to this integral spirituality. They do this as individual groups or as a collective whole. Monthly meetings of RUN offer refreshing opportunities for prayer and reflection. And RUN also organizes an annual retreat just for this purpose. The value of those graced moments is often indescribable. Such opportunities are not presently available within the lay groups. The only opportunity they had was lost with the closure of ICO.

Above all this, the real challenge we envisage in adopting the alternative witnessing proposed in our paradigm would be dealing with a dominant theology underlying many Catholics which still creates a dichotomy between private charity and activism for systemic change. This tendency leads to a pathology well described as a socially dormant conscience with its various symptoms, such as ignorance, inadequacy and apathy that view socio-political activities like a UN apostolate as an irrelevant distraction for a religious person. If they do not defeat these attitudes or at least confront their influence, Catholic NGOs may not succeed in winning the support of their constituencies to advance their work or to enlist them in advocacy to influence UN member states. Thus, these NGOs must frequently organize education sessions with their constituencies. Again, as we observed in the concluding part of our work, we can already see some positive signs in this direction.

Catholic UN NGOs are already organizing education programs. NGOs of religious congregations often hold seminars and workshops around UN issues to educate their constituencies about their UN ministry. They emphasize the significance of such activities as witnessing their call to follow Christ as religious today. Since 1999, IMCS-Pax Romana, "a Catholic Confederation of students from all over the world," has brought the UN human rights agenda to both its members and to diocesan promoters of justice and peace through its two annual internship programs. On these occasions for on-going formation, theologians are often invited to interact with UN resource people. Participants assume responsibility for organizing similar events at their local campuses. Our suggestion is that such educational events are good opportunities too for education concerning UN structural issues and the need for a coordinated advocacy on behalf of the organization's reform.

Dialogical Confrontation & the Internal Dynamics of the Catholic NGOs & the Church

Apart from its use as a paradigm for UN ministerial presence, dialogical confrontation also serves as an attitude of critical self-reflexive engagement with one's own institutional systems. It empowers the NGOs to critique their own systems, ensuring efficiency and effectiveness. Though Augustine would identify the "city of God" with the Church, but only in some aspects, he also teaches that the society of the just can quickly revert to the level of the city of man. The "city of God," as Gregory Baum interprets Augustine, is "present wherever people love and serve one another, but it gives way to the 'city of man,' the proud city, when people become self-centered, pursue their own advantages and abandon solidarity."[58]

Catholic NGOs and their respective parent institutions are not necessarily free from the evils of UN systemic sinfulness they must challenge. The 1971 Synod of Bishops statement *Justitia in Mundo* (*Justice in the World*) recommends critical self-reflexive engagement as a Church responsibility required for the role of protagonist and witness to justice. "While the Church is bound to give witness to justice, she recognizes that anyone who ventures to speak to people about justice must first be just in their eyes. Hence we must undertake an

---

[58] Gregory Baum, "The Meaning of Hope in Evil Times," *ARC* 20 (1992): 82.

examination of the modes of acting and of the possessions and life style found within the church itself."[59]

Thus, Catholic NGOs need to search their own organizations for similar weaknesses and limitations, embracing the challenge of transforming them. It is appropriate and necessary that these NGOs give serious consideration to accusations leveled against them. Some accusations, especially against international NGOs, include unequal terms of collaboration between their expatriate western agents and their local agents. Most of them have an employment structure that "establishes a vertical distinction, or hierarchy, between the two groups, [expatriates and locals] to accommodate different standards of living in the North and the South."[60] Their administration may have some issues of insufficiency or a total lack of transparency and accountability. Sometimes their leadership exhibits highhandedness and condescending attitudes. While these particular accusations are not specifically leveled against the Catholic groups, it is not rash criticism simply to observe that some Catholic groups suffer accusations similar to those suffered by most international NGOs.

Further, some Catholic NGOs, especially those related to traditional institutions, are still locked in "orthodox thinking and inflexible bureaucratic structures"[61] that do not allow their staff the creative experimentation and in-depth adaptation to tackle issues effectively. Several do not allow adequate lay collaborator participation in decision-making. Within their parent institutions, power imbalances still affect ways decisions are made and applied, demonstrating the paternalism and maternalism that are sure signs of hierarchical proclivities. Again, as earlier mentioned, in some male institutions of priests and brothers, the brothers are still marginalized and denied election to some higher leadership positions. Catholic NGOs not standing up against these

---

[59]World Synod of Catholic Bishops, 1971, *Justice in the World*, III.40

[60] Naoki Suzuki, *Inside NGOs: Learning to Manage Conflicts Between Headquarters and Field Offices* (Warwickshire, UK: Intermediate Technology Publications, 1998), xvi.

[61] Ibid.

institutional ills, even if critical of UN structures, risk being challenged – "healer, heal yourself."

Dialogical confrontation demands and prepares Catholic-inspired NGOs to engage the Holy See on its choice to remain neutral in voting on *all* UN matters, which critics interpret as a betrayal of key aspects of incarnational solidarity. Regarding its General Assembly participation, the Holy See has of its own volition chosen Permanent Observer status over full membership and thus refrains from exercising the right to vote or even to recommend a candidate of its own.[62] The Holy See makes it clear that its representatives in the UN and its agencies are simply observers.[63] It deems this choice to remain neutral in all UN votes consistent with its role as spiritual and moral guide to the organization. Nevertheless, it may, and has, signed and ratified multilateral treaties.[64] These actions are not contrary to its non-voting situation at the UN which it took on with the observer status option. Also, though it may, and has, influenced some decisions at the UN and its conferences, such influence in these decisions are not effects of direct action associated with the voting right but rather of its use of the diplomatic lobbying of its allies.

True, to some extent neutrality has worked to the Holy See's advantage, as the Rev. Vittorio Guerrera of the Holy See Mission pointed out during my interview with him in November 2008. He pointedly referred to Holy See success in conflict resolution and mediation between adversaries, many of whom regard the Holy See as an honest broker. He also believes that the neutral, nonvoting option empowers the Holy See more than any other nation to respond to issues on the

---

[62] See Number 10 of the Annex to UNGAResA/58/314, "Participation of the Holy See in the Work of the United Nations;" "A Short History of Holy See's Diplomacy," *www.holysee.org*.

[63] https://holyseemission.org/contents//mission/our-history.php.

[64] This observation can be strengthened by a survey of Vatican bilateral treaties or concordats. *http://www.holyseemissiongeneva.org/index.php?option=com_content&view=article&id=23301&Itemid=103*.

floor of the General Assembly honestly and without fear or hint of favoritism.

The Holy See Mission's reasons for choosing the observer status and the neutrality option are valuable as presented. The nonvoting option is a pragmatic Holy See choice. We should assume it is based upon what is judged best for the overall mission of the Church, as evidenced in the interview with the Holy See mission cited above. If the Holy See were to exercise voting rights, it might damage its respected long-standing record as a non-political participant, thus jeopardizing its role in service to states, especially who see it as an honest broker of peace.

Nevertheless, from the standpoint of solidarity with the poor and witnessing to the truth, this option still remains problematic. It could lead to the perception that the option for neutrality is in effect a refusal to take decisive and public positions on specific issues or concrete instances of injustice suffered by people around the world. It calls into question the credibility of the Church's pledge of solidarity with, and in support of, the poor. Some social justice activists argue that no one should ever remain neutral in any case regarding the poor. Neutrality is itself a position, for it is a yes vote in favor of the *status quo*.

The periodic non-vote position of member states, which is known as absenteeism, is different from the complete neutrality option of the Holy See Mission. Our call for a deep reflection on this option, especially on account of its myriad implications from the standpoint of incarnational solidarity that underpins our theological argument, challenges the choice of observer status in place of a full membership, since it is clear that this choice is of the Holy See's own volition.[65] Critiquing this option cannot be dismissed as idealistic wishful thinking. In fact, representatives of the Holy See have also mulled over the possibility of revisiting this option as changes in time continue. This has come up again and again within Catholic circles, an example of which

---

[65](https://holyseemission.org/contents//mission/our-history.php.

can be seen in the 2003 and 2004 discussions of the Holy See making UN membership application, which the Vatican Secretary of State implicitly welcomed.[66] Whether such an application would be accepted or rejected is a different matter. Again, we reiterate that we base our criticism on the Holy See's claim that the non-member observer status option is simply its choice. Fear either of rejection or of implications of taking public stands is not a sufficient reason to avoid considering the change in membership status and a voting option.

It is also important to note that for the Holy See to register its decision by a vote is not unchristian nor should it be compared to the situation of hating the sinner instead of the sin as some Christians may insinuate. This is provided for by the theological principle of solidarity with and for the poor and moral justification of witnessing to the truth. It does not necessarily matter how it votes and neither are we suggesting what the vote of the Holy See would have been on all or any of the votes taken in the latest complete session of the UN General Assembly, including all resolutions and decisions passed by acclamation or consensus.

The same theological principle and moral justification of the common good and the impact on the wellbeing of the most disadvantaged of society should be the guide for how the vote of the Holy See should go. Solidarity in Jesus' model explained in chapter three of our work is a matter of continuous choosing of the other even at the cost of risking his identity as the sinless one, as John the Baptist's hesitation to baptize him illustrates. In his Baptism episode, rather than standing aloof (neutral) in the crowd, Jesus joined the people wailing, yearning, seeking their God and longing to cross over the threshold to the new life offered through the Baptist.

Choosing and exercising the right to vote are considered here as concrete and visible expressions of the Church's continuous choosing and identifying with the poor and standing up for the truth at whatever

---

[66] See *https://zenit.org/articles/vatican-diplomacy-a-force-to-be-reckoned-with*.

the cost. The Holy See does take positions like this as it lobbies or registers reservations on some issues at the UN such as between a pro-life or a pro-choice stance on abortion.

An example of this is the Holy See's reservation on some sections of the SDGs on the account of what it considered lack of clarity on some terms used in the Agenda, such as "sexual and reproductive health," "sexual and reproductive rights," "reproductive rights," "contraception," "family planning," "gender," and "education" or "information on sexuality." This situation is why some Christian social critics would actually consider a neutrality option as willful choice by the Holy See for which it should be called to answer when those decisions are harmful to the common good especially affecting the most vulnerable of the world.

In particular individual cases, to refrain from voting could obscure the option for the poor and hinder projects challenging unjust structures. As an example, the Church's concern for Palestinians plus any good effects of its nonvoting option might all be offset by the Holy See Mission's neutrality on Palestine UN membership.

Such is the outrageous situation of the poor and oppressed of Palestine. It is known that the Holy See diplomatically recognizes the two-state solution for the Israeli-Palestinian conflict and had started referring to the state of Palestine instead of the Palestine Liberation Organization (PLO) as it was formerly identified. The recent decision of Holy See under Pope Francis to formally sign a treaty recognizing the State of Palestine is welcome development in the right direction.[67] Yet without corresponding action at the UN to support the membership of Palestine in the organization, an action of significant symbolism, the people of Palestine and their sympathizers would still question Holy See's already bold step in this direction.

---

[67] "Joint Statement of the Bilateral Commission of the Holy See and the State of Palestine at the conclusion of the Plenary Meeting," (13.05.2015),
http://www.news.va/en/news/253815, retrieved on May 28, 2015.

Furthermore, the Holy See's position can even arouse suspicion of hidden ulterior motives, perhaps the desire to save face or to preserve positive standing among certain nations with Holy See bilateral relations. These charges against neutrality also apply to the Holy See refusal to initiate any effective challenge to unjust UN structures.

We may cite as further examples the growing global demand for UN Charter review, reformation of the Security Council and revitalization of the General Assembly. To begin any of these processes requires a majority vote, and in some cases a consensus of the General Assembly. Finally, the Holy See's nonvoting option could smother the Church's vocal criticism of unjust UN structures raised in several papal UN addresses. The Church may be blamed for not matching its action to its words.

The choice for neutrality, which is also how we interpret NGO silence or inaction over UN structural sin, is inconsistent with theological, ecclesiological self-understandings of Vatican II that support Church activities in the socio-political realm. Neutrality properly belongs instead to practices from pre-conciliar Church obsession with identity preservation. The pre-conciliar Church did not get involved in anything that would detract from its image, no matter how noble the cause. But today this neutrality bolsters the criticism that, even though the Vatican II Church has openly announced compassion for the poor, it has not shown conclusive evidence of solidarity with them.

This shortcoming is well expressed by Gregory Baum's analysis of the unresolved struggles in human institutions between the *logic of maintenance* and *logic of mission*—between a desperate desire to protect itself and the burden of doing what it was founded to do—and how the former often takes precedence over the latter.[68]

Although the two logics should harmoniously work together for both institutional survival and institutional goal attainment, all too often

---

[68]Gregory Baum, *Theology and Society* (New York: Paulist Press, 1987), 239, 243.

unjustified precedence is granted to maintenance. Good programs are frequently sacrificed to protect the institution, as institutional status is obsessively chosen over the very purpose for which the institution was established in the first place. The Church, like any institution, can be overwhelmed by exaggerated attention to maintenance logic. For the sake of its dignity, it sometimes passes over an action that might place its self-image at risk in the sight of the nations, even when that action would benefit the poor. Both the nonvoting option of the Holy See and the blind eye that Catholic-inspired NGOs turn to UN structural sin betray the prophetic character of incarnational solidarity which demands *being-with* even in the face of risk.

Pope Benedict XVI clearly saw tension between maintenance logic and mission logic. He also observed that the former is often chosen over the latter. On the occasion of his visit to Germany, he spoke at Freiburg September 25, 2011 to representatives of Catholic associations active in the life of the Church and society, saying "In the concrete history of the Church, however, a contrary tendency is also manifested... She gives greater weight to organisation and institutionalisation than to her vocation to openness."[69]

In his discussion, the Pope focused upon Church worldliness, criticizing a Church too settled in this world, adapting to worldly standards, conforming to worldly values and seeking self-sufficiency. He urged the pressing need for the Church to "constantly rededicate herself to her mission, [of] filling the world with God's word and in transforming the world by bringing it into loving unity with God."[70] To accomplish this task adequately, the Church must commit anew to detachment from worldliness such as the proclivities to logic maintenance that we identified — self-preoccupation, self-centeredness and self-

---

[69]See Pope Benedict XVI, "It is Time for the Church to Set Aside Her Worldliness," A Speech to Representatives of Catholic Society Active in the Life of the Church and Society, Freiburg, September 25, 2011. PV-GERMANY/ VIS 20110926 (750) Pope Benedict XVI message in Germany.
[70]Ibid.

preservation. Without this liberation, Church missionary activity, especially in the context of the new evangelization that supports UN participation, will not maintain its credibility.

From the example of Christ's sinlessness as solidarity there emerge renewed insights into human spirituality dynamics: sin is what prevents us from experiencing or exercising solidarity with others. It is fundamentally a choice of self over others and over God, examples of such defects being the aforementioned self-preoccupation, self-centeredness and self-preservation. The Church and religious institutions working in UN ministry through NGOs still struggle against these faults.

To be the chosen of Christ implies that we are loved and are enabled to choose others and God. But the selfishness of a deformed self-love keeps us from our vocation of living for others. It degrades our dignity and revokes our identity as a compassionate Church. To continue such a contradiction while simultaneously telling other institutions to act justly is hypocritical of religious groups offering themselves as models of justice. They manifest arrogance and abuse power. To live their professed vision in the light of the theological self-understandings of their UN mission, the Holy See and Catholic-inspired NGOs must take to heart the soteriological implications of solidarity, for in the final analysis obsessive self-preservation leads to its own demise. Christ warns us of this in John's gospel. "Whoever loves his life will destroy it, and whoever despises his life…keeps it" (John 12: 20-27).

The core problem with obsessive maintenance logic is that it creates a divide between what the institution says and what it does. The Church's official social teaching promotes the logic of mission, yet in practice this teaching is beset with contradictory actions such as the nonvoting option. Situations like this lead some onlookers to wonder whether the Church applies its social teaching to itself. How else can we evaluate neutrality after hearing Benedict XVI's insistence that defending, articulating and witnessing to the truth are the exacting and indispensable forms of our charity?[71]

Further, voting is a unique opportunity to demonstrate and articulate our love for truth as well as our commitment to defending and witnessing to it. It even happens at times that the way we vote matters less than that we vote at all, for our vote is our voice. This further consideration renders Holy See neutrality more problematic to critics who would speculate that either the Holy See remains unimpressed with the seriousness of UN decisions or that it simply fears to stand for the truth in or out of season. For a few, a third possibility is that the Holy See is serving some ulterior motives. Diplomacy and its dynamics and intricacies—knowing how to play the game—which some loyal supporters offer as a justification for Holy See neutrality, persuade fewer and fewer critics.

It is fitting that groups like Catholic-inspired NGOs encourage the Holy See to re-evaluate its neutrality. Further, a call for such a critical re-evaluation is pertinent since this decision is still open to discussion, as indicated by former Permanent Observer Archbishop Celestino Migliore. The example of Christ remains the foundation for our solidarity with and for the poor. It is the ultimate criterion of our authenticity and our credibility. As Richard Gaillardetz writes, "The Church is a Church of the poor to the extent that it stands in solidarity with the powerlessness of the poor in this world and looks to the crucified Christ, who embraced powerlessness on the cross and effected its transformation in the resurrection."[72]

This re-evaluation may also sharpen the dilemma of the Holy See remaining both the Church and the government of a state. To vote may jeopardize the Holy See's non-biased diplomatic power, but to remain

---

[71] Benedict XVI, *Caritas in Veritate*, #1 (Washington, D.C.: United States Conference of Catholic Bishops, 2009), 1.

[72] Richard Gaillardetz, *Ecclesiology for a Global Church: A People Called and Sent* (Maryknoll, New York: Orbis Books, 2008), 191.

neutral may compromise its prophetic role as UN spiritual and moral guide. We have identified a similar dilemma of NGOs, particularly those of Catholic inspiration, whose prophetic roles of protesting the dominant culture and criticizing unjust structures are undermined by UN regulations for their participation.

Further Theological Import
of Catholic NGOs/UN Relationship

Finally, we consider the value this paradigm of Catholic NGOs' UN relationship brings to the Church's fundamental responsibility of faithfully caring for revelation itself. We have steadily maintained that these UN-related reflections greatly contribute to the wider theological enterprise, extending the boundaries of theology itself, "making faith connections"[73] more broadly and bringing UN issues into faith perspectives. Academic theology itself is thereby enriched as it struggles to interpret and evaluate UN ministry in specifically Christian categories and as intrinsic to the economy of salvation. The Church's UN mission of its essence continues the saving word and work of the risen Lord in space and time. As such it is a fabulously rich, if not utterly unique, opportunity for theological activity.

An example of theology enriched by reflection on Catholic UN presence involves the Christian social responsibility tension between inclusivist and exclusivist perspectives. This tension is illustrative of, and instructive for, both the Catholic UN presence in general and the collaboration advocated by the paradigm of dialogical confrontation. Inclusivists readily collaborate with others in contributing to a better and more just society. Exclusivists see such collaboration as abandoning the unique and overarching normative function of revelation and thus of theology as well.

---

[73] See Howard W. Stone and James O. Duke, *How to Think Theologically,* second edition (Minneapolis: Fortress Press, 2006), 13, 14, 15.

Gregory Baum, a major inclusivist figure, does not set aside revealed Gospel values mandating for Christians active concern for peoples' social, economic and political conditions. Yet he holds that only when theology enters critical dialogue with social science can it bring revelation to "a new fidelity to its nature and mission."[74] Developing this position, critical theologians maintain that authentic Christian theology and life demand interaction with others.[75]

However, the exclusivist John Milbank sees modern theological dialogue with other disciplines, especially social theories, as surrendering any claim to be comprehensive since theology must then conform to secular standards and to scientific objectivity. Milbank insists that theology and Christianity itself should neither borrow from the outside nor partner with other disciplines but should maintain their own historically specific faith. Only then would they render their own account of the ultimate causes at work in human history.[76] If there is to be any cross-conversation, "it must articulate Christian difference in such a fashion as to make it strange."[77]

Gregory Baum and John Milbank both work out of an Augustinian perspective. Their opposition shows the varied ways Augustine was and continues to be a foundation on which opposing theological positions can be built—a frequently observed paradox. Baum interprets the Augustinian dynamics of city of God and the earthly city, especially a Christian's role therein, as validating Christian participation in projects of universal solidarity and common value. Milbank leads contemporary post-modern Augustinianism undergirding the current radical reform movement use of city of God as separated from the earthly city with no justifiable collaboration. Again paradoxically,

---

[74] Gregory Baum, *Theology and Society* (New York: Paulist Press, 1987), 160.

[75] See Mary Jo Leddy, "Foreword," *Intersecting Voices: Critical Theologies in a Land of Diversity*, Don Schweitzer and Derek Simon, eds. (Ottawa: Novalis, 2004), 7.

[76] See John Milbank, *Theology and Social Theory* (New York: Routledge, 1999, reprint 2006), 382.

[77] Ibid., 383.

some thinkers detect inconsistency in exclusivist withdrawal attitudes since they depend on alienation theories of sociologists like Max Weber and Peter Berger. These sociologists criticize modernity, locating its dehumanizing trends in the growing power of technology and bureaucracy.[78] Baum observes that Milbank's opposition to theology partnering with other disciplines is itself based upon social theories.[79]

Exclusivists support the status quo. By rejecting critical solidarity, they discourage alignment with social change groups challenging unjust and unequal institutional structures. Admittedly growing technology and bureaucratic power heavily contribute to dehumanization, and as structural evil they should be criticized. As a matter of fact, they are also observable in structural evils lurking in the UN system. Yet it is no remedy for these evils to abandon global partnerships or reject global solidarity for the common good of all. Rather, and especially, for Catholic UN NGOs, participation in universal solidarity goes together with criticizing the glaring deficiencies of the UN and with taking on initiatives pressing for UN reform.

Rather than constructing a new theology of Christian social or political action, our process is a theological critique recognizing signs of hope uncovered by an attentive but cautious examination of these seemingly secular activities in the light of faith. In this we use as hermeneutical tools the implications of some of these already accepted theologies of Christian social or political action. As maintained in chapter three, the theology or theologies of Christian social or political action are already constructed and developed in various Catholic social teachings derived from the Scripture and the Church's rich tradition, such as the Second Vatican Council pastoral constitution on the Church in Modern World.

---

[78] Gregory Baum, *Theology and Society,* 164-166.

[79] Gregory Baum, *Essays in Critical Theology* (Kansas City, MO: Sheed and Ward, 1994), 19.

However, we believe that dialogical confrontation in the way we suggest here would not only encourage Christians to take seriously their role in the socio-political sphere but has already provided them with the "how." This "how" highlights the validity of critiquing the structures of the institutions in which we participate without necessarily abandoning them. Such a critique must also be executed in our own institutions. Recall that we cited the example of the NGOs' need to make use of the values gained from their UN work to look into their own institutions and into the Church at large. Far from advocating that the NGOs leave their own institutions or the Church, we urge — as we urge regarding the UN--that they take on their faithful responsibility to ensure that their various institutional structures do not obstruct God's love. Such was the challenge confronted above where we explained the unresolved tension between logic of mission and logic of maintenance.

CONCLUSION

& RECOMMENDATIONS

A fundamental insight proposed by this entire work is that Roman Catholic-inspired NGO UN ministry is a harbinger of a "radically different ecclesiology that reflects the Church's call to mission in a post-Christendom and postmodern [or post-secular] context."[1] UN ministry is not simply new. It is among the providentially dynamic gifts of the Holy Spirit infusing with grace a new consciousness that Church must now embark into a new world. The issues of these UN NGOs are not just strategic nor are they simply theological in an academic sense. They cannot be glossed over without serious consequence. They are theological in the sense of theology as a charismatic gift and philosophical as well, signaling the crumbling of self-confident modernity and the rise of a new world the Church must seriously deal with.

The NGO UN presence is considered here as residing in what Jürgen Habermas calls "public space," and in this space they fill the vacuum, they respond to the hunger, to the inner longing left by secularization's attempt to undermine religion by denial of the transcendent and by bestowing on science the role of omnipotent custodian of all

---

[1] Eddie Gibbs and Ryan K. Bolger, *Emerging Churches: Creating Christian Community in Postmodern Cultures* (Grand Rapids, MI.: Baker Academic, 2005), 65.

knowledge. The NGO UN reflective experience unites various prob-lematic systemizations and classifications modernism has intruded into the inner life of the Church: natural versus supernatural, public facts versus private values, faith versus reason and body versus soul. In other words, by tearing down dualism—the wall of division be-tween the secular and the sacred—our theological venture serves not only the narrow need of validating the Church-UN relation. It also contributes to the restoration of wholeness in the entire living Church—liturgy, identity, ministry and mission. For in the words of Madeleine L'Engle the deepest message of the incarnation is that "there is nothing secular that cannot be sacred."[2]

Finally, every Catholic, irrespective of role or rank, has a part to play in improving this activity so that it may bear the desired fruits that witness to the basic theological and pastoral principle of solidarity that gives foundation to them. The first step is attending to the limited awareness ordinary Catholics have about this mission of their Church. That demands empowering them to appreciate the "social question" as a world-wide issue impacting their everyday faith life where they live. In other words, this mission brings to the today's Christians, and Catholics in particular, a new kind of United Nations consciousness: the awareness that we are now always living in a global world, within ourselves and within our immediate neighborhoods. Contemporary existence propelled by globalization brings us in constant contact with people, cultures, needs, languages and ecology as never before. In each moment of this encounter we have the challenge of responding as patriots and citizens and as loving Christians. In fact, Church doc-uments before the Second Vatican Council had already begun to see the "social question" as a world-wide issue.

Concurrently, popes have gradually but progressively brought their teaching into global context. Pope Paul VI made the key visit to the UN bringing the Second Vatican Council itself (1965). Letters by Pope

---

[2] See Madeleine L'Engle, *Walking on Water,* in ibid.

John Paul II to youth (1985), families and children (1994), and the elderly (1999) were written to mark special UN celebratory years. This same Pope also spoke of work in his 1982 address to the UN's International Labor Organization (ILO). Pope Benedict XVI spoke on hunger in 2009 to the UN's Food and Agriculture Organization (FAO). Pope Francis spoke on international cooperation and care for the poor in an address to the FAO in June 2013.

These concerns for universal solidarity are always held in harmony with the principles of subsidiarity. John Paul II observes in *Sollicitudo Rei Socialis* that concern for the global should not diminish concern for the local, but both levels of concern should complement each other. Without such unity of complementarity, solidarity may give way to a demeaning paternalistic social assistance, and subsidiarity to social privatism.

Further examples of the UN as occasion or context for specific Church teaching could be multiplied over and over. So, could examples of the gradual, progressive shifting within the Church of the "social question" into a world-wide issue. We cannot predict how much time it will take for the ordinary person in the pew, for pastoral ministers and for the Church as a whole to integrate fully this world-wide shift of the "social question." Many obstacles stand in the way like excessive nationalism, anti-UN ideologies and an over-concern of the legitimate need to focus intently upon what is local. The lack of sufficient catechetical materials on this issue shows how far we have to go.

But we can already see some positive signs. Education programs are being organized by Catholic NGOs working with the UN. Those of religious congregations hold series of seminars and workshops around UN issues to educate their constituencies about their UN work. They emphasize the significance of such activities as witnessing to their call to follow Christ as religious today. Since 1999, IMCS-Pax Romana, a Catholic Confederation of students from all over the world, has brought the UN human rights agenda to both its members and to diocesan promoters of justice and peace through its two annual internship programs. On these occasions for on-going formation, theologians are often invited to interact with UN resource people. Participants assume responsibility for organizing similar events at their local campuses.

Church teaching is clear and emphatic: the social question as a constituent part of preaching the Gospel is now world-wide. Myriad factors of Church life, renewal and pastoral activity promote increased awareness of this reality. But a particularly glaring missing "piece of the puzzle" is a more prophetic UN presence of Catholic-inspired NGOs.[3]

Is Dialogical Confrontation a Fundamental Contradiction?

We appreciate that our recommendation of dialogical confrontation for Catholic NGOs as an alternative way of witnessing or being present at the UN might not only be somewhat difficult. It may even seem contradictory in our insistence that these NGOs should not withdraw or stand aside from the UN but yet must not identify themselves with the structural sins evident in the UN institutions and systems. The reason why we do not create a fundamental contradiction rests upon an underlying Catholic morality issue that is at times difficult, and even contentious, to apply. This underlying issue is the Catholic position on the morality of cooperation with evil or with structures in which sin abides, such as the case we made of the UN and Catholic participants.

Catholic morality is solidly based upon the twin mandates to do good and to avoid evil. Catholic morality does not allow the justification of the means by the end. Catholic morality does not allow doing good with a bad intention nor does this morality allow doing evil with a

---

[3] Part of this is adapted from my earlier article, "The Holy See in the United Nations: An Assessment and Critique," *New Theology Review*, vol.26, no.1 (September, 2013): 41 of 29-41.

good intention. However, Catholic morality does not demand avoiding each and every entanglement with evil that may be forbidden by rigorist demands of a purist who stays clean from any and all contact with evil, for our Catholic morality does allow cooperation with evil under some conditions.

A reflection on these conditions reveals how this book can recommend collaboration with United Nations structures, policies and practices and at the same time criticize particular aspects of those UN structures, policies and practices. This insight applies to the essence of dialogical confrontation and explains why it is not self-contradictory. In Catholic theology, dialogical confrontation as this work describes means cooperation with evil that is clearly allowed for the technically expressed moral reason that this cooperation with evil is material, mediate and remote. We will explain these terms as set forth in typical Catholic moral theology manuals.

Catholic morality fundamentally distinguishes cooperation with evil into formal and material. Formal cooperation with evil means a concurrence with the bad will of the principal agent of the act, occurring usually when the evil is intended by the cooperator as an end or means, Formal cooperation with evil is always to be avoided. Material cooperation, as opposed to formal, is that which contributes in some way to the performance of the act by the principal agent. Material cooperation with evil is allowed in some circumstances.

Material cooperation with evil is distinguished into immediate and mediate. Immediate cooperation with evil is that which cooperates with the evil act itself. Mediate cooperation is that which merely prepares in some morally neutral manner for the evil act or assists in some morally neutral tangential aspects of its execution. Immediate material cooperation with evil is always to be avoided. Mediate material cooperation with evil is allowed in some circumstances.

Mediate material cooperation with evil is distinguished into proximate and remote. Proximate mediate material cooperation is close in causality to the evil act of the principal agent. Remote mediate material cooperation with evil is operationally distant from the causality of the evil act of the principal agent. It is certainly allowed by Catholic morality for a good reason that is in proportion to the evil caused by the act of the principal agent.

An example of such material, mediate remote cooperation with evil allowed by Catholic morality is the general approval by the Holy See UN Mission of the Sustainable Development Goals (SDGs) especially regarding eradication of poverty and promotion of integral development while this Holy See UN Mission criticizes any support for abortion among the SDGs. Excessively purist Catholic rigorists have criticized the Holy See UN Mission for supporting the SDGs because the SDGs include some inclination toward abortion. Nevertheless, the Holy See UN Mission's general affirmation of the SDGs is clearly within Catholic morality of cooperation with evil – it is material, mediate and remote. The Holy See accepts the SDGs while criticizing the aspects of the SDGs it opposes, such as abortion. There is no contradiction in the position of the Holy See. This is dialogical confrontation, which is a term synonymous with dialogical engagement.

Consistent with this example of the Holy See UN Mission and far from being self-contradictory, our book's affirmation of dialogical confrontation exemplifies the internal consistency of criticizing aspects of the United Nations while remaining and working within the UN system as an NGO. The remarks of each of the four popes who have spoken at the UN support this position. As we may recall from the discussion in chapter two of our work, Benedict XVI so recognized the enormous pressing need for UN reform that, in his perspective, healing the UN organizational power imbalance would itself facilitate a faster and more lasting recovery from the economic recession.

The popes see the realization of this healing as the task for every actor in the UN including the Church, thus by implication, chastising all these actors for not yet doing enough in this regard. This is the step we are taking in our approach of dialogical confrontation based on our claim above in the Introduction that being positive and hopeful about the world or any institution cannot be seen as being "naively optimistic," nor would refraining from often quite critical remarks on imbalances and failures in the modern world be at all helpful.[4] Rather, it is the duty of Christian social actors to seek to "preserve an uneasy tension between affirming legitimate human endeavors and insisting on the world's need for transformation."[5]

We have used as guide to deal with these tendencies St. Augustine's assessment of problematic human institution tendencies—the competing interplay of love for solidarity clashing with inclinations toward domination. These are contrary realities with and within which a Christian participant must work to increase the space for the former and limit the opportunities for the latter.

Like the popes, we are encouraging Catholic NGOs to participate in the UN while drawing attention to negative aspects of their participation. We want to see the Catholic NGOs at the UN to be as bold as the popes in calling the UN to the realization of its blind spots and to do so more often. It is especially as the "third UN" that they enjoy the privileged rare audacity that neither Member State delegates nor UN staff dare to approach in raising issues of justice. Also, we recall that the NGOs claim, and rightly so, that there is no program that the UN has undertaken that did not first start with NGOs advocacy. So, we believe that if they see this as important as the four pontiffs who have spoken at the UN did, then they would utilize their privilege and persistence in putting the issues of UN reform prominent among the items of UN agendas.

---

[4] See Joseph Komonchak, "The Significance of Vatican Council II for Ecclesiology," *Gift of the Church: A Textbook on Ecclesiology,* Peter C. Phan, ed. (Collegeville, Minnesota: The Liturgical Press, 2000), 89.
[5] Richard R. Gaillardetz, "The Ecclesiological Foundations of Modern Catholic Social Teaching," 75.

Finally, we reiterate our position that this alternative witnessing is consistent with Jesus' paradigm illustrated in the theology of incarnational solidarity — the mystery of God entering into history, becoming one like us and chastising us even while gently leading us to full glory. Indeed, this reality did appear to some people either as folly or contradiction, as Paul will say, yet that is the crux of salvific reality and its success.

ABBREVIATIONS & ACRONYMS

AARP	American Association of Retired Persons
ACISJF	International Catholic Association for Girls
APA	American Psychological Association
ASPnet	Associated Schools Project Network
AU	African Union
BINGOs	Business international Non-Governmental Organizations
CAIP	Catholic Association for International Peace
CCFD	Comité Catholique contre la Faim et le Dévelopment
CFC	Catholics for a Free Choice
CICO	Conference des Organizations Internationales Catholiques - Conference of International Catholic Organizations
CONGO	Conference of Non-Governmental Organizations in Consultative Status with ECOSOC
CSocD	Committee on Social Development
CV	*Caritas in Veritate*
CWSI	Center for Women Studies and Intervention
DESA	Department of Economic and Social Affairs
ECOSOC	Economic and Social Council
EN	*Evangelii Nuntiandi*
ENGOs	Environmental Non-Governmental Organizations
EU	European Union
FAO	Food and Agriculture Organization

FOWAL	Federation of World Peace and Love
G4	Germany, Brazil, Japan and India - while advocating an increase in the number of permanent members, also require that they, plus two others from Africa, possibly Nigeria and South Africa, be included in the present arrangement as permanent members
GCM	Global Compact for safe, orderly and regular migration
GONGOs	Government operated Non-Governmental Organizations – which may have been set up by governments to look like NGOs in order to qualify for foreign aid
GS	*Gaudium et Spes*
HIV/AIDS	Human Immunodeficiency Virus/Acquired Immune Defi ciency Syndrome or Acquired Immunodeficiency Syndrome
IAAC	Independent Audit Advisory Committee
IALANA	International Association of Lawyers Against Nuclear Arms
IASC	Inter-Allied Suffrage Conference
ICC	International Criminal Court
ICJ	International Court of Justice
ICMICA-IMCS	International Catholic Movement for Intellectual and Cultural Affairs, which together with the International Movement of Catholic Students, forms Pax Romana
ICO	International Catholic Organizations
IFAD	International Fund for Agricultural Development
ILO	International Labor Organizations
IMF	International Monetary Fund
INGOs	International Non-Governmental Organizations
IOM	International Organization for Migration
IPPNW	International Physicians for the Prevention Nuclear War
IUCWL	International Union of Catholic Women's League

JM	*Justitia in Mundo*
LU	Latin Union
MDGs	Millennium Development Goals
MM	*Mater et Magistra*
MSF	Médecins Sans Frontiéres
NCWC/USCC	National Catholic Welfare Conference/ United States Catholic Conference
NEPAD	New Program for African Development
NSAs	Non-state actors
OA	*Octogesima Adveniens*
OAS	Organization of American States in Washington
OSA-UN/NGO	Order of St. Augustine-United Nations / Non-governmental Organization
PC	*Perfectae Caritatis*
PGA	Parliamentarians for Global Action
PLO	Palestine Liberation Organization
PP	*Populorum Progressio*
PT	*Pacem in Terris*
QUANGOs	Quasi-Non-Governmental Organizations – those that are at least partially created or supported by states
RCCINGOs	Roman Catholic Church-inspired Non-Governmental Organizations
RINGOs	Religious International Non-Governmental Organizations
RN	*Rerum Novarum*
RSH	Religious of the Sacred Heart
RUN	Religious at the UN
SAPs	Structural Adjustment Programs

SIPRI	Stockholm International Peace Research Institute
SND	Sisters of Notre Dame
SP	*Summi Pontificatus*
SS	*Sollicitudo Rei Socialis*
UDHR	Universal Declaration of Human Rights
UFC	Uniting for Consensus
UNCHR	United Nations Commission on Human Rights
UNCHS	United Nations Centre for Human Settlements
UNCPRMW &MF	United Nations Convention on the Protection of the Rights of All Migrants Workers and Members of their Families
UNDCP	United Nations International Drug Control Program
UNDP	United Nations Development Program
UNDPI	United Nations Department of Public Information
UNEP	United Nations Environment Program
UNESCO	United Nations Educational, Scientific and Cultural Organization
UNGA/GA	United Nations General Assembly
UNHRC	United Nations Human Rights Council
UNIAEA	United Nations International Atomic Energy Agency
UNICEF	United Nations International Children's Emergency Fund (otherwise known since 1953 as the United Nations Children's Fund)
UNICO	UN International Conference
UN-NGLS	United Nations-Non-Governmental Liaison Service
UNPA	United Nations Parliamentary Assembly
UNSC/SC	United Nations Security Council
UNSG	United Nations Secretary-General

UNTC	United Nations Trusteeship Council
UNWTO	World Tourism Organization
USAID	United States Agency for International Development
WATUN	World Alliance to Transform the United Nations
WEF	World Economic Forum
WFDY	World Federation of Democratic Youth
WFP	World Food Programme
WHO	World Health Organization
WIDF	Women's International Democratic Federation
WSF	World Social Forum
WTO	World Trade Organization
WWI	World War I
WWII	World War II

GLOSSARY

Anthropology – understanding of the human person in his/her entirety from ultimate perspectives such as theology or philosophy.

Anti-Christ – the false Christ or false prophet who denies the father and the son and works against them, whose appearing will precede the second coming of the lord.

Apocalyptic – derived from, and an adjective of, apocalypse – the revelation or unveiling of things unknown - mostly associated with the end times and presented in terms of a prophetic warming of impending catastrophe.

Apostolate – the activities of all the faithful, members of Christ's body seen as partaking in the original mission entrusted by the Savior to the twelve apostles and thus to the Church to "make disciples of all nations" (Matthew 28:19). These activities, inspired by grace and though temporal, are intended to bring people to the knowledge and love of Christ.

Armageddonites – those who believe that they alone will get a quick, free pass when they are "raptured" to paradise; used allegorically for those who believe no one else is elected or destined for salvation.

Atlantic Charter – a joint declaration released by U.S. President Franklin D. Roosevelt and British Prime Minister Winston Churchill on August 14, 1941 outlining the allied post-war goals.

Catechism – summary of the belief, teachings, practices and traditions of the Catholic Church used for the instruction of the Catholic faithful and teaching of new converts.

Catholic-inspired NGO – an NGO whose work and reason for being are based upon Catholic teaching and practice. These are apostolates of Catholic individuals and groups but not official representatives of the Catholic Church.

Catholicity – the character of being in conformity with the Catholic Church.

Charism – charisma - gifts. The charism of a religious congregation refers to the distinct spirit that animates a religious community and gives it a particular character. (*http://www.nashvilledominican.org/our-vowed*)

Christology – theological study of the person and life of Jesus drawn from the accounts of him in the Scriptures.

Civilization of Love – used as a synonym for the "City of God", the community of those who strive for a world-wide inclusive and nurturing humanity working for the universal common good.

Clash of Civilizations – belief propagated by Samuel Huntington that people's cultural and religious identities are the primary source of conflict in the post-Cold War world. However, it is used here to refer to the continuous battle of self-interests undermining arriving at global solidarity visible in international communities like the UN.

Common Good – defined in Catholic social teaching as "the sum total of social conditions which allow people, either as groups or as individuals, to reach their fulfillment more fully and more easily."

Congregation – an assembly of persons brought together for common religious worship. It is also used in a specific way to refer to groups of men and women committed to a religious life by public or monastic vows.

Cosmology – the study of the universe and its components, how it formed, how it has evolved and what its future is, from ultimate perspectives such as theology or philosophy.

"Deterritorialization" and "Reterritorialization" – a historical imperial attitude now prevalent in supranational tendencies of multinational corporations where "the center is everywhere, and the circumference is nowhere."

Ecclesiology – the theological study of the Christian Church, its origin, its nature, constitution, ordinances, and activities and doctrines.

Economy of salvation also called the Divine Economy, — God's salvation plan for the world ultimately expressed in Christ especially through the cross and accomplished through the Church.

Encyclical – an official document of high authority treating particular themes related to the universal welfare of the Church, years past sent by the pope to the bishops and the entire faithful of the Catholic Church and now to the world.

End time – a future time-period described variously in several world religions where world events achieve a final climax.

Eschatology – branch of theology that deals with the final events of history, or the ultimate destiny of humanity, commonly referred to as the "end of the world" or "end time."

Evangelization – bringing the Good News of Jesus into every human situation and seeking to convert individuals and society by the divine power of the Gospel itself. At its essence are the proclamation of salvation in Jesus Christ and the response of a person in faith, which are both works of the Spirit of God (*Evangelii Nuntiandi*, no. 18).

Fundamentalist and Fundamentalism – a conservative movement in theology among nineteenth- and twentieth-century Christians. **Fundamentalists** – believe that all the statements in the Bible are literally true. Such a tendency exists in the Catholic Church in the various groups that stretch conservatism to the limit and also hold on the theory of *sola scriptura*. But more so in those Pope Francis recently referred to as Roman Catholics who believe they have "absolute truth."

Global Forum on Migration and Development (GFMD) — an initiative of the United Nations Member States to address the migration and development interconnections in practical and action-oriented ways, in an informal non-binding process, outside the UN system.

Grace – the unmerited divine saving presence or divine helping accompaniment we receive as pure gift.

Hermeneutical – pertaining to a method or theory of interpretation.

Holy See – the supreme administrative body of the Catholic Church under the pope and his cabinet, known as the Roman Curia. It has the responsibility of discharging the duties of the Vatican State as provided in the Lateran treaty of 1929, which recognized its sovereignty by granting it the geographical territory of Vatican City. It is on the basis of this sovereignty that the Catholic Church enjoys in the UN the singular and unique privilege that no other religion has in its status of Permanent Observer State.

Immanent – existing or operating within; inherent; used in theology to refer to God as permanently pervading and sustaining the universe.

Missiological – pertaining to the mandate, message, and mission or role of the Christian Church in time and space.

Mythos – set of traditional or recurrent narrative themes having a significant truth or meaning for a particular culture, religion, society or other groups.

Natural law – in Catholic philosophy, the rational creature's participation in God's wisdom, the directive norm of all movement and action.

Neo-Scholasticism – a revival and development of medieval scholasticism in Roman Catholic theology and philosophy which began in the second half of the 19th century. It claims that philosophy does not vary with each passing phase of history; that the truth of seven hundred years ago is not only still true but also operative today.

Ontological Relatedness – the believe that it belongs to the nature of a people to be related or maintain relationships; used in this work to refer to a typical African uniqueness as expressed in the African philosophy "I exist because I relate."

Pneumatology – in Christian theology, the study of the Holy Spirit.

Religious (a person) – a person who commits himself or herself to public or monastic vows as a nun or brother

Religious Institute – a group in which members...pronounce public vows and lead a life of brothers or sisters in common.

Sacerdotal – of or relating to priests or priesthood; priestly

Salvific – having the intention or power to bring about salvation or redemption.

Sin – an evil act against the law of God; a disruption of the moral order.

Original Sin – sin contracted simply by birth in sinful humanity.

Personal Sin – sin committed knowingly and freely by a person or by a group of persons.

Structural Sin – socially and morally significant enduring results of original and personal sin.

Solidarity – the ties in a society that bind people together as one. It is used in theology as special identification with the conditions of the suffering expressed in practical actions for and on their behalf. Solidarity is about valuing our fellow human beings and respecting who they are as individuals.

Soteriology – the doctrine or nature of salvation in and through Christ.

Triumphalist – excessive pride in one's belief or particular church membership, with a feeling of superiority towards others and a dominating tendency.

Universality of Reason – the notion that no one has a monopoly on reason and that every person has the right to contribute from their standpoint.

Via Negativa – (negative way or by way of denial) method, a conscious attempt to describe a concept by rescuing it from what it is not so that its true meaning may emerge.

SELECTED BIBLIOGRAPHY

BOOKS & PUBLISHED ARTICLES

Abdullah, Yasmin. "The Holy See at United Nations Conferences: State or Church?" *Columbia Law Review*. Vol. 96, no. 7 (1996).

Alberigo, Giuseppe. *A Brief History of Vatican II*. New York: Orbis Books, 2006.

Annan, Kofi. *In Larger Freedom: Towards Development, Security and Human Rights for All*. New York: United Nations, 2005.

Appleby, R. Scott. "Global Civil Society and the Catholic Social Teaching." John A. Coleman and William F. Ryan. Eds. *Globalization and Catholic Social Thought: Present Crisis, Future Hope*. Ottawa: Novalis, 2005. 130-140.

Augustine. *City of God*. Trans. Henry Bettenson. London: Penguin Group, 2003 Edition.

Bascio, Patrick. *The U.N. was my Parish: Experiences of a Priest-Diplomat*. Denville, New Jersey: Dimension Book, 1977.

Baum, Gregory. *Signs of the Times: Religious Pluralism and Economic Injustice*. Ottawa: Novalis, 2007.

_____. *Religion and Alienation: A Theological Reading of Sociology* 2nd Edition. Ottawa: Novalis, 2006.

_____. "Critical Theologies in Canada: From Solidarity to Resistance." Don Schweitzer and Derek Simon. Eds. *Intersecting Voices: Critical Theologies in a Land of Diversity*. Ottawa: Novalis, 2004. 49-66.

_____. *Karl Polanyi on Ethics and Economics*. Montreal: McGill-Queen's University Press, 1996.

_____. "The Meaning of Hope in Evil Times." *ARC XX* (Spring 1992): 79-83.

_____. *Theology and Society*. New York: Paulist Press, 1987.

Bell, Daniel and Jean-Marc Coicaud. "The Ethical Challenges of International Human Rights NGOs." *Policy Brief*. November 9 (2006): 2-5.

Bell, P. M. H. The Origins of the Second World War in Europe. Harlow: Pearson Education Limited, 2007.

Bendell, Jem. *Debating NGO Accountability*. New York: NGLS, 2006.

Bergant, Dianne. "Salvation." Carroll Stuhlmueller. Ed. *The Collegeville Pastoral Dictionary of the Bible Theology*. Collegeville, Minnesota: The Liturgical Press, 1996. 867

Berger, Julia. "Religious Nongovernmental Organizations: An Exploratory Analysis." *Voluntas: International Journal of Voluntary and Nonprofit Organizations*. Vol. 14, No. 1 March (2003):15-39.

Boff, Leonardo, *Church: Charism and Power: Liberation Theology and the Institutional Church*. New York: Crossroad, 1985.

Bok, Sissela. "Foreword." *Gandhi: An Autobiography, The Story of My Experiments with Truth*. Trans. Mahadev Desai.Boston, Massachusetts: Beacon Press, paperback edition, 1957. xiii-xviii.

Bonhoeffer, Dietrich. *Discipleship*. Trans. Barbara Green and Reinhard Krauss. Minneapolis: Fort Press, 2003 edition.

Bornstein, Erica. *The Spirit of Development: Protestant NGOs, Morality, and Economics in Zimbabwe*. New York: Routledge, 2003.

Brown, Peter. "Augustine and a Crisis of Wealth in Late Antiquity." *Augustinian Studies* 36 (2005): 6-30.

Brown, Robert McAfee. "Toward a Just and Compassionate Society: A Christian View." *Cross Current* (summer 1995).

Bryant, Raymond L. *Nongovernmental organizations in Environmental struggles: Politics and the Making of Moral Capital in the Philippines*. New Haven: Yale University Press, 2005.

Burnaby, John. *Augustine: Later Works*. Philadelphia: Westminster Press, MCMLV.

Burt, Donald X. "Peace." *Augustine Through the Ages: An Encyclopedia.* Allan D. Fitzgerald. Ed. Grand Rapids, Michigan: William B. Eerdmans Publishing Company, 1999. 629-632.

Bussanich, John. "Happiness, Eudaimonism." *Augustine Through the Ages.* 412-414.

Buttler, Richard. "Toward the Next Fifty Years." *The Community of Nations,* Mai Adjali and Deborah Storms. Eds. New York: Friendship Press, 1995. 24-30.

Cavanaugh, William T. *Theopolitical Imagination: Discovering the Liturgy as a Political Act in an Age of Global Consumerism*. New York: T & T Clark, 2002, 2004 reprint.

Chatfield, C. "Intergovernmental an Nongovernmental Associations to 1945." J. Smith, Et. Al. Eds. *Transnational Social Movements and Global Politics: Solidarity Beyond the State.* Syracuse, New York: Syracuse University Press, 1997.

Children in Armed Conflict: Everyone's Responsibility. New York: Path to Peace Foundation, 2002.

Chopp, Rebecca S. *The Praxis of Suffering: An Interpretation of Liberation and Political Theologies.* Maryknoll, New York: Orbis Books, 1992.

Clarke, Gerard. *The Politics of NGOs in South-East Asia: Participation and Protest in the Philippines.* London: Routledge, 1998.

Clark, J. *World Apart: Civil Society and the Battle for Ethical Globalization.* Connecticut: Kumarian Press, 2003.

Cnaan, Ram. "Commentary." *Nonprofit Management and Leadership.* Vol. 7. No. 2(1996): 221-225.

Colson, Charles. *Kingdoms in Conflict: An Insider's Challenging View of Politics, Power, and the Pulpit.* New York & Grand Rapids, MI.: William Morrow and Zondervan Publishing House, 1987.

Coleman, John A. "Making the Connections: Globalization and Catholic Social Thought." John A. Coleman and William F. Ryan. Eds. *Globalization and Catholic Social Thought: Present Crisis.* Ottawa: Novalis, 2005. 9-27.

Congar, Yves *Lay People in the Church.* Trans. Donald Attwater. Westminster, MD: The Newman Press, 1965.

Coriden, James A. Et. Al. Eds. *The Code of Canon Law: A Text and Commentary.* New York: Paulist Press, 1985.

Crawford, James. *The Creation of States in International Law.* Oxford: Clarendon Press, 1979.

Dolbeau, Francois. Ed. *Vingt-six sermons au people d'Afrique, Collection des Etudes Augustiniennes, Antique,* 147. Paris: Instut des Etudes Augustininnes, 1996.

Douglas A. *Inequality and Christian Ethics.* Cambridge, UK: Cambridge University Press, 2000.

Dorr, Donald. *Option for the Poor: A Hundred Years of Vatican Social Teaching,* Revised Edition. Maryknoll, New York: Orbis Books, 1992.

Drayton, W. "Words Matter." *Alliance Magazine.* Vol. 12. No. 2 (June 2007).

Dupuy, André. Ed. *Pope John Paul II and the Challenges of Papal Diplomacy: Anthology (1978-2003).* New York: Path to Peace Foundation, 2004.

_____. Ed. *Words that Matter: The Holy See in Multilateral Diplomacy, Anthology (1970-2000)*. New York: Path to Peace Foundation, 2003.

Ebrahim, A. "Accountability in Practice: Mechanisms for NGOs." *World Development* Vol. 31. No. 5(2003): 813-829

_____. "Making Sense of Accountability: Conceptual Perspectives for Northern and Southern Nonprofits." *Nonprofit Management and Leadership*. Vol. 14. No. 2(2003): 191-212.

Ederer, Rupert J. "Solidarity." *Encyclopedia of Catholic Social Thought, Social Science, and Social Policy*. Vol. 2. Michael Coulter. ET. Al. Eds. Lanham, Maryland: Scarecrow Press, 2007. 1010-1011.

Editorial commentary. "In Defense of Politics." *Commonweal* Volume CXXXVI, Number 14 (August 14, 2009).

Edwards, Michael. ET. Al. David Lewis and Tina Wallace, Eds. *New Roles and Relevance: Development NGOs and the Challenge of Change*. Bloomfield, Connecticut: Kumarian Press, 2000.

Edwards, M. and D. Hulme. "Too Close for Comfort? The Impact of Official Aid on Non-governmental Organizations." *World Development*. Vol. 24. No. 6(1996): 961-973.

Elshtain, Jean Bethke. "Why Augustine, Why Now?" *Augustine and Postmodernism: Confession and Circumfession*. John D. Caputo and Michael J. Scanlon. Eds. Bloomington, Indianapolis: Indiana University Press, 2005.

_____. *Augustine and the Limit of Politics*. Notre Dame, Indiana: University of Notre Dame Press, 2003.

Eugene, Hyginus. *The Holy See and the International Order*. Gerrads Cross, Buckinghamshire, England: Colin Smythe, 1976.

Fasulo, Linda. *An Insider's Guide to the UN*. New Haven, Yale University Press, 2004.

Flannery, Austin. Ed. *Vatican Council II: The Conciliar and Post Conciliar Documents*. Vol. 1. New Revised Edition. Northport, New York: Costello Publishing Company, 5th reprint, 2004.

Forrester, Duncan. *Christian Justice and Public Policy*. New York: Cambridge University Press, 1997.

French, William. "Greening Gaudium et Spes." William Medges. *Vatican II*, 196-207.

Gaillardetz, Richard. *Ecclesiology for a Global Church: A People Called and Sent*. Maryknoll, New York: Orbis Books, 2008.

_____. "The Ecclesiological Foundation of Modern Catholic Social Teaching." Kenneth Himes Et. Al. *Modern Catholic Social Teaching: Commentaries and Interpretations*. Washington D.C., Georgetown University Press, 2005. 73-98.

Gartlan, Jean. *At the United Nations: The Story of the NCWC/USCC Office for United Nations Affairs 1946-1972*. Baltimore: Gateway Press, INC., 1998.

Gibbs, Eddie and Ryan K. Bolger: *Emerging Churches: Creating Christian Community in Postmodern Cultures*. Grand Rapids, MI.: Baker Academic, 2005.

Giddens, A. "The Role of the Third Sector in the Third Way." *CAF Focus*. No. 2, (1999):8.

Gladwell, Malcolm. *The Tipping Point: How Little Things can make a Big Difference*. Boston: Back Bay Books, 2002.

Gold, Dore. *Tower of Babble: How the United Nations has Fueled Global Chaos*. New York: Crown Forum, 2004.

Goldie, Rosemary. *From a Roman Window, Five Decades: The World, the Church and the Catholic Laity*. Blackburn: HarperCollins 1998.

Goldring, Natalie "The 2006 Review Conference on Small Arms and Light Weapons: A Study in Frustration," *Disarmament Diplomacy* no. 84 (Spring, 2007). *http://www.acronym.org.uk/old/archive/dd/dd84/84ng.htm*.

Goodrich, Leland M. and Edvard Hambro. *Charter of the United Nations: Commentary and Documents*. Boston: World Peace Foundation, 1946.

Greene, Bonnie M. "Building the Conditions for Peace: Beyond the Blue Helmets." *The Community of Nations*, Mia Adjali and Deborah Storms. Eds. New York: Friendship Press, 1995. 31-48.

Gutierrez, Gustavo. *A Theology of Liberation: History, Politics, and Salvation*. Trans. Sister Caridad Inda and John Eagleson. Revised Edition. Maryknoll: Orbis Books, 1989.

Habermas, Jurgen. *Jurgen Habermas on Society and Politics: A Reader*. Boston: Beacon Press, 1989.

_____. *Communicative Action*. Vol. 1. Boston: Beacon Press, 1984.

Haney, Eleanor H. *The Great Commandment: A Theology of Resistance and Transformation*. Cleveland Ohio: The Pilgrim Press, 1998.

Hanhimäki., Jussi M. *The United Nations: A Very Short Introduction*. New York: Oxford University Press, 2008.

Hanson, Eric O. *The Catholic Church in World Politics*. Princeton, New Jersey: Princeton University Press, 1987.

Hart, Liddell. *History of the First World War.* London: Pan Books, 1976 reprint.

Hauerwas, Stanley and William H. Willimon. *Resident Aliens.* Nashville, TN: Abingdon Press, 1989.

Hayward, J. E. S. "Solidarity: The History of an Idea in Nineteenth Century France." *International Journal of Social History* 4:2 (1959): 261-284.

Hellwig, Monika K. *Public Dimensions of a Believer's Life: Rediscovering the Cardinal Virtues.* New York: Rowman and Littlefield Publishers, 2005.

Higgins, George G. "The U.N. and its Critics." *Worldview Magazine Archive* Vol. 12. No. 10 (October 1969):5-8.

Himes, Michael. "'The Church and the World in Conversation:' The City of God and 'Inter Urban' Dialogue." *New Theology Review*, 18.1 (February 2003): 27-35.

Higgins, George G. "The U.N. and Its Critics." *Worldview Magazine Archive*, vol. 12, no, 10, October (1969):6.

Hinze, Christine Firer. "Straining Toward Solidarity in a Suffering World: *Gaudium et Spes* 'After Forty Years.'" William Madges, ed., *Vatican II: Forty Years Later.* Maryknoll, New York: Orbis Books, 2006. 165-195.

Hochhuth, Rolf. *The Deputy.* New York: Grove Press, Inc., 1964.

Holland, Joe and Peter Henriot. *Social Analysis: Linking Faith and Justice.* Maryknoll, New York: Orbis Books, 1983 Edition.

Hollenbach, David. *The Global Face of Public Faith: Politics, Human Rights, and Christian Ethics.* Washington D.C.: Georgetown University Press, 2003.

Hudson, A. "Making the Connection: Legitimacy Claims, Legitimacy Chains and Northern NGOs' International Advocacy." D. Lewis and T. Wallace. Eds. *After the 'New Policy Agenda?' Non-governmental Organizations and the Search for Development Alternatives.* Connecticut: Kumarian Press, 2000.

"International Campaign Calls into Question Vatican's Seat at the UN." *Catholic for A Free Choice: News Release,* March 24, (2000):1-6.

Johnson, Elizabeth. *Consider Jesus: Waves of Renewal in Christology.* New York: Crossroad, 1999.

Jones, Arthur. "Catholics were There at the Start." *National Catholic Reporter* (1 October 1999): 1-4.

Jones, Arthur. "Nuns at the U.N." *National Catholic Reporter,* online edition (October 1, 1999): 1. *http://www.natcath.com/NCR_Online/archives/100199/100199d.htm,* visited February 04, 2009.

Jordan and Van Tujil. "Political Responsibility in Transnational NGO Advocacy." *World Development*, vol. 28, no. 12(2000): 2051-2065.

Kaldor Mary and Helmut Anheier. Et. Al. Eds. *Global Civil Society 2006/7.* London: Sage 2005.

Kawamura, Noriko. Turbulence in the Pacific: Japanese-U.S. Relations During World War I. Westport, CT: Praeger, 2000.

Kennedy, Paul. *The Parliament of Man: The Past, Present, and Future of the United Nations.* New York: Vintage Books, 2006.

Ketelers, John. "A Synthesis of the Discussion." *Forum of Catholic-inspired NGOs.* Rome November 30 – December 2 (2007): 1-8.

Kirkpatrick, Frank. *Community: A Trinity of Models.* Washington, D.C.: Georgetown University Press, 1986.

Komonchak, Joseph. "The Significance of Vatican Council II for Ecclesiology." Gift *of the Church: A Textbook on Ecclesiology.* Peter C. Phan, Ed. Collegeville, Minnesota: The Liturgical Press, 2000.

Lakeland, Paul. *The Liberation of the Laity: In Search for an Accountable Church.* New York: Continuum, 2004.

Leddy, Mary Jo. "Foreword." *Intersecting Voices: Critical Theologies in a Land of Diversity.* Don Schweitzer and Derek Simon. Eds. Ottawa: Novalis, 2004.7.

_____. *Radical Gratitude.* Maryknoll, New York: Orbis Books, 2002.

Lewis David and Tina Wallace. Eds. *New Roles and Relevance: Development NGOs and the Challenge of Change.* Bloomfield, Connecticut: Kumarian Press, 2000.

Loconte, Joseph "The United Nations' Disarray." *Christianity Today* (February 2007): 1-3.

Lyon, F.S.L. *Internationalism in Europe 1815-1914.* Leiden: A.W. Sijthoff, 1963. Macmurray, John. *Persons in Relation.* New York: Humanity Books, 1999.

Malone, James W. (Bishop). "The Church in the Modern World: a 30-Year Perspective – 'Problems of Special Urgency.'" *Woodstock Report.* 42 (June 1995): 3-8.

Markus, R.A. *Saeculum: History and Society in the Theology of St. Augustine.* Paperback Edition. New York: Cambridge University Press, 1988, reprinted 2007.

Martino, Renato R. (Archbishop). "Foreword." André Dupuy, *Words that Matter: The Holy See in Multilateral Diplomacy Anthology (1970-2000).* New York: Path to Peace Foundation, 2003.

McCormick, Richard A. "The Social Responsibility of the Christian." *Blueprint for Social Justice,* Vol. LII, No. 3 (November 1998): 1-6.

McFadyen, Alistair. *Bound to Sin: Abuse, Holocaust and the Christian Doctrine of Sin.* New York: Cambridge University Press, 2000.

McGrath, Alister. *Christian Theology: An Introduction.* Malden, MA.: Blackwell *Publishing,* 2007.

McKenzie, John L. *Dictionary of the Bible.* New York: Bruce Publishers, 1965.

Mickens, Robert. "The Whole Truth is only found Together." *The Tablet* (July 6, 2002).

Milbank, John. Et. Al. Eds. *Radical Orthodoxy.* New York: Routledge, 1999, reprint 2006.

_____. *Theology and Social Theory: Beyond Secular Reason.* 2nd Edition. Malden, MA.: Blackwell Publishing, 2006.

Miller, Vincent. *Consuming Religion: Christian Faith and Practice in a Consumer Culture.* New York: Continuum, 2005.

Muravchik, Joshua. *The Future of the United Nations: Understanding the Past to Chart a Way Forward.* Washington, D.C.; The AEI Press, 2005.

Murray, John Courtney and Wilfrid Parsons: *International Co-operation.* Washington, D.C.: Catholic Association for International Peace, 1943.

Myers, Ched. *Binding the Strong Man: A Political Reading of Mark's Story of Jesus.* Maryknoll, New York: Orbis Books, 2005, 15th printing.

Najam, A. "NGO Accountability: A Conceptual Framework." *Development Policy Review,* Vol. 14(1996): 339-53.

_____. "The 4 C's of Third Sector Government Relations: Cooperation, Confrontation, Complementarity and Co-Optation." *Nonprofit Management and Leadership,* vol. 10, no. 4(200): 375-96.

Nash, Ronald H. *Social Justice and the Christian Church.* Michigan: Mott Media, 1984.

Negri, Antonio and Michael Hardt. *Empire.* Cambridge, Massachusetts: Harvard University Press, 2000.

Nicholson, Patrick, "Window on the World," *Tablet,* 12 April (2008): 4-5.

Northedge, F. S. The League of Nations: Its Life and Times, 1920–1946. New York: Holmes & Meier, 1986.

Nossel, Suzanne "US Joins Russia and China in Trying to Weaken Arms Trade Treaty" (July, 13, 2012) *http://blog.amnestyusa.org/us/us-joins-russia-and-china-in-trying-to-weakenarms-trade-treaty/.*

Nouwen, Henri J.M. Et. Al. *Compassion: A Reflection on the Christian Life.* New York: Doubleday, 1983.

Obiezu, Emeka Christian. "Community Versus Empire: The Catholic NGOs/ United Nations Relations in an Augustinian Perspective." *Journal of Catholic Social Teaching.* vol.11, no.1 (winter, 2014): 151-177.

_____. "The Holy See in the United Nations: An Assessment and Critique." *New Theology Review.* vol.26, no.1 (September 2013): 29-41.

_____. *Towards a Politics of Compassion: Socio-political Dimensions of Christian Responses to Suffering.* Bloomington, Indiana: AuthorHouse Publishers, 2008.

O'Gara, Margaret. "Openness and Gift: Themes from Rahner's Theology." *Science et Espirit* 59/2-3 (2007): 373-386.

Path to Peace: A Contribution, Documents of the Holy See to the International Community. New York: Liturgical Publications in partnership with the Permanent Observer Mission of the Holy See to the United Nations, 1987.

Pécoud, Antoine and Paul De Guchteneire. "Introduction: The Migration Without Borders Scenario." *Migration Without Borders.* 4, 5.

Pei-heng, Chiang. *Non-Governmental Organizations in the United Nations: Identity, Role and Function.* New York: Praeger, 1981.

Petty, Michael W. *A Faith That Loves the Earth: The Ecological Theology of Karl Rahner.* New York: University Press of America, 1996.

Pfeiffer, James. "Civil Society, NGOs, and the Holy Spirit." *Human Organization* Vol. 63. No. 3 (2004): 359-372.

Pietilä, Hilkka. *The Unfinished Story of Women and the United Nations.* New York: NGLS, 2007.

Presence. Vol. 7. Issue 1, Fall (2008): 1-3.

Rahner, Karl. *Foundations of Christian Faith: An Introduction to The Idea of Christianity.* Tran. William V. Dych. New York: Crossroad, 1978, reprinted 2007.

_____. "The Abiding Significance of the Second Vatican Council." *Concern for the Church: Theological Investigation.* Vol. 20. Tran. Edward Quinn. New York: Crossroad, 1981. 90-102

_____. "Basic Theological Interpretation of Vatican II." *Concern for the Church: Theological Investigation.* Vol. 20. 77-89.

_____. "Diaspora Community," *Theological Investigations.* Vol. X. New York: Seabury, 1977. 84-102

_____. *Christian Commitment: Essays in Pastoral Theology.* New York: Sheed and Ward, 1963.

Rahner, Karl, Ingrid Maisch and Klaus Berger. "Salvation." Karl Rahner. Ed. *The Concise Sacramentum Mundi.*New York. The Seabury Press, 1975. 1449-1530.

Rao, John C. "Ultramontanism." *Encyclopedia of Catholic Social Thought, Social Science, and Social Policy.* Lanham, Maryland: The Scarecrow Press, 2007. 1087-9.

Reiser, William. *Jesus in Solidarity with His People: A Theologian Looks at Mark.* Collegeville, Minnesota: The Liturgical Press, 2000

Roche, Douglas. "The Case for a United Nations Parliamentary Assembly." *A Reader on Second Assembly and Parliamentary Proposals.* Eds. Saul Mendlovitz and Barbara Walker. New York: Center for UN Reform Education, April 2003. 1-33.

_____. B*read not Bombs: A Political Agenda for Social Justice.* Edmonton: University of Calgary Press, 1999.

_____. *United Nations: Divided World.* Toronto: NC Press Limited, 1984.

Rolheiser, Ronald. *Again an Infinite Horizon: The Finger of God in our Everyday Lives.* New York: Cross Publishing Co., 2001.

Rossi, Joseph. "Two American Catholic Women at the UN, 1947-1972." *The Catholic Historical Review* 93.2 (April 2007): 300-324.

_____. *Uncharted Territory: The American Catholic Church at the United Nations, 1946-1972.* Washington D.C.: The Catholic University of America Press, 2006.

_____. *American Catholics and the Formation of the United Nations.* Lanham, MD.: University of   America Press, 1993.Ryall, David. "How Many Divisions? The Modern Development of Catholic International Relations." *International Relations.* vol. xiv. no. 2 August (1998): 21-33.

Salamon, L. M. and H. K. Anheier, Et. Al. Eds. *Global Civil Society: Dimensions of the Nonprofit Sector.* Baltimore: John Hopkins University, 1999.

Sane, Pierre. "Foreword." *Migration Without Borders: Essays on the Free Movement of People.* Antoine Pécoud and Paul De Guchteneire. Eds. Paris: Unesco Publishing, 2007. ix-x.

Scarnecchia, D. Brain and Terrence McKeegan. "The Millennium Development Goals: In the Light of Catholic Social Teaching." *International Organizations Research Group: White Paper* no. 10 (September 04, 2009): v-95. *www.c-fan.org/docLib/20090904_IORG_W_Paper_Number10.pdf.*

Schreiter, Robert J. "Changes in Roman Catholic Attitudes Towards Prose-
lytism and Mission." Martin E. Marty and Frederick E. Greenspahn.
Eds. *Pushing the Faith: Proselytism and Civility in a Pluralistic World.* New
York: Crossroad, 1988. 93-108.

Seary, Bill. "The Early History: From the Congress of Vienna to San Fran-
cisco." Peter, Willetts. Ed. *The Conscience of the World: The Influence of
NON-Governmental Organizations in the UN System.* Washington D.C.:
Brookings Institution Press, 1996. 15-30.

*Serving the Human Family: The Holy See at the Major United Nations Confer-
ences.* New York: Path to Peace foundation, 1997.

Shelley, John. "Introduction." Dorothee Soelle. *Political Theology.* Philadelphia: Fortress Press, 1974. vii-xviii.

Sirico, Robert A. and Maciej Zieba, O.P. *The Social Agenda: A Collection of
Magisterial Texts.* Vaticano: Pontifical Council for Justice and Peace and
Libreria Editrice, 2000.

Sobrino, Jon. "Foreword." Dean Brackley. *Divine Revolution: Salvation and
Liberation in Catholic Thought.* Maryknoll, New York: Orbis Books, 1996.
viii-xv.

Sobrino, Jon and Juan Hernandez Pico. *Theology of Christian Solidarity.*
Maryknoll: Orbis Books, 1985.

Stedjan, Scott "US Opposes Small Arms 'Ammunitions' within a Global Arms
Trade Deal," *The World Post,* (2011), *http://www.huffingtonpost.com/louis-bel-
anger/us-opposes-small-arms-amm_b_829908.html.*

Stone, Howard W. and James O. Duke. *How to Think Theologically.* Second
edition. Minneapolis: Fortress Press, 2006.

Stoutzenberger, Joseph. *The Christian Call to Justice and Peace.* Winona, Minnesota: St Mary's Press, 1987.

Sturm, Douglas. *Solidarity and Suffering: Toward a Politics of Relationality.* New
York: State University of New York Press, 1998.

Suzuki, Naoki. *Inside NGOs: Learning to Manage Conflicts Between Headquarters and Field Offices.* Warwickshire, UK: Intermediate Technology Publications, 1998.

Sybesma-knol, R.G. *The Status of Observers in the United Nations.* Brussels:
Brussels University Press, 1981.

Szura, John. "The Augustinians: Promoters of Justice and Peace." John Paul
Szura and Robert Dodaro, O.S.A., *Augustine: Promoter of Justice and
Peace.* Rome: Augustinian Secretariat of Justice and Peace, 2003. 15- 35.

"The Catholic Church at the United Nations," and "Catholic Church Abuses its Position at the UN. *National Secular Society,* February 4, (2004):1-8.

The ILO: What it is. What it Does. Geneva: International Labor Office Department of Communication.

Thompson, Milburn J. *Justice and Peace: A Christian Primer.* Maryknoll: Orbis Books, 2003.

Traub, John. *The Best Intentions: Kofi Annan and the UN in the Era of American World Power.* New York: Picador, 2007.

Van Bavel, T.J. *Christians in the World: Introduction to the Spirituality of Augustine.* New York: Catholic Books Publishing Co., 1980.

Van Rooy, Alision. *The Global Legitimacy Game: Civil Society, Globalization and Protest.* London: Palgrave Macmillan, 2004.

Viénot, Denis. "Message from the President and Secretary General of Caritas Internationalis." *Globalising Solidarity: 2005 Activities Report, Caritas Internatioanlis.* Vatican City, Rome: Caritas Internationalis, 2005.

Ward, Graham. "Modernism." *The Oxford Companion to Christian Thought: Intellectual, Spiritual, and Moral Horizons of Christianity.* Adrian Hastings, Alistair Mason and Hugh Pyper. Eds. New York: Oxford University Press, 2000. 442.

Weiss, Thomas. G. Et. Al. *United Nations and Changing World Politics.* Boulder, Colorado: Westview Press, 2014

_____. Global Governance and the UN: An Unfinished Journey. Indiana: Indiana University Press, 2010.

_____. *What's Wrong with United Nations and How to fix It.* Cambridge, Malden, MA: Polity Press, 2008.

Whitehead, Kenneth D. "The Pope Pius XII Controversy." *The Political Science Reviewer.* Volume XXXI (2002): 283-387.

White, L. C. *International Non-Governmental Organizations.* New Brunswick: Rutgers University Press, 1951.

Willetts, Peter. Ed. *The Conscience of the World: The Influence of NON-Governmental Organizations in the UN System.* Washington D.C.: Brookings Institution Press, 1996.

Williams, Colin W. *Where in the World?: Changing Forms of the Church's Witness.* London: The Epworth Press, 1966.

Wink, Walter. *The Powers That Be: Theology for a New Millennium.* New York: Galilee-Doubleday, 1998.

_____. *Engaging the Powers: Discernment and Resistance in a World of Domination*. Minneapolis: Fortress Press, 1992.

_____. *Unmasking the Powers: The Invisible Forces that Determine Human Existence*. Philadelphia: Fortress Press, 1986.

_____. *Naming the Powers: The Language of Power in the New Testament*. Philadelphia: Fortress Press, 1984.

Young, Nick. "NGOs: The Diverse Origins, Changing Nature and Growing Internationalization of the Species." *China Development Brief, online edition* (Dec. 31, 2004). *http://www.chinadevelopmentbrief.com/node/297*.

CHURCH DOCUMENTS

UN-related documents

Benedict XVI, "Address of His Holiness Pope Benedict XVI to the 62nd session of the United Nations General Assembly 95th plenary meeting New York, 18 April 2008," *http://www.holyseemission.org/Pope%20Benedict%20XVI%20GA%20English.html*.

John Paul II, "Address to the 50th General Assembly of the United Nations, (1995).

John Paul II, "Address to the NGOs gathered as the UN Headquarters, New York: 1979.

Paul VI, "Address to Holy See Representatives to International Organizations." (4 Sept, 1974).

Paul VI, "Address to the 20th Session of the General Assembly of the United Nations" (Oct. 4, 1965).

Holy See Mission, *http://www.holyseemission.org/index2.htlm*.

Encyclicals, Letters, Addresses, Vatican II & Synod documents

Benedict XVI. *Caritas in Veritate*, "Love in Truth" (2009).

_____. "Vatican: Activity in Favour of Solidarity and Common Good" AC/ANNIVERSARY VATICAN CITY STATE/..., VIS 090216 (440), Vatican Information Service NINETEENTH YEAR - N. 30 - MONDAY, 16 FEBRUARY 2009, *http://212.77.1.245/news_services/press/vis/dinamiche/d1_en.htm*.

John Paul II. *Vita Consecrata*, "On Consecrated Life" (1996).

_____. *Centesimus Annus,* "On the Hundredth Anniversary of *Rerum Nonarium*" (1991). xxx

John Paul II. *Sollicitudo rei Socialis,* "On Social Concern" (1988).

Paul VI. *Evangelii Nuntiandi,* "Evangelization in the Modern World" (1975).

Paul VI. *Octogesima Adveniens,* "A Call to Action on the Eightieth Anniversary of *Rerum Novarum* (1971).

Synod of Bishops. *Justitia in Mundo,* "Justice in the World" (1971).

Second Vatican Council. *Ad Gentes* "Decree on the Church's Missionary Activity" (Dec. 7, 1965).

_____. *Apostolicam Actuositatem,* "Decree on the Apostolate of Lay People" (Nov. 18, 1965).

_____. *Dei Verbum,* "Dogmatic Constitution on Divine Revelation" (Nov. 18, 1965).

_____. *Gaudium et Spes,* "Pastoral Constitution on the Church in the modern World" (Dec. 7, 1965).

_____. *Lumen Gentium,* "Dogmatic Constitution on the Church" (Nov. 41, 1964).

_____. *Perfectae Caritatis,* "Decree on the Up-to-Date Renewal of Religious Life (Oct. 28, 1965).

John XXIII. *Pacem in Terris,* "Peace on Earth" (1963).

_____. *Mater et Magistra,* "Christianity and Social Progress" (1961).

Pius XII. *Summi Pontificatus,* "On the Unity of Human Society" (1939).

_____. "Christmas Eve Message" (1942).

Leo XIII. *Rerum Novarum,* "The Condition of Labor" (1891).

Other Church Documents
Arranged according to Year of Publication

Rule and Constitutions: Order of St. Augustine. Rome: Pubblicazioni Agostiniane, 2008.

Pontifical Council for Justice and Peace. *Compendium of the Social Doctrine of the Church.* Ottawa: Canadian Conference of Catholic Bishops, 2005.

The Order of Prayer in the Liturgy of the Hours and the Celebration of the Eucharist for the Order of St. Augustine: North American Provinces. Mahwah, New Jersey: Paulist Press, 2004.

Document and Decisions of the Ordinary General Chapter 2001 of the Order of St. Augustine. Roma: Pubblicationi Agostiniane, 2001.

Rule and Constitution of the Order of Saint Augustine. Villanova, PA: Augustinian Press, 1991.

Code of Canon Law. Latin-English Edition. Washington D.C.: Canon Law Society of America, 1983.

United Nations & National Official Documents

"H.E. Father, Miguel d'Escoto Brockmann: Acceptance Speech upon His Election as President" 4 June 2008. New York: UN/DPI, August 2008, 08-42680-August 2008-3,000-DPI/2516A.

UK-France Summit Declaration, March 27, 2008. Accessed 10/05/10.

"Sixtieth General Assembly Plenary, GA/10484." *http://www.un.org/News/Press/docs/2006/ga10484.doc.htm*, 07/20/06. Accessed on 01/10/10.

2005 World Summit Outcome." *Journal of the United Nations. http://daccess-dds ny.un.org/doc/UNDOC/GEN/N05/510/94/PDF/N0551094.pdf?OpenElement*, 09/14/05. Accessed 01/10/10.

Report of the International Commission of Inquiry on Darfur to the United Nations Secretary-General, United Nations, 25 January 2005.

"NGOs and the United Nations Department of Public Information." *DPI/NGO Section: Brochure*. New York: UN-Department of Public Information, 2005.

United Nations Convention on Migrants' Rights: Information Kit. Paris: UNESCO, 2005. US, Bureau of Public Affairs, June 20, 2005. Accessed, 01/05/10.

World Bank, *Issues and Options for Improving Engagement Between the World Bank and Civil Society Organizations*. Washington, D.C.: Dept. of External Affairs, Communications and United Nations Affairs, World Bank, 2005.

Basic Facts – About the United Nations. New York: News and Media Division of United Nations Department of Public Information, 2004.

"G4 Nations Bid for Permanent Security Council Seat." *Deutsche Welle. http://www.dw-world.de/dw/article/0,1564,1335522,00.html*, 09/22/04, accessed on 01/10/10.

Intergovernmental Negotiations and Decision Making at the United Nations: A Guide. New York: NGLS, 2003.

"The Question of Observer Status in the United Nations: The Case of Non-Member States." United Nations Public Information Office. February 4, 2000.

General Assembly Resolution 49/75 K, "Request for an Advisory Opinion from the International Court of Justice on the Legality of the Threat or use of Nuclear Weapons," 15, 16. *http://daccessdds.un.org/doc/UN-DOC/GEN/N95/760/03/PDF/N9576003.pdf?OpenElement,* accessed August 02, 2009.

International Court of Justice. "Legality of the Threat or Use of Nuclear Weapons, Advisory Opinion, I.C.J. Reports, 1996, p226." (ICJ, General List no., 95, July 8, 1995), 266, pdf-44, *http://www.icj-cij.org/docket/files/95/7495.pdf,* accessed August 02, 2009.

CHR 54th 4/22/1998E/CN.4/RES/1998/77" (United Nations Human Rights, Office of the High Commissioner for Human Rights, 1998), *http://ap.ohchr.org/documents/sdpage_e.aspx?b=1&se=10&t=11.*

Earth Summit Agenda 21: The United Nations Programme for Action from Rio. New York: UN DPI/1344, April 1993. 219-245.

General Assembly resolution (A/RES/45/158) December 18, 1990.

UN System Engagement with NGOs, Civil Society, The Private Sector, and other Actors: A Compendium.

United Nations Webcast, www.un.org/webcast.

General Assembly resolution, 55/2, para. 30.

Unpublished Works & Other Online Sources

A Brief History of IMCS-Pax Romana (1887-2006). Online Edition, *www.cccm.ca/stage/files/uploads/docs/ABriefHistoryofIMC.pdf.*

Ahern, Kevin. "The Role of International Catholic Organizations in Promoting the Gospel in the Community of Nations." 1-17.

_____. "Catholic NGOs Working Closely with the Holy See." An address to a forum on Catholic Non-Governmental Organizations at the Vatican. Vatican City, November 30 – December 2, 2007.

China's Involvement in Sudan: Arms and Oil." Human Rights Watch. 2007-12-23. *http://www.hrw.org/reports/2003/sudan1103/26.htm.*

Dance, Kevin. "The Mystery of the Cross and the Work of the United Nations," *http://www.cptryon.org/compassion/75/un.html.*

"Darfur genocide charges for Sudanese president Omar al-Bashir". Guardian. *http://www.guardian.co.uk/world/2008/jul/14/su-dan.warcrimes1?gusrc=rss&feed=worldnews,* accessed, 12/11/09.

Havel, Vaclav. "The Need for Transcendence in the Postmodern World." Speech delivered in the Independence Hall, Philadelphia, July 4, 1994.

_____. "Reflecting on Hope…." From *Disturbing the Peace,* written or spoken while he was in prison.

Leddy, Mary Jo. "On Naming the Present," Address to Colloqium on *North American Theology.* San Antonio, Texas: Oblate School of Theology, Oct. 2002.

Marchione, Margherita. "The Truth About Pope Pius XII." *Catholic League for Religious and Civil Rights.* Online Edition.

McElroy, Wendy. "Victims Versus Victimhood." Oct. 11, 2005, 2 http://lewrockwell.com/mcelroy94.html.

Results of the Mapping-Questionnaire. Rome: Catholic-inspired NGOs Forum, Forum des ONG d'inspiration Catholique, March 2009.

Scholte, J.A. "Protecting the Rights and Addressing the Responsibilities of Non-governmental Organizations." Summary Report, unpublished paper. Coventry, UK: Warwick University, 2003.

Seffrin, John R. "Non-Governmental Organization." *Encyclopaedia of Public Health,* Lester Breslow. Ed. Gale: Cengage, 2002. *eNotes.com,* (2006). *http://www.enotes.com/public-health-encyclopedia/nongovernmental-organiza-tions-united-states.*

Shah, Anup. "World Military Spending," *Global Issues* (March 1, 2008). *http://www.globalissues.org/article/75/world-military-spending.*

SIPRI Arms Transfers Data for 2007", *SIPRI,* 2008.

Stephenson, Carolyn. "Non-Governmental Organizations (NGOs)." *Beyond Intractibility.* Guy Burgess and Heidi Burgess. Eds. Boulder, Colorado, Research Consortium, University of Colorado, January 2005. *http://www.beyondintractiblity.org/essay/role_ngo/.*

Tauran, Jean-Louis. "The presence of the Holy See in the International Organizations." Public Lecture (Monday April April 22, 2002).

The African Executive, "64th UN General Assembly Speeches," *http://www.afri-canexecutive.com/modules/magazine/news.php?id-_news=76&id_news_main=6&magazine=257,* published 09/24/2009, accessed, 12/11/09.

"The Christmas Editorials." *Catholic League for Religious and Civil Rights.* Online Edition. *http://www.catholicleague.org/pius/nyt_editorials.htm.*

The Increasing Importance of African Oil." Power and Interest News Report. 2007-03-20. *http://www.pinr.com/report.php?ac=view_report&report_id=460.*

"The United Nations is Terminally Paralyzed: The Democratic World needs a Forum of Its Own." Intelligence Square Date January 22, 2009, *http://www.intelligencesquared.com/. Accessed on 05/20/09.*

International, *http://www.unanima-international.org/english/index.htm.*

Urso, Ida. "The New World Order and the Work of the United Nations." A talk given at the World Goodwill Symposium. *Let the Future Stand Revealed: Envisioning the World We Choose.* New York City: October 28, 1995. 1-6.

_____. "Let Purpose Guide the Little Wills of Men: The Spiritual Impulse Behind the United Nations." A talk at the Arcane Scholl Conference. Saturday, May 13, 1995, New York. 1-10.

VIVAT International, http://www.vivatinternational.org/. *Franciscans International* has even included non-Catholic groups in their network.

"What is an NGO?" January 5 (2007). *http://www.indianngos.com/ngosection/newcomers/whatisanngo.htm.*

Willetts, Peter. "What is a Non-Governmental Organization?" *UNESCO Encyclopedia of Life Support Systems, Section 1 Institutional and Infrastructural Resource Issues, Article 1.44.3.7, Non-Governmental Organizations. http://www.staff.city.ac.uk/p.willetts/CS-NTWKS/NGO-ART.HTM.*

World Alliance to Transform the United Nations. *http://www.transformun.org/.*

Newspaper & Radio Sources

Anheier Et. Al. "Global Civil Society 2001" (2001); "U.S. on Russia N-G-O Law Voice of America January 27 (2006) *http://www.voanews.com/uspolicy/archive/2006-01-27-voa2.cfm;*

Arab Times, (Thursday, September 4 (2008),1. *http://www.arab-timesonline.com/pdf08/sep/4/page%2009.pdf.*

"D&P on Funding Leash." *Catholic Register* (Weeks of July 26-August 2, 2009): 3.

"Poll shows Power of AIPAC drops slightly." *Jewish News Weekly* (December 19, 1999), retrieved on (June 25, 2007).

Schoetzau, Barbara. "United Nations elects Ex-Sandinista as Assembly President." *Voice of America,* June 4, 2008. *www.voanews.com/english/archive.*

Interviews: Arranged Alphabetically
& by Date of Interview

Dance, Kevin. Passionist International. 62nd UN DPI/NGO Conference, Mexico (Sept. 2009).

Deegan, John of the Order of Augustine. UN OSA-NGO Course, Mexico (Sept. 2009).

Kirby, Joan of the Religious of the Sacred Heart (RSH) and immediate past president of the DPI/NGO committee. 62nd UN DPI/NGO Conference, Mexico (Sept. 2009)

Uti, Ngozi of Center for Women Studies and Intervention (CWSI), Nigeria. 62nd UN DPI/NGO Conference, Mexico (Sept. 2009).

Guerrera, Vittorio. The personal Secretary of Archbishop Celetino Migliore, Holy See Permanent Observer at the UN, the Holy See UN Permanent Observer Mission, New York (November 12, 2008).

Burke, Joan of Sisters of Notre Dame de Namur and Chairperson of ECOSOC/NGO Committee on Social Development. New York (Nov. 10, 2008).

Farley, Dorothy of Dominican Family International and past leader of International Catholic Organization's Information Centre, New York (Nov. 10, 2008).

Forley, Joseph Vincentian Family's Commission for Promoting systemic Change. New York (Nov. 10, 2008).

Malano, Christopher of International Movement of Catholic Student, a subsidiary of PAX-ROMANA. 61st UN DPI/NGO Conference, Paris (Sept. 2008).

Representative of *Comité Catholique contre la Faim et le Dévelopment (CCFD)*. France (Sept. 2008).

Roche, Douglas. Former Canadian Ambassador to the United Nations. Toronto (Feb. 2008).

Szura, John. A founding member of the Order of St. Augustine's NGO at the UN and a Member of the American Psychology Association. Toronto (May 2008).

Wilson, Lester. Staff of United Nations DPI and Professor of United Nations Studies, Long Island University. United Nations Headquarters New York (2007).

ABOUT THE AUTHOR

EMEKA XRIS OBIEZU is a Roman Catholic priest of the Order of St. Augustine. He was the immediate past permanent representative of Augustinians International at the United Nations (UN), New York. In that post, he was a special consultant to the UN Economic and Social Council, he was a regular speaker at major UN events in New York, Geneva, and around the world, and he contributed to the various UN policies and decision-making processes. He is an expert in policy advocacy, international migration and development, and United Nations and global governance, as well as religions' interface with international organizations.

He is a contributor in the global network on Migration and Development with focus on global governance of migration. He is the coordinator of African Network for Safe Migration, as well the convener of national collaboration on Migration and Development in Nigeria – a forum for interactive sharing by all stakeholders in migration dynamics in Nigeria, including government, international agencies, civil society and the private sector. He is also a co-founder and the coordinator of Civil Society Network on Migration and Development.

On various aspects of migration management, he consults for different agencies and organizations, including the International Organization for Migration (IOM), the International Center for Migration Policy Development (ICMPD), and the United Nations High Commissioner for Refugees (UNHCR). He is an expert adviser to the Technical Working Group of the Nigerian Migration Mechanism under the co-ordination of the National Commission for Refugees, Migrants and Internally Displaced Persons (NCFRMI).

Fr. Obiezu earned a Ph.D. in Political Theology from the University of St. Michael's College in the University of Toronto, Canada. He also holds a certificate in International Migration Law; Peace Studies and Conflict Resolution, and another certificate in Understanding Societal Change, from the United Nations Institute for Training and Research, Geneva, and from United Nations University of Peace, Costa Rica.

He has lectured, presented and published on these and other major issues of his interest in both academic and popular settings.

OTHER BOOKS
FROM PACEM IN TERRIS PRESS

ROMAN CATHOLIC CLERICALISM
Three Historical Stages in the Legislation of a Non-Evangelical,
Now Dysfunctional, and Sometimes Pathological Institution
Joe Holland, 2018

CATHOLIC PRACTICAL THEOLOGY
A Genealogy of the Methodological Turn to Praxis,
Historical Reality, & the Preferential Option for the Poor
Bob Pennington, 2018

SAINT JOHN OF THE CROSS
His Prophetic Mysticism in the Historical Context
of Sixteenth-Century Spain
Cristóbal Serrán-Pagán y Fuentes, 2018

BRETTON WOODS INSTITUTIONS & NEOLIBERALISM
Historical Critique of Policies, Structures, & Governance of the International Monetary Fund
& the World Bank, with Case Studies
Mark Wolff, 2018

THE WHOLE STORY:
The Wedding of Science & Religion
Norman Carroll, 2018

PADRE MIGUEL
A Memoir of My Catholic Missionary Experience in Bolivia
amidst Postcolonial Transformation of Church and State
Michael J. Gillgannon, 2018

POSTMODERN ECOLOGICAL SPIRITUALITY
Catholic-Christian Hope for the Dawn of a Postmodern Ecological Civilization Rising
from within the Spiritual Dark Night of Modern Industrial Civilization
Joe Holland, 2017

JOURNEYS TO RENEWED CONSECRATION
Religious Life after Fifty Years of Vatican II
Emeka Obiezu, OSA & John Szura, OSA, Editors, 2017

THE CRUEL ELEVENTH-CENTURY IMPOSITION OF
WESTERN CLERICAL CELIBACY
A Monastic-Inspired Attack on Catholic Episcopal & Clerical Families
Joe Holland, 2017

LIGHT, TRUTH, & NATURE
Practical Reflections on Vedic Wisdom & Heart-Centered Meditation
In Seeking a Spiritual Basis for Nature, Science, Evolution, & Ourselves
Thomas Pliske, 2017

THOMAS BERRY IN ITALY
Reflections on Spirituality & Sustainability
Elisabeth M. Ferrero, Editor, 2016

PETER MAURIN'S
ECOLOGICAL LAY NEW MONASTICISM
A Catholic Green Revolution Developing
Rural Ecovillages, Urban Houses of Hospitality,
& Eco-Universities for a New Civilization
Joe Holland, 2015

PROTECTION OF RELIGIOUS MINORITIES
A Symposium Organized by Pax Romana at the United Nations
and the United Nations Alliance of Civilizations
Dean Elizabeth F. Defeis & Peter F. O'Connor, Editors, 2015

BOTTOM ELEPHANTS
Catholic Sexual Ethics & Pastoral Practice in Africa:
The Challenge of Women Living within Patriarchy
& Threatened by HIV-Positive Husbands
Daniel Ude Asue, 2014

CATHOLIC LABOR PRIESTS
Five Giants in the United States Catholic Bishops Social Action Department
Volume I of US Labor Priests During the 20th Century
Patrick Sullivan, 2014

CATHOLIC SOCIAL TEACHING & UNIONS
IN CATHOLIC PRIMARY & SECONDARY SCHOOLS
The Clash between Theory & Practice within the United States
Walter "Bob" Baker, 2014

SPIRITUAL PATHS TO
A GLOBAL & ECOLOGICAL CIVILIZATION
Reading the Signs of the Times with Buddhists, Christians, & Muslims
John Raymaker & Gerald Grudzen, with Joe Holland, 2013

PACEM IN TERRIS
Its Continuing Relevance for the Twenty-First Century
(Papers from the 50th Anniversary Conference at the United Nations)
Josef Klee & Francis Dubois, Editors, 2013

PACEM IN TERRIS
Summary & Commentary for the Famous Encyclical Letter
of Pope John XXIII on World Peace
Joe Holland, 2012

100 YEARS OF CATHOLIC SOCIAL TEACHING
DEFENDING WORKERS & THEIR UNIONS
Summaries & Commentaries for Five Landmark Papal Encyclicals
Joe Holland, 2012

HUMANITY'S AFRICAN ROOTS
Remembering the Ancestors' Wisdom
Joe Holland, 2012

THE "POISONED SPRING" OF ECONOMIC LIBERTARIANISM
Menger, Mises, Hayek, Rothbard: A Critique from
Catholic Social Teaching of the Austrian School of Economics
Pax Romana / Cmica-usa
Angus Sibley, 2011

BEYOND THE DEATH PENALTY
The Development in Catholic Social Teaching
Florida Council of Catholic Scholarship
D. Michael McCarron & Joe Holland, Editors, 2007

THE NEW DIALOGUE OF CIVILIZATIONS
A Contribution from Pax Romana
International Catholic Movement for Intellectual & Cultural Affairs
Pax Romana / Cmica-usa
Roza Pati & Joe Holland, Editors, 2002

This book and other books from Pacem in Terris Press,
are available for purchase at:

www.amazon.com, amazon.de, amazon.es,
amazon.fr, and amazon.it